What Would Buffy Do?

What Would Buffy Do?

The Vampire Slayer as Spiritual Guide

Jana Riess

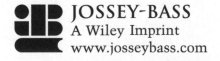

JOSSEY-BASS
A Wiley Imprint
www.josseybass.com

Published by Jossey-Bass
A Wiley Imprint
989 Market Street, San Francisco, CA 94103-1741   www.josseybass.com

Jossey-Bass books and products are available through most bookstores. To contact
Jossey-Bass directly call our Customer Care Department within the U.S. at
800-956-7739, outside the U.S. at 317-572-3986, or fax 317-572-4002.

Jossey-Bass also publishes its books in a variety of electronic formats. Some content
that appears in print may not be available in electronic books.

Cover and interior photos copyright © Durham, Delmas, Sarandrea, Caine,
O'Conno/ZUMA. Photo on page 8 copyright © Corbis.

Scripture quotations, unless otherwise noted, are from the New Revised Standard
Version of the Bible, copyrighted ©1989, by the Division of Christian Education of the
National Council of Churches of Christ in the United States of America. Used by
permission. All rights reserved.

The fact that an organization or Web site is referred to in this work as a citation and/or
a potential source of further information does not mean that the author or the pub-
lisher endorses the information the organization or Web site may provide or recom-
mendations it may make. Further, readers should be aware that Internet Web sites
listed in this work may have changed or disappeared between when this work was
written and when it is read.

Library of Congress Cataloging-in-Publication Data

Riess, Jana.
  What would Buffy do?: the vampire slayer as spiritual guide / Jana K. Riess.—1st ed.
    p. cm.
Includes bibliographical references.
  ISBN 0-7879-6922-2 (alk. paper)
  1. Spiritual life—Christianity. 2. Buffy, the vampire slayer
(Television program) I. Title.
  BV4501.3.R54 2004
  791.45'72—dc22

                                                              2003026454

Printed in the United States of America
FIRST EDITION
PB Printing   10 9 8 7 6 5 4 3 2 1

Contents

For Jerusha, my resident Potential Slayer

Introduction

A Savior in a Micro-Mini?

In the early days, I was a little embarrassed to admit that I enjoyed watching *Buffy the Vampire Slayer*, a popular TV series about a young woman who (quite literally) stakes out the undead. The first time I ever saw the show, I was hooked by its clever dialogue, surprising plot twists, and personable characters. I soon discovered that a host of critics shared my view that the program was "the most original, witty, and provocative television show of the past two decades," as the British newspaper *The Independent* put it. But there was even more to the series than first met my eye. Over time I also came to see that *Buffy* offered strong spiritual values that came, ironically enough, in a vampire-ridden package that people of faith often dismissed out of hand. Some individuals objected to the show's violent premise (vampire slaying, after all, is not for the faint of heart) and depictions of emerging adolescent sexuality, but they often missed its deeper spiritual connotations and powerful message about the triumph of good over evil.

In fact, *Buffy* is a classic medieval morality play—only with skimpier clothes, wittier dialogue, and cutting-edge alternative music. During its seven-season run from March 1997 to May 2003, it was easily one of the most moralistic programs on TV, depicting a world in which evil never goes unpunished and doing good is its own reward. It also offered one of TV's strongest and most intelligent female heroines, a savior in a micro-miniskirt who courageously battled the evil powers of demon-packed Sunnydale, California. The show's creator, Joss Whedon, says that the lead character—whom he intentionally named Buffy to highlight the incongruence of her superficial appearance and her unique destiny as her generation's chosen Slayer—reversed the stereotype of young pretty women in film and TV. Buffy was blonde but never a victim, vulnerable but also tough as nails, sexy and sensual but also in a manner untouchable. "I wanted . . . Barbie with Kung Fu grip," says Whedon of the show's gender-bending premise. In Buffy's character Whedon quite intentionally created a feminist icon, and he changed the face of TV by making "girl power" a viewer draw.

But *Buffy* did more than give us a heroine who could kick some dastardly derriere. It asked probing metaphysical questions and often dared to leave them unanswered. It stubbornly resisted the temptation to tie everything up with a neat, made-for-TV ending. This very ambiguity, this willingness to allow viewers to think for themselves, is what some audience members found so disturbing about the show and others found so enlightening. *Buffy* was provocative in every sense of the word, especially for people of faith. As *Relevant* magazine admiringly wrote, *Buffy* and its spin-off series, *Angel*, are "perhaps the two most occultic shows on the air. . . . Vampires, demons, paganism—these shows are the gristle religious watchdogs love to chew, and rightly so. They're dark, broody, fascinated with life's shadows. Their characters couldn't care less about God. Yet, thematically, these are two of the most religious programs on network TV, secular universes saturated with grace."

Although the series often expressed ambivalence about organized religion, and was created by a self-professed atheist, it offered powerful depictions of core spiritual values at work in the lives of its major characters. This book explores some of the show's most central spiritual and religious ideas, from redemption and self-sacrifice to the need for humor and forgiveness in fighting our spiritual battles. Buffy and the show's other characters have valuable spiritual lessons to impart, offering wisdom for the faith journey, the courage to make ethical choices, and forgiveness when our actions have harmed others. As Xander tells Buffy at the beginning of the fourth season, "When it's dark and I'm all alone and I'm scared or freaked out or whatever, I always think, 'What would Buffy do?' You're my hero" (4.1). This book starts from the premise that she is a worthy one and that we could all learn something from the Slayer and her friends.

Where's "the Lord"?

The fourth-season episode "Who Are You?" (4.16) hinges on a climactic scene in which several vampires have taken over a Sunnydale church, holding the parishioners hostage and threatening to devour them. One of them is surprised that the church, a holy place he's feared for so long, turns out to be innocuous and not at all threatening: "I've been avoiding this place for so many years, and it's nothing," he sneers. "It's nice! It's got the pretty windows, the pillars, *lots* of folks to eat. Where's the thing I was so afraid of . . . you know, the Lord?" The vampire concludes that he should start killing off the people to see whether the Lord will show up.

Like this vampire, some people who have watched *Buffy* conclude that God seems to have no place in the Buffyverse—that God is powerless, if present at all. It's certainly true that the show depicts a mostly God-neutral universe. It does not posit an all-powerful creator who set the world in motion—a view challenged as early as the second half of the pilot episode, when Giles speaks of the "myth" of origins in the biblical book of Genesis (1.2). The Buffyverse contains no God to pray to (although in one very funny scene Cordelia utters a desperate and comical prayer of self-preservation in a school closet; 2.3) and no explicitly stated belief in a higher benevolence or spirit. On the other hand, one might expect that *Buffy*'s fairly dualistic universe, which takes for granted the existence of a First Evil, the primordial force that engenders all evil creatures, would also assume the existence of a corresponding First Good. But on such matters, the Buffyverse is largely silent. On *Angel* we see the closest thing resembling a personal god in the Powers That Be, beings that often assist Angel in his quest to help others. But these beings are sometimes capricious and not without their own motivations for intervening. In general, the Buffyverse assumes a mostly nontheistic universe.

Should we agree, then, with the Christian contemplative Thomas Merton, who taught that "agnosticism leads inevitably to moral indifference"? Seven years of this series suggest that on this issue, Merton may have been mistaken. Buffy and her friends, despite their unanswered questions about God, never cease to *do their job:* saving the world at whatever personal cost. Rather than being indifferent, they care passionately about right and wrong, good and evil. So although *Buffy* shows a good deal of ambivalence about the existence of God (Buffy says that we know "nothing solid" on that question; 7.7), the show offers a deep spiritual core that is based in ethical behavior.

Also, despite its reservations about God, *Buffy* has always assumed an afterlife, with untold numbers of hells and heavenly paradise dimensions (one of the latter of which was home to Buffy after her second death). As the ex-demon Anya tells us, there are even shrimpless dimensions and a land of perpetual Wednesday. In other words, the show makes clear that the "matrix" of what we think we know on this earth is just a drop in the bucket of spiritual experience. As the Christian apostle Paul puts it, we see through a glass darkly—there is far more to life than can be glimpsed here on earth. Writer and producer Marti Noxon has said that the show's creators have tried to make its concepts of heaven and hell fairly fuzzy and "inter-denominational. . . . We're not going to get too specific about what exactly the ruling forces are." Although the details of the afterlife on *Buffy* remain a bit blurry, the show expresses a longing for transcendence. As Noxon said in another interview, Joss Whedon's work "is full of yearning for belief. And . . . the show speaks to people who also have that yearning."

If the Buffyverse does contain an active God, divine interventions and messages are most clearly visible through the courageous choices of human beings. It's interesting to return to that fourth-season scene in which vampires have taken over a Sunnydale church (4.16). Just after the gibe that "the Lord" is absent from the building, the Vampire Slayer Faith (in Buffy's body) strides in to save the day. The vampire, who has just started to feed off a man in the front pew, is forced to abandon his would-be victim and deal with Faith, who says she has "just come to pray" but is actually there to slay. As she does her job—dusting one of the bloodsuckers with the wood from a hymn rack—we are left to understand that on *Buffy*, praying and slaying may well be the same thing. "Have you accepted Jesus Christ as your personal savior?" Buffy is asked when strolling across campus on her first day at UC Sunnydale. "Uh, you know, I meant to, and then I just got really busy," she replies (4.1). What has kept her busy is saving the world, time and time again. Like the biblical heroine Esther, Buffy is a young woman who feels the burden of preserving her people. And just as God is nowhere mentioned in the book of Esther, God is merely implicit in the Buffyverse, present every time the characters put their own lives on the line to save others.

'Note to Self: Religion Freaky'

In the episode "Tabula Rasa" (6.8), a spell renders Buffy and her friends temporarily incapable of remembering their identities. When vampires attack and the end seems near, Xander is left to figure out how to do his own last rites, not remembering what religion he is. "Now I'm not sure what I am, so bear with me here," he says desperately, falling to his knees with hands clasped. "And now I lay me down to sleep, uh, Shema Israel, uh, om, om. . . ."

Just as Xander very entertainingly covers all the bases with regard to the world's belief systems, the show has always adopted an eclectic and wonderfully cheeky approach to religion. Its uncertainty about God extends to its treatment of organized religion, which is usually regarded with distance and, at times, irreverence. In the show's final weeks on the air, the Parents' Television Council—never big fans of Buffy—protested the fact that one of the villains of the seventh season was shown to be a former Roman Catholic priest, still wearing his clerical collar. Some conservative viewers were upset that the series would depict a member of the clergy as having so clearly allied himself with the forces of darkness by serving as the chief agent for the First Evil (the biggest and baddest Big Bad that Buffy had yet encountered). But they must have been sleeping through the third season, which had an episode with a similar theme. In "Anne" (3.1) Buffy has fled to Los Angeles and finds that a runaway acquaintance, Lily, has been taken in by the street ministry of a caring pastor. Naturally, though, he turns out to be a heinously evil sort, who preys upon runaways and makes them work as his slaves, removing all traces of their individuality and identity. Clearly, religious figures in the Buffyverse can be working for the powers of darkness, and their claim to authority is suspect.

Sometimes, though, they are depicted as good folks who are trying to help but may be just a little removed. At the funeral for Buffy's mother, Joyce, for example, the minister who intones the familiar "ashes to ashes, dust to dust" liturgy and commends Joyce's soul to God is essentially a disembodied voice (5.17). We hear him speaking, but the camera pans only fleetingly across his face. It's an apt metaphor for the way the series treats religion: religion is an offstage voice that informs the action but is not integral to that action. Even in the best of circumstances, Buffy holds organized religion at arm's length. As Buffy observes early in the series, "Note to self: religion freaky" (2.9).

That's not to say that organized religion is not incorporated into the show, which is often Christian in its outward trappings. Christian crosses have the power to repel vampires, and Buffy often wears one around her neck when she slays, especially in the first few years. (Note that at the end of the first season, when she announces she's quitting in order to avoid her prophesied death, the first thing she does is snatch off her cross and fling it to the floor; 1.12.) Christian holy water can harm vampires, and some rituals need to take place in churches. Interestingly, though, it's not Christianity but Buddhism that drives the show's central themes: consequences (or karma), redemption through one's own efforts, the pervasive nature of suffering, the need for self-sacrifice. It's even a pastiche of different kinds of Buddhisms. Inwardly, the show is intensely Zen in its determination to privilege experience over teaching (dharma)—on *Buffy*, personal experience is the best dharma to be found anywhere. But outwardly, the show more closely resembles Tibetan Buddhism, with its elaborate, exotic rituals and pantheon of supernatural beings. The figure of the Slayer herself has echoes in Tibetan Buddhist tradition: the Slayer is a kind of lama, one individual chosen in her generation to lead others. In the original *Buffy* film, Buffy even shares the dreams of past Slayers, feeling almost as though their personal experiences are her own—reflecting shades of the Tibetan *tulku* tradition, in which each lama is the incarnation of previous lamas and is endowed with their knowledge and experience. This idea is developed further in the *Angel* episode "Damage" (A5.11).

So *Buffy* offers Christian symbols, Buddhist themes, a generous helping of Wiccan ethics, and some sprinkled references to Judaism, among other traditions. Rather than adopting the worldview of any one religion, *Buffy*'s general approach is one voiced by its star, Sarah Michelle Gellar: "I believe in an idea of God, although it's my own personal ideal. I find most religions interesting. . . . I've taken bits from everything and customized it." This customizing is the key to understanding the show's approach and appeal. *Buffy* might be paradigmatic of Generations X and Y because it is so spiritually eclectic, borrowing freely from several different religious traditions at the same time. The power lies not with religious institutions but with spiritual individuals who forge their own paths. One of the catchphrases of Generation X has been, "I'm not religious, but I'm very spiritual." The same might be said for the show as well. It's not religious per se—meaning that it allies itself to no particular institution and sometimes seems at odds with organized religion. But it is deeply spiritual, and at its heart *Buffy* understands the real purpose of religion. Religion is more than creeds and dogmas and institutions—all things that can be a real turnoff to the kinds of mavericky people who love *Buffy*. At its heart, religion is actually about community. As Rabbi Harold Kushner points out, even the very word *religion* is grounded in community, because the Latin root *lig* implies joining things together (think *ligament* or *ligature*). Religion is about making connections, forging unity and community. And community is something that Joss Whedon understands remarkably well.

About This Book

Although this book will be best appreciated by those fans of the show who are already familiar with *Buffy*'s basic plot contours and characters, don't panic if you're not in that category. Several seasons are already available on DVD, and the others are coming soon. At the end of the book, you'll find a season-by-season plot summary and a character guide to bring you up to speed on who's who in the Buffyverse. Although most of the book's examples are taken from *Buffy*, some come from *Angel*, the spin-off show that concluded its fifth season in 2004. This is especially true in the chapter on redemption (Chapter Eleven), which has always been a key theme on *Angel*.

This book is arranged thematically, with chapters organized into three parts, gradually broadening our perspective by moving from the individual to the world. The first part addresses issues of the reader's own spiritual journey, with themes like self-sacrifice, embracing change as a spiritual teacher, learning from the reality of death, balancing emotions, and maintaining a sense of humor. The second part widens the net to include relationships with families, friends, and mentors. *Buffy* prompts us to ask: How can we learn to choose forgiveness over vengeance? What does it mean to share power? When is *disobedience* a spiritual virtue? The third section explores the next step— a socially engaged spirituality. How can we live with the consequences of our actions and find redemption for poor choices? What does it mean to live in service of the world? Ultimately, the message of both *Buffy* and *Angel* seems to be that although it's great for us to have our own quests and spiritual journeys and all that ("blah, blah, bliddy blah," as Buffy would say), it doesn't mean anything unless it's in service of others. We can be enlightened until the cows come home, but our own nirvanas won't do anyone any good unless we turn around and give something back. Buffy's tombstone (the second time she died) proclaimed that she saved the world. A lot. Can we say the same?

The title of this book, as I stated earlier, comes from Xander's touching and funny declaration to Buffy in the fourth-season opener, when he helps her regain some of the confidence she has lost in suddenly finding that she is a small fish in the big pond of college. But the second half of the quote ("OK, sometimes when it's dark and I'm all alone, I think, 'What is Buffy wearing?'") is actually just as important. Although *Buffy* is a deeply spiritual and often very profound show, it is also meant to make us laugh, and one of its perennial messages is that we need to avoid taking ourselves too seriously. As Oscar Wilde wrote, "A little sincerity is a dangerous thing, and a great deal of it is absolutely fatal." So as you read this book, it is my hope that you have fun with it. I certainly had a terrific time writing it.

One last thing. Through exactly 144 episodes—the biblical number of fullness and completeness—*Buffy* encouraged viewers to do the right thing and to support one another along the path. In the fourth and fifth seasons, a phrase is repeated that I have come to think of as a mantra for the show and for my own spiritual growth: "You think you know what you are, what's to come. You haven't even begun." Or as Giles summarizes in "Restless" (4.22), "It's all about the journey."

What Would Buffy Do?

Personal Spirituality

CHAPTER 1

Be a Hero, Even When You'd Rather Go to the Mall

The Power of Self-Sacrifice

In the season-one finale, "Prophecy Girl" (1.12), Buffy discovers that vampire activity has increased in Sunnydale and that the vampires seem to be cockier and more numerous than ever before. She is irritated that Giles, her Watcher, doesn't seem to be evincing more interest in the escalating situation. ("Look, I broke a nail, OK? I'm wearing a press-on," Buffy complains.) But Giles knows something that he is trying to conceal from his Slayer: he has read about her imminent death in the Codex prophecy book. He can't keep this a secret for long. When Buffy first overhears Giles and Angel discussing the prophecy in the school library, she is horrified and quits her job as the Slayer. She is furious with Giles for not telling her sooner and also with Angel, if only because he is immortal and will never have to face the moment she now realizes is at hand: she is doomed to die. Buffy tells them she doesn't care whether the Master rises. "Giles, I'm sixteen years old," she says simply. "I don't want to die."

> May I be a guard
> for those who are
> protectorless,
> A guide for those
> who journey on
> the road;
> For those who wish
> to go across
> the water,
> May I be a boat,
> a raft, a bridge.
> —*Bodhisattva vows*

3

In the space of a day, however, Buffy goes from resigning as Slayer to feeling resigned to her dire fate—a shift that happens because she cares so much for other people. She changes her mind after fellow students Willow and Cordelia discover the aftermath of a deadly vampire attack at the school. Willow, traumatized by the deaths of students she knew, later asks Buffy what they're going to do about it. "What we have to," Buffy replies grimly. She knows what she needs to do and ventures out with a crossbow to do it, despite Giles's objections. And she does die, fulfilling the prophecy and sacrificing herself to save others. It won't be the last time that such a sacrifice is required of her. It's interesting that when she is revived, Buffy comes back slightly different, stronger than before. Her willingness to relinquish her power through death has made her more powerful; after sacrificing her life, she emerges with a more forceful sense of authority and self.

Throughout the show's seven seasons, Buffy wrestles with the weight of the world on her bony, spaghetti-strapped shoulders. For her the evil just keeps coming. "When I saw you stop the world from, you know, ending, I just assumed that was a big week for you," Riley tells her in "A New Man" (4.12). "Turns out I suddenly find myself needing to know the plural of *apocalypse*." Buffy's sacrifices aren't just onetime events (though they do seem to coincide with the annual May ratings sweeps) but represent an ongoing decision to place others first. She and other characters in the show—most notably Angel and Xander—choose to be heroes when they could instead opt for selfish, and possibly more fulfilling, lives. There is holiness in these kinds of sacrifices, great and small. In fact, the word *sacrifice*, literally translated, means to "make sacred"—it is the discovery and perpetuation of holiness through selfless acts and compassionate moments. Buffy and her friends force us to ask ourselves: What does it mean to save the world—a lot?

'She Is the Chosen One': Buffy

Buffy's sacrifices are most obvious when she is dealing with life-and-death matters, risking her life every night to patrol the cemetery and rid the world of undead undesirables. But Buffy makes a hundred other smaller sacrifices that need to be recognized too. In the first season, we see her struggle with the desire to have a normal boyfriend and social life, resulting in the very funny episode "Never Kill a Boy on the First Date" (1.5). She explains to Giles that, at age sixteen, a date with a cute guy seems more important than saving the world from a new vampire threat: "If the apocalypse comes, beep me," she tells him before heading out with Owen, her love interest *du jour*. Giles reluctantly agrees and lets her try to have this semblance of an ordinary life; but naturally things go awry, and Owen is almost killed. The end of the episode sees Buffy making a very responsible, grown-up, but heartbreaking decision: she gives Owen up so as not to place him in danger again. This is self-sacrifice of a different sort, of laying aside her dream of a "normal" boyfriend because a mere mortal is too likely to get killed in the fray.

Buffy's desire for normalcy is hardly over, however, and the first two seasons are taken up with her ongoing identity crisis. She longs to be popular, but Cordelia and others have labeled her a freak because of the strange things that always seem to happen when Buffy is around. She yearns to be a good student, and she is certainly intelligent enough to do well in school, but the time she needs to spend slaying prevents studying or even regular sleep. She wants to have a good relationship with her mother, Joyce, but believes that family secrets are necessary components of

> Strong is the soul, and wise, and beautiful:
> The seeds of godlike power are in us still:
> Gods are we, bards, saints, heroes, if we will.
> —Matthew Arnold, *Written in Emerson's Essays*

her life as the Slayer. (It's interesting that Buffy really seems to be wrong about this last bit; by the third season, she is more comfortable with her identity, and that is due in no small part to her finally being forced to let Joyce in on the secret.) Above all, she desires to be "destiny-free," as she puts it when she first receives her call to be the Slayer (an event we witness in flashback in 2.21). She'd like to have it all—Buffy says she wants to "date and shop and hang out and go to school and save the world from unspeakable demons. You know, I wanna do girlie stuff!" (3.3). That's easier said than done, however. Even in the third season, when Buffy's social life and Slayer duties are more integrated, she has to let go of some of her individual desires—pursuing a relationship with Angel, planning to attend college away from the Hellmouth—to serve the greater good.

Being the Slayer is not an easy gig, and throughout the series Buffy struggles with wanting a different, simpler kind of life. (It's a good thing, Faith and Buffy agree in the seventh season, that they are hot chicks with superpowers. It kind of takes the edge off the burden of Slayerhood; 7.21.) Despite her wishes, Buffy knows what she has to do: her job is to fight evil, even when it requires tremendous personal sacrifice. As she tells the Potential Slayers in the series finale "Chosen" (7.22), "I hate this. I hate being here. I hate that *you* have to be here. I hate that there's evil, and that I was chosen to fight it." But Buffy knows she always has a choice. *They* have a choice. And like Buffy, all of the Potentials choose to join the battle, laying down their lives if necessary.

The first-season finale is not the only time Buffy dies; there's another, even more powerful, sacrifice in "The Gift" (5.22), the fifth season's last episode. At some level Buffy has always known that this moment was coming; in fact, Joss Whedon had dropped an oblique hint of it two years earlier, in "Graduation Day (Part Two)" (3.22). In that episode's dream sequence, Faith says that Buffy is counting down to 730. Exactly 730 days later in the Buffyverse, the Slayer gives up her life to save the world. By that time, Buffy has had other intimations as well, including a vision quest in which the spirit of the First Slayer informed her that death was her gift. After initially rejecting this, Buffy resolves that even if the fight against Glory is hopeless and the world comes to an end, she'll leave it trying to save her sister. (This is an interesting contrast to Ben, who in the same episode chooses to do precisely the thing Buffy refuses to do—sacrifice Dawn to save his own skin.) Buffy's plan to stop Glory before the bloodletting ritual begins is shattered, however, so she seizes upon Plan B: to forfeit her life and use her own blood to close the portal. When Buffy realizes that she can avert the apocalypse in this way, she has a moment of utter clarity: this is the work she has to do. She dives off a high platform, arms extended in a cruciform position, and lays down her life in everyone's stead.

Buffy's most dramatic sacrifices are not always in choosing to die; one of her most demanding sacrifices came when she had to choose to kill. After Angel loses his soul in "Innocence" (2.14), becoming the dark Angelus once more, he starts killing again, tormenting Buffy by attacking her friends. (Joss Whedon has said that the episode is a thinly disguised metaphor for the way that some men become evil monsters after a sexual conquest.) But the emotionally vulnerable Buffy finds that she cannot slay Angelus when she has a golden opportunity. Stake in hand, facing a weakened foe (whom, in a moment of utterly poetic justice, she has disabled with a kick to the groin), Buffy chooses not to kill him. "You can't do it," he taunts her. "You can't kill me." She walks away, saying simply, "Give me time."

But by the end of the season, having endured his emotional torture and the grisly murder of high school teacher Jenny Calendar, Buffy is ready to do what she knows she must. In the season finale "Becoming (Part Two)" (2.22), Buffy has to kill Angel just moments after he has regained his soul and become her caring lover again. His human transformation has occurred moments too late (of course), because the Hellmouth has already been opened and Angel's blood is the only thing that can close it. She tells Angel to close his eyes—echoing the same words that Darla said to him when she first sired him as a vampire (2.21)—and then stabs him with all her might, sending him to hell. In having to destroy Angel, Buffy is nearly destroyed herself; the end of the episode sees her fleeing Sunnydale for a burdenless life of anonymity in Los Angeles. Giving her own life is one thing, but asking her to obliterate her greatest love is almost more than Buffy can bear. This sacrifice tests the very limits of her sense of identity.

"He Is Not a Lower Being": Angel

Of course, Buffy is not the only character who risks her life—and her own happiness—to serve others. Angel eventually returns from hell and continues to find his redemption in good works in Los Angeles, where he goes after he tells Buffy that they don't have a future together. In *Angel's* first season, he experiences a surprise response to the blood of a demon he has killed ("I Will Remember You," A1.8). The demon's blood, it turns out, has restorative properties that bring Angel back to life. He finds he has a heartbeat and can walk in broad daylight for the first time in more than two centuries. He is fully human again in every respect and can have what he's dreamed of having (a night with Buffy without losing his soul) and what he would have dreamed about had he been aware of its existence (a pint of cookie-dough fudge mint-chip ice cream). But when he realizes that he is of more use in saving the world as a melancholy, superhuman vampire than as a happy but comparably weak human being, he returns to the capricious Powers That Be and asks the oracles to restore his vampire state. The male oracle rather dismissively calls Angel "a lower being" and refuses to be concerned with his request, but the woman says this rebuff is wrong: "This one is willing to sacrifice every drop of human happiness and love he has ever known for another," she explains. "He is *not* a lower being." When Angel "swallows the day," turning back time twenty-four hours and carrying its memory

Angel (David Boreanaz), a brooding bodhisattva in black leather.

while all others, including Buffy, cannot recall it, he sacrifices his own joy and hopes of a future with the woman he loves. Before the time is reversed, he tries to explain his decision to Buffy, who is appalled by this news. But Angel doesn't want to be a liability to her or to the cause: "How can we be together if the cost is your life? Or the lives of others?" he asks her. After one last passionate kiss, the scene reverts to twenty-four hours earlier.

The female oracle is quite right: Angel is clearly not a lower being. In Mahayana Buddhist terms, his actions would qualify him as a bona fide bodhisattva, a being who has achieved an enlightened state but has chosen to sacrifice his own well-deserved nirvana for the good of others. Mahayana Buddhist art sometimes depicts the bodhisattva with one arm extended toward heaven and one reaching down to help other people, representing the bodhisattva's noble decision to seek enlightenment for all. Famous bodhisattvas include Kuan-Yin, a demigoddess of compassion, and—interestingly enough—one named Tara, probably the most popular Tibetan female deity. Tara, incidentally, is probably the character on *Buffy* who is the least self-centered and most conscious of others: she is, for example, the compassionate, nonjudgmental friend to whom Buffy confesses her ill-advised sexual relationship with Spike in "Dead Things" (6.13). Tara's whole being is suffused with kindness for others. Even her last words—"your shirt"— reflect her gentle concern that her blood has spattered onto Willow's blouse (6.19).

In Buddhism individuals strive to become bodhisattvas by asking themselves the same kind of question that Angel obviously posed to himself when he considered the possibility of a "normal" life. The question is not, "What will make me happiest?" but "How can I best be of service to others?" For Angel the answer lies in the lonely, gritty "City of Angels." He's a brooding bodhisattva in black leather, on a mission to save the lost in L.A.

'The One Who Isn't Chosen': Xander

Although they are the central figures in *Buffy* and *Angel*, Buffy and Angel are not the only characters who give of themselves to save others. Even in *Buffy*'s first episodes, Xander proved himself to be a courageous figure, risking his life to save his friend Jesse and help Buffy in "The Harvest" (1.2) or marching down to the Master's Lair in "Prophecy Girl" (1.12). Xander's heroism is all the more moving because he lacks Buffy's Slayer strength, Willow's skill in witchcraft, or Giles's extensive knowledge—he's an Everyman with heart. As Cordelia famously taunts him in "The Zeppo" (3.13), he seems like a fourth wheel, blundering along while Buffy attempts to keep him "fray-adjacent." In that same episode, however, Xander secretly saves the whole town of Sunnydale from a zombie gang and asks for neither credit nor reward. His friends don't even realize what he has done. Xander's style is to do his good works quietly—as when he anonymously buys a poverty-stricken Cordelia the prom dress she's been eyeing—rather than call attention to himself. As he points out to Dawn in "Potential" (7.12), the Scoobies who have special powers "never know how tough it is . . . to be the one who isn't chosen. To live so near to the spotlight and never step in it.

But I know. I see more than anybody realizes because nobody's watching me."

In "Triangle" (5.11) Xander valiantly hurls himself at the troll who is going to kill Anya and Willow in the Magic Box. Olaf the troll, impressed by this chivalry, offers Xander the chance to choose which of his women will be saved: his best friend, Willow; or his paramour, Anya. Just as Xander refused to side with either of the women in one of their fiery squabbles earlier in the episode, he declines to show any partiality now, although his noncompliance seems to spell certain death for all three of them. "That's insane troll logic," he snaps at Olaf, who becomes angry and attacks Xander instead. It's interesting that one act of self-sacrifice sparks another—just as Xander had risked his life to save Anya from the troll, she now offers her life in Xander's place, a surprising move for an ex-vengeance demon. Xander's love, and his willingness to die for his friends, increases the bonds between all of them.

On another occasion Xander's deep love saves not just his friends or the town of Sunnydale but the entire world. At the end of season six, when Willow has fully embraced the dark side and allowed her anger at Tara's death to consume her, she sets out to incinerate the planet (6.20-6.22). (It can be argued that this is a morally ambiguous act. Not purely evil, it may come out of a sense of misguided altruism: she seeks to end the terrible misery and suffering of others.) Xander, who has spent much of the last couple of episodes feeling inadequate—he couldn't stop Warren from shooting Tara, is confused about his feelings for Anya, and tells Dawn that he feels like running from a crisis —steps up to the plate in a major way. Placing himself in the path of the lightning bolts that snake out of Willow's fingers, Xander first tries to crack jokes to defuse the situation: "You're not the only one with powers, you know. You may be a hopped-up über-witch, but . . . this carpenter can drywall you into the next century." He says he knows that he is powerless to stop her from ending the world, but she is his best friend: "World gonna end. . . . Where else would I want to be?" he asks. "Is this the master plan?" Willow sneers. "You're gonna stop me by telling me that you *love* me?" Undeterred, Xander reminds his friend of their first day of kindergarten, when she broke a yellow crayon and was too ashamed to tell anyone. He has loved her ever since. "I loved crayon-breaky Willow and I love scary-veiny Willow. So if I'm going out, it's here. You wanna kill the world? Well, then start with me. I've earned that."

Willow reaches out her hand and magically wounds him without touching, lacerating his face and chest. Doubled over in pain, he still insists that he loves her and tries to step toward her. Each time Xander declares his love for his friend, her power to harm him diminishes, until finally Willow is unable to injure him and she crumples to the ground in tears. Xander, the show's gentle carpenter, has saved the world with his demonstration of unconditional love, echoing the sacrifice of another gentle carpenter of another time. And it's not just a warm, fuzzy, generic kind of love; this is person-specific and intimate. In one of the show's most explicitly Christian

> Our remedies oft in ourselves do lie
> Which we ascribe to heaven.
> —Shakespeare, *All's Well That Ends Well,*
> Act I, Scene I

references, the Prayer of Saint Francis of Assisi is sung after Xander's moving display of heroism. As Buffy and Dawn crawl out of a grave and Xander cradles the weeping Willow, singer Sarah McLachlan croons the saint's timeless invocation. Xander has been an instrument of peace, offering hope and forgiveness when he has been injured. His compassion and love for Willow, it turns out, are the strongest remedy of all for fighting evil.

Being a Bodhisattva

For Xander, Angel, Buffy, and other characters, self-sacrifice is not a sign of weakness but of strength: their altruism extends from a desire to see justice accomplished for others as well as themselves. It's not a heroism that is out of reach but an everyday heroism born of compassion. As Joss Whedon told an audience of fans in the summer of 2003, "We don't need heroes so much as recognizing ourselves as heroes."

We live in a culture that tends to put the individual first and chides those people who put their own desires aside to assist others. Some of these critiques are certainly valid; feminists, for example, raise important points when they note that historically women have been told that their needs were supposed to come last in the hierarchy of importance. This kind of gender imbalance easily leads to exploitation. But on *Buffy* it's not just women who give of themselves: Xander, Angel, Giles, and other male characters—even Spike—are willing to make tremendous sacrifices when it counts.

Buffy sends the message that when individuals choose to sacrifice themselves for others, it's a powerful good. That doesn't mean, however, that they can make the same choice for others. In the second season, we're treated to two back-to-back episodes in which people have wrongly tried to force someone into self-sacrifice: in "Inca Mummy Girl" (2.4), we encounter the heartache of a sixteen-year-old girl who was compelled to become a human sacrifice centuries ago. The very next episode, "Reptile Boy" (2.5), shows an eerily similar theme, as we see a fraternity make annual sacrifices of beautiful young women to appease a snake monster that grants them prosperity and success. Clearly, the series argues that it is wrong to make sacrifices, whether literal or metaphorical, of others against their will—but that there is great power when individuals selflessly make this decision on their own. One theme of the Buffyverse is that for human beings to realize their full potential and make the world a better place, an element of sacrifice is essential. It's just part of the human experience.

How, then, do we become bodhisattvas, beings who are more concerned with the welfare of others than we are with our own? In Buddhism this is not a onetime act

Lord make me an instrument of
  your peace;
Where there is hatred, let me
  sow love;
Where there is injury, pardon;
Where there is doubt, faith;
Where there is despair, hope;
Where there is darkness, light;
And where there is sadness,
  joy.
O divine master, grant that I
  may not so much seek to be
  consoled as to console—
To be understood as to
  understand,
To be loved as to love.
For it is in giving that we
  receive,
It is in pardoning that we are
  pardoned,
And it is in dying that we are
  born to eternal life. Amen.
  —Prayer of Saint Francis of Assisi

that emerges out of nowhere but the ongoing result of a lifelong discipline of compassion. Buddhists talk about cultivating *bodhicitta*, a method of developing loving-kindness in our relations with others and our understanding of ourselves. It's the idea that we can consciously seek to remove suffering from others on a daily basis, because as the Dalai Lama puts it, all persons desire happiness and do not desire suffering. In Buddhism those who are on the road to becoming bodhisattvas take a vow to remove suffering from all sentient beings (not just the ones they like or agree with, mind you, but *all* beings). They seek to put the vow into practice by consistently demonstrating virtues such as compassion, selflessness, and wisdom—and by staying in the dreary world rather than escaping into bliss.

Our own self-sacrifice will probably not involve saving the world by laying down our lives in a literal sense. But on *Buffy* the real pain, as Buffy tells Dawn, is often simply to live in the world. Buffy is called on to live for others, not just die for them: in the fifth season, for example, she has to push aside her own pain to help Dawn, who is in desperate need of guidance after Joyce's death (5.16ff.). Buffy doesn't want to do this and at times is downright surly about her responsibilities to Dawn, but she does it nonetheless. In the sixth season, she has to make a similar decision, choosing to remain with Dawn in the pain-filled world rather than trying to regain the paradise she lost before being wrenched back to earth. This is self-sacrifice too. Although it's certainly crucial that Buffy dies twice and risks her life countless times to save others, this sacrifice—to choose to embrace the pain of life in order to help her sister every day—may be the one we can most relate to.

Our own sacrifices may be far less visible than Buffy's, but like hers, they will spring from our decision to have compassion for others. Fundamentally, this begins with recognizing that others are in pain. As Philo said two thousand years ago, "Be kind, for everyone you meet is fighting a great battle." Or as Buffy puts it to Jonathan when she saves him from suicide in "Earshot" (3.18), even she understands about his pain. "Oh, right," he retorts. "'Cause the burden of being beautiful and athletic, that's a crippler." Buffy calls him an idiot for not realizing that he's not the only one who suffers: "My life happens to, on occasion, suck beyond the telling of it," she tells him. "Sometimes more than I can handle. And it's not just mine. Every single person down there is ignoring your pain because they're too busy with their own." Even the beautiful and popular ones are lonely and confused. "It looks quiet down there," Buffy says. "It's not. It's deafening." The pain of the world is overwhelming; as the First Noble Truth of Buddhism states, life is suffering. What remains is for us to show compassion for one another and to be heroes every day. Like Xander, we may not be Chosen with a capital *C*, but we always have the power to choose; and more often than not, we will surprise ourselves.

CHAPTER 2

Change Makes Us Human

Embracing the River of Change

"I haven't seen you in the killing fields for an age!" Spike tells Angelus when they meet after an absence of many decades (2.3). After a brief conversation, Spike becomes suspicious that Angelus is really Angel-with-a-soul, posing as Angelus, since he hasn't yet taken out the Slayer. "You're not . . . *housebroken?*" Spike says in horror. He punches Angel and launches into a verbal attack. "Things change," Angel says simply. The idea is abhorrent to Spike, who responds, "Not us! Not demons." Of course, the scene is ironic in hindsight because Spike becomes one of the characters on *Buffy* who most embodies change, as we will see. But in general, his statement is true for most demons: even if circumstances change, demons and vampires remain essentially stagnant. By extension, then, human beings are defined by change—it is an intrinsic feature of what makes us human. For the characters on *Buffy*, as well as for us, change is an opportunity for growth and greater spiritual maturity.

> Life is its own journey, presupposes its own change and movement, and one tries to arrest them at one's eternal peril.
> —*Laurens Van der Post,*
> Venture to the Interior

The Unchanging Demon . . . and Spike

In the Buffyverse a vampire is literally a walking corpse in which a demon has taken up residence. As Christopher Golden and Nancy Holder explain in the official *Watcher's Guide*, what makes vampires seem human is their "*capacity* for feeling emotion," but what makes them demons is their "inability to change. . . . They are what they are, and they remain that way." Although demons are sometimes morally valiant or sympathetic (Whistler in the second season or Clem in the sixth and seventh), most are slaves to some kind of self-centered "static goal," whether it is finding a tasty victim for the daily feeding, creating chaos, or attempting to dominate the world. Those goals don't usually change. Sometimes evil creatures' powerlessness to change is the very cause of their downfall: in a hilarious exchange in "The Harvest" (1.2), Buffy identifies vampires in a crowd of dancing people just by their "carbon-dated" clothing. ("Deal with that outfit for a moment. . . . Trust me. Only someone living underground for ten years would think *that* was still the look.") And in the second season, she is able to destroy the seemingly unconquerable Judge because of rocket-launcher technology that was not available six hundred years before, when he last enjoyed a reign of terror (2.14). Clearly, a refusal to keep pace with the times can be a serious liability.

Buffy continually stresses the idea that change, however painful and difficult, is necessary and good. Sometimes the changes we face are so distressing that we entertain an unthinkable alternative, which is simply to avoid change at all costs. A demonic sense of suspended animation actually begins to look appealing. In "Lies My Parents Told Me" (7.17), for example, we learn a bit more of Spike's history through flashbacks to his nineteenth-century life as William, who writes awful poetry that only a mother could love. His mother adores him, with a devoted and protective attachment that is unparalleled in William's life. But her health is failing, which is a source of grave concern to him. So when William joins the ranks of the undead, his first real act is a siring that has disastrous consequences: he makes his mum a vampire. "Think of it," he coaxes her. "No more sickness, no more dying. You'll never age another day. Let me do this for you. . . . It's all right, Mother. It's only me. We'll be together forever." This last line is particularly telling. Spike tries to use the siring as an opportunity to preserve the status quo for all time—loving mama and faithful son, infinitely bonded together. They will not grow old. What he has not foreseen is that the theft of her soul has also robbed her of any love for him—or the ability to love at all. She is planning to leave him. (She says of his poems, "You honestly thought I could bear an eternity listening to that twaddle?") Her taunts and cruel barbs are intolerable for him, and he stakes her. Spike's attempt at keeping things forever the same backfires so badly that he apparently does not sire another person until more than a century later, and even then only because he's under the influence of the First Evil.

Changelessness may seem superficially appealing, but the show consistently makes the point that to be human is to evolve. Again, Spike is (ironically enough) an excellent example: his character begins as a one-off villain, an insolent brute who is almost a caricature of a James Dean–style vampire maverick. But fans responded to the renegade bad boy that James Marsters played, and the character began a slow transformation that inched him ever closer toward humanity. This evolution is one of the show's defining story arcs—

> There is nothing permanent except change.
>
> —Heraclitus

and refreshingly subtle for TV. *Buffy* and *Angel* are so interesting because they posit the twist that very few demons are wholly evil; because "pure" demons are rare, most combine demonic and human qualities. Demons, including vampires, can vary considerably along the demonic-human continuum. The lives of some vampires, like Luke in the first season, are an unchanging litany of feeding times and bloodletting, the gorier the better. (Don't remember Luke from the first season? Well, that's precisely the point—predictable, purely evil vampires just don't make for very interesting TV.) But others, such as Harmony, are distinguished by just how much humanity they have retained. Well, *humanity* for Harmony may be a bit of a stretch, because even as a high schooler she was more known for cruel barbs than kindness; but as a vampire she still desires relationships, can be generous, and feels something like love for Spike.

If an ability to change is what makes us human, then Spike is definitely on the road to full humanity. Even before he decided to regain his soul, other changes had already humanized him, starting with his century-long love for Drusilla. In fact, in their first episode ("School

Hard," 2.3), Spike does his opening sequence in vamp face, bragging to the other vampires about Slayers he has killed. He seems at first glance to be all demon. But his face transforms into a human countenance when his beloved Drusilla enters the room; he expresses concern for her health, places his coat around her shoulders, and calls her "Princess." He's still an evil killer but one with shades of tenderness. Spike's humanity evolves further through losing Drusilla, getting the chip, working alongside Buffy, falling in love with her, and—perhaps most importantly—being rejected by her. Change is painful and slow, and sometimes it takes descending to rock bottom before we recognize the need for further transformation. Spike only comes to understand why he needs a soul after he comes close to raping Buffy near the end of the sixth season (6.19). "Things change," his demon friend Clem tells him. "They do," Spike responds, realizing something. "If you make them." He decides to make change happen and undergoes a painful quest for reensoulment in order to become the kind of man that Buffy deserves.

> Do not pursue the past. Do not lose yourself in the future. The past no longer is. The future has not yet come.
>
> —The Buddha

Through the last several years of the series, Spike is transformed from a soulless, blood-sucking vampire to a central character whose motivations are almost impossibly complex. He goes through stages of doing the right things for the wrong reasons (fighting demons in the fourth season because he needs an outlet for his violence and can no longer harm humans) to doing the right things for slightly better reasons (fighting demons in the fifth season because he's fallen in love with the Slayer) to doing the right things for reasons that are almost selfless. By the seventh season, the reensouled Spike is fighting demons because it's the moral thing to do. It's a sea change for him, and a courageous one, punctuated by his willingness to die for others in the series finale. On *Angel*, where his character first appears as a ghost, Spike learns that although he has changed tremendously, he still has more work ahead. For him a willingness to change by continuing to help others is not just the key ingredient in a better life. It is the only thing that seems to be keeping him out of the jaws of hell.

Change as a Catalyst for Growth: Willow, Xander, and Giles

In contrast to the usual demon, humans are in a constant state of flux. *Buffy*'s writers have always placed a premium on having their characters go through real changes, however painful: these kids would not be barren sitcom teens who find themselves stuck in high school for the better part of a decade. They would grow up and experience substantial heartache. Change is difficult, but change is good. "Nobody is what they are forever," Joss Whedon has said. "They change; their alliances change and sometimes dissolve."

In the fourth season, we see this most clearly in the lives of three central characters: Willow, Xander, and Giles. At the beginning of the season, Willow is the most excited at the prospect of the changes before them: she felt that in high school, "knowledge was pretty much frowned upon," but college finds her mind "just opening up" (4.1). She relishes the idea that college is going to be a challenge, but she does not yet realize that it will be most challenging emotionally, not intellectually. Willow goes through significant changes that year, losing her boyfriend Oz and then finding pure love in an entirely unexpected place—the arms of another woman. Willow also becomes more powerful in her ability to do witchcraft. As she attempts increasingly difficult spells, we see her struggling with her own confidence and defining her role. In "Fear, Itself" (4.4), a Halloween episode in which several of the principal characters have to confront their worst fears, Willow seems terrified of failure. When Buffy questions her competence to perform a complicated conjuring spell, Willow spits out, "I'm not your sidekick!" She is anxious to demonstrate her ability to save the gang and to prove her identity as an individual without Buffy. But the spell fails; her lack of decisiveness about where to direct the lights she conjured causes the lights to attack her instead. Willow does not quite know what she wants.

For Xander life after high school is a series of dead-end jobs and insecurity about his future. It begins promisingly with his taking a cross-country road trip to see all fifty states. (Buffy to Willow: "Did you explain about Hawaii?") But upon his return—having not gotten very far before the engine fell out of his car—the demands of grown-up life weigh on him acutely. He tries stints as a pizza delivery guy, bartender, candy salesman, ice cream truck driver, and construction worker. Throughout the season he is paying rent to his parents to sleep in their basement and not yet able to afford a place of his own. He also feels superfluous to his best friends, Willow and Buffy, who have moved on to college without him. In "Fear, Itself," that insecurity is manifested as actual invisibility: he becomes invisible to his friends. Xander's worst fear is that the people he cares about, who seem to be growing distant from him, will put him aside and ignore him.

For Giles the fourth season is all about his new role in relation to Buffy. After her graduation from high school (and his own sacking by the Council), Giles initially enjoys a heady period of freedom from responsibility. Willow calls him a "gentleman of leisure," and he seems to revel in his liberty: he brings a woman back to his apartment, takes up jogging, and even subscribes to a motorbiking magazine. But it isn't long before he feels underutilized, even pointless, as Buffy takes seriously Giles's pronouncement that she can handle things without him. He finds himself out of touch with the Scoobies and is the last to know about the Initiative and about Buffy's relationship with her new boyfriend Riley. In "The Yoko Factor" (4.20), Spike taunts Giles about being irrelevant, saying that Buffy treats him "very much like a retired librarian." Giles succumbs to this mocking because he feels unwanted, and he wonders about the next step.

Although these changes are agonizing for *Buffy*'s characters, almost all of them prove to be positive. Willow emerges in the fifth season as a stronger, more self-assured young woman who is in a stable and loving relationship. Xander settles on a career in construction and turns out to have a genuine talent for it: after boarding up Buffy's living room window after a robot attack, Xander prattles on about how the "The jamb can be shimmed to be square" (5.15). Buffy is amused and taken aback by his expertise. "Shimmed?" she teases him. "Is that even a real word? Do you have any idea what you're talking about?" Xander smiles. "Yeah, I do. Scary, isn't it? I think I've actually turned into someone you want around after a crazed robot attack." Xander's changes aren't just professional but personal, as he allows his relationship with Anya to deepen and snags a terrific apartment for them to share. Giles, bereft of formal duties as Watcher, moves on to a second career as a shopkeeper, finding satisfaction in his new small business, the Magic Box. None of these developments would have been possible without the angst-ridden growth of the fourth season.

No matter how difficult change is, we often see (usually later, with benefit of hindsight) that the far more alarming prospect is that of standing still. Interestingly, in the fourth-season finale "Restless" (4.22), this theme is highlighted in the dreams of all three characters. Willow's dream takes her back to high school (where else?), where we see her underlying fear that despite her newfound power, confidence in love, and maturity, at some level she remains an insecure high school kid. (Ever mindful of continuity, the show's writers even put her in an outfit similar to the one she wore in the pilot episode.) Willow is terrified—not of change but of not having changed at all. The same theme echoes in Xander's dream, where no matter what he does, he always finds himself back in his parents' basement. And Giles seems torn between moving ahead with his own future—represented by Olivia and the baby carriage—and his old duties as Watcher. ("Gotta make up your mind, Rupes," Spike tells him.) Clearly, the real terror is not change but stagnation.

Impermanence as an Opportunity

The theme of change as a catalyst for growth is present not only in *Buffy*'s story arc but also behind the scenes. Joss Whedon and other writers were disappointed, for example, when popular actor Seth Green (Oz) elected to leave the show in the fourth season to pursue a film career. However, his departure gave the writers "an opportunity to make changes that might not have otherwise happened," Whedon explained. "It gave a chance to bring in Amber [Benson, who played Tara] who turned out to be a wonderful addition to our show." That unanticipated casting change made way for a story development that no one had predicted: Willow's emerging self-understanding as a lesbian.

In the world of TV-as-usual, formulas are comforting: the guy gets the girl; the heroine saves the day; the villain gets his comeuppance. *Buffy*, by contrast, follows no such formula. Central characters suddenly bite the dust, and once-evil miscreants sometimes engage in selfless acts. There are no sacred cows, no arenas into which the writers will not venture. The *only* constant on this show is change. Writer

James Collier says that *Buffy*'s goal has always been "to keep the characters in a state of constant evolution." But fans are often uncomfortable with the show's sudden shifts in direction. For example, many fans were upset about Willow's coming out, mourning the loss of Oz and wondering aloud about her new direction. Writer and producer Marti Noxon remarked, "People are resistant to change, and the ironic part of that is good drama only comes through change."

In our own lives as well as in TV writing, the best growth usually happens because of change. The challenge is to remain open to what change has to teach us rather than simply rejecting it outright and remaining forever in our comfort zones. Change is an opportunity, jump-starting us for maturity and further development. Buddhism, which emphasizes the dangers of attachment (generally, this means attachment to circumstances, not to people), offers a helpful perspective on this. In traditional Buddhist parlance, this notion of the shifting nature of the world is called impermanence. Buddhism does not require that people become stoic or emotionless in the face of inevitable change; it demands that they recognize the impermanence of all things and welcome the advent of new experiences. Suffering is caused by believing that the way things are is the way they will or should always be; Buddhism teaches that we can alleviate our suffering when we let go of that illusion of permanence.

> God changes not what is in a people, until they change what is in themselves.
>
> —Qur'an 13:11

Vietnamese monk Thich Nhat Hanh says that instead of viewing impermanence as an obstacle or something to fear, we should see it as an opportunity: "If a grain of corn is not impermanent, it can never be transformed into a stalk of corn," he reminds us. Change helps us recognize that we are not ultimately in control of our circumstances and that we have to relinquish the illusion of control. Change can move us forward to new levels and show us the seeds of greater things that may lie in the future.

In fact, unexpected change—usually in the negative form of a loss or an illness—often propels many of us to undertake the spiritual path in the first place. In *Letting Go of the Person You Used to Be*, Lama Surya Das reminds us that it was only when Siddhartha was exposed to suffering and injustice for the first time that he decided to seek spiritual enlightenment, thereby gaining nirvana and becoming the Buddha. The change and loss all around him acted as a catalyst to bring him to spiritual awakening. Although Das points out that such aphorisms as "Time heals all wounds" and "What doesn't kill us makes us stronger" are shallow and even infuriating, it is true that we need to find mature, enlightened ways of dealing with change and transitions. "No one asks for their life to change, not really," says the demon Whistler in "Becoming (Part One)" (2.21). Although we don't usually appreciate change when it comes, we have to learn to trust the process and allow for growth. As the pre-Socratic philosopher Heraclitus said, we cannot step into the same river twice, for other waters are constantly flowing on to us. When we embrace the river of change and flow with its currents, we will recognize that it is not just the river that is fluid— we are changing as well.

Death Is Our Gift

What Death Can Teach Us About Living

It is good to have a reminder of death before us, for it helps us to understand the impermanence of life on this earth, and this understanding may aid us in preparing for our own death.

—*Black Elk*

Every person reading this book has something in common, something most of us prefer not to acknowledge: we are all going to die. Each of us will someday face the moment of our own death, which may come as a long-awaited friend, an intensely feared enemy, or an unwelcome surprise visitor. When Buffy, searching for answers about her life and heart, goes on a vision quest in the desert, she is told that death is her gift (5.18). She rejects this immediately: "Death is not a gift," she protests. "If I have to kill demons because it makes the world a better place, then I kill demons. But it's not a gift to anybody." Buffy fears death and renounces the notion that it can be beneficial. But in the fifth season, we also see her coming to terms with the fact that some part of her actually longs to die, to lay down the lonely burden of being the Slayer and find some peace. When she grills Spike about his past murders of two Slayers, he reveals that this secret yearning was their fatal flaw: a part of every Slayer is always

24

"just a little bit in love with" the idea of death, a weakness he has twice exploited (5.7).

Like Buffy in the fifth and sixth seasons, most of us feel some mixture of dread and longing about our own deaths. Death awaits us with a stark inevitability, a seemingly indisputable finality. Most of the world's religions have taken up the idea of death and what, if anything, lies beyond it. *Buffy* certainly posits that there are heavens and hells—untold dimensions about which we know very little. For such a deeply metaphysical show, *Buffy* says surprisingly little about the afterlife that it presumes to exist. However, the show has quite a bit to say about how the ultimate reality of death should inform the human experience here and now. For spiritual growth an important and immediate question is: What can we learn from the knowledge that we are going to die? It is essential that we permit the truth of our fleeting nature to animate our lives while we are here. Or as Buffy says to Willow in the very first episode of the series, "Life is short. . . . Seize the moment. 'Cause tomorrow, you might be dead!"

Death as the Enemy

Buffy has always been one of the more death-obsessed shows on television. In the pilot episode Buffy is tossed into a coffin next to a decaying body and has to fight her way out by defeating an attacking vampire. This early scene foreshadows the show's ongoing preoccupation with death: Buffy dies twice; Spike and Angel died long ago; Joyce dies suddenly and unexpectedly. Joyce's death may be the most instructive for us, because "The Body" (5.16) is one of the only episodes that is almost devoid of supernatural villains, mirroring our own situation. (I'm guessing that you and I are far more likely to die of natural causes than from a vampire bite or a plunge into a portal of mystical energy.) Until Buffy slays one token vampire in the morgue at the end of the episode, there are no monsters, no creatures to fight. There is only death, the monster that has taken her mother so abruptly—and it's the one monster that Buffy can't overcome. The episode is brilliant in its depiction of the shock, confusion, and rage that people might experience in the hours immediately after a death: Buffy engages in a couple of fantasy sequences in which she imagines herself having saved Joyce's life in the nick of time. Willow has a breakdown and an identity crisis about being a grown-up, all centered around choosing a shirt. Giles remains outwardly strong for Buffy and the Scoobies, keeping his grief private until the next episode, when he can sit alone with his music and his memories. Xander refuses to believe that the death was natural and wants to find someone to blame—Glory, the doctors who let Joyce come home from the hospital, anyone. "We don't have enough monsters in this town that doctors have to help them out?" he fumes. In a rage, Xander punches his hand through a wall.

Perhaps the most poignant reaction comes from Anya, who has only recently reentered the realm of mortality herself and is having a hard time grasping what death is: "I mean I don't understand . . . how we go through this," she says. "I mean, I knew her, and now she's . . . There's just a *body*. And I don't understand why she just can't get in it and not be dead anymore." Anya is disturbed and terrified by the irrevocability of Joyce's death. "I was having fruit punch," she mourns, "and I thought, well, Joyce will never have any more fruit punch, ever. And she'll never have eggs, or yawn, or brush her hair, not ever. And no one will explain to me why!"

In typical fashion, the transparent Anya voices the pain and anxiety that the others are experiencing but don't discuss openly. She wants life to return to the way it has been, and she articulates the familiar refrain of many people when a death brushes their lives: a lament that the deceased person will never again enjoy the ordinary pleasures of mortality. Death comes as an enemy, removing the ones we love and snatching us away from the life we know. It is appallingly permanent. Even religions that teach a resurrection of the body do not posit that we will simply return to the old life unscathed. (Jesus, for example, seems to have been so physically changed by the experience that even his disciples did not recognize him when he returned.) Even when we are deeply comforted by our beliefs about the afterlife, when we lose those we love, death feels immutable. It is the ultimate and apparently final change—and as we saw in Chapter Two, change is often difficult to face. "Death is change, and change is always fearful as well

> What benefit is there in being frightened and scared of that which is unalterable?
>
> —The Buddha

as challenging," writes novelist and poet Madeleine L'Engle. "Until we can admit the fear, we cannot know the assurance, deep down in our hearts, that indeed, we are *not* afraid."

Death as a Teacher

Because she has not been as close to Joyce as some of the other characters, Anya begins recovering relatively quickly from the shock of the death. She also allows it to make its mark in her life. In "Forever" (5.17) Anya turns from grief and loss with a renewed zest for living. After she and Xander make love, he comments that the experience was more intense than usual, and she responds that this is "because of Joyce." Anya has been thinking quite a bit about death and about how birth and death are interrelated. Reflecting this way, she says, "makes death a little less sad, sex a little more exciting." Xander does not initially understand her point ("Again I say: 'Huh?'"). "It's just that I think I understand sex more now," she explains. "It's not just about two bodies smooshing together. It's about life. It's about making life." She knows she's not ready to make life yet—which is a relief to Xander—but she enjoys knowing she could. "It all makes me feel like we're a part of something bigger. Like I'm more awake somehow, you know?"

Joyce's death has made Anya "more awake" and has driven her to appreciate the gift of life. In subtle ways other characters are also moved to cherish life while they are immersed in it. Willow, we find, is now keeping a journal. "Life goes by so fast," she tells Tara. "If you don't write stuff down, it just gets lost. And I want to remember." Every detail is important, she now realizes—even what she and Tara ate for breakfast.

Willow's determination to record and relish everyday events encapsulates the chief lesson we all need to learn from death: appreciation. The knowledge of eventual death can deepen our enjoyment of every impermanent delight we encounter. When lilacs bloom gorgeously for only ten days, their very transience means that we are sure to put other things aside and drink in their scent while we have the chance. Every parent knows this lesson well: as our children grow up, time seems to accelerate, and we find ourselves thinking longingly of the days when they were learning to walk or struggling with their first words. Every change in a child is both a celebration and a loss. We mourn the passing of babyhood even as we cheer our children on to new accomplishments. And as we watch them grow, the lessons of our own mortality seem to be brought into sharper relief. We know we had better pay attention to this child, and this moment, because the instant will soon disappear, never to return.

The knowledge that death is coming, whether imminently or eventually, can help us express our deepest feelings to those we love. The end of the fourth season contains a comic but poignant instance of this. As they gear up for their ultimate battle with Adam, Buffy and Willow are thrilled to see Xander safe and sound, and they embrace him heartily (4.21). "You know we love you, right?" Buffy asks. "We totally do!" Willow chimes in. "Oh God," says Xander fearfully. "We're gonna die, aren't we?" He suspects that their affectionate greeting means the end must be near. Knowing that death might be imminent forces the Scoobies, who have been at odds with one another through much of the season, to put aside their differences and embrace one another for what may be the last time.

Death is a teacher, a reminder of impermanence. It calls us to a heightened awareness of the world around us. As Thich Nhat Hahn explains, "If we really understood and remembered that life was impermanent, we would do everything we could to make the other person happy right here and right now." If we let it, death can be our greatest instructor, reminding us of why we are here and the higher purpose we serve.

Preparing for Death

Learning from death begins with our acknowledgment of its eventual reality: as Buffy tells Giles, "it's OK to use the *D* word" (5.7). Many people stubbornly refuse to recognize their own mortality, which means that they forfeit the possibility of fruitful and rich reflection on life. We spend a lot of energy convincing ourselves that death does not exist. As the Christian writer Philip Yancey says, "We dress up our corpses in new clothes, embalm them, and bury them in airtight caskets and concrete vaults to slow natural decay. We act out a stubborn reluctance to yield to this most powerful of life experiences." Many people recoil from death to such an extent that they cannot spiritually prepare for it.

It's no accident that both Buddhist and Christian monks have been trained for centuries to meditate on death. Great paintings often depict Saint Jerome with a skull and a crucifix, reminders of his future death and the past death of his Lord. Other symbolic warnings of life's fleeting nature—a half-burned candle, an hourglass—often surround the aged saint. The point of these paintings is to demonstrate how Jerome, one of the Christian tradition's most vibrant intellects, regularly contemplated his own passing—and to encourage us to do the same. In a similar vein, many Buddhists find it helpful to meditate on impermanence. Some Tibetan monks actually use bone fragments in their prayer beads to remind themselves of mortality. Although the practice may appear strange to us, it is not morbid; it is realistic. As Lama Surya Das explains, "Tibetan practitioners regularly prepare for death. Yet this does not mean that they are fatalistic and negative about life." No person on the spiritual path should deny that death is coming.

> Never send to know for whom the bell tolls; it tolls for thee.
>
> —John Donne, *Devotions Upon Emergent Occasions*, no. 6

However, it is also not good to dwell on death or be so paralyzed by fear of it that we cannot function. Time and again in the series, Buffy must overcome her fear of death just to fulfill her duty as the Slayer. In the first season, she sets aside her dread and accepts the prophesied showdown with the Master, even though the prophecy says she will be killed in the conflict (1.12). In the fifth season, she realizes that she can't run from Glory and has to come face-to-face with her. Buffy is able to confront her fear of death and let it improve her fighting. She does not deny that the terror exists, but she has learned to overcome it. In contrast, the observant villain Adam notes in "Who Are You?" (4.16) that the creatures who seem to fear death the most are those who have once cheated it: vampires. "Being immortal, you fear it more than those to whom it comes naturally," he comments. "Demon in a human body, you walk in both worlds and belong to neither." It's an astute observation. Vampires fear death because their very existence as "undead"—neither living nor dead—undermines the natural order. As Angel puts it, he's "dying to get rid of" immortality, because "a lot of things that seem strong and good and powerful . . . can be painful" ("Earshot," 3.18).

Buffy soon has her own experience of cheating death, which unleashes a host of ambiguities and emotional issues. At the close of the fifth season, as we've seen, she nobly sacrifices her life to seal off the mystical energy portal that Glory opened, knowing that it would have destroyed the world (5.22). Although Buffy once rejected the idea that death would be her gift, when the time comes, she discovers that she knows exactly what to do and is at peace with herself. "This is the work that I have to do," she tells Dawn before diving into the portal. The season ends with scenes of her friends, including a devastated Spike, sobbing. We see a final shot of Buffy's tombstone. She is gone.

But Willow, Xander, Tara, and Anya are not content to let her rest in peace; so Willow conducts a dangerous spell to raise Buffy from the dead (6.1). After spending four months in heaven, returning to earth seems like hell for her. Buffy has to deal with numerous real-world responsibilities: finding a job (and a rotten one at that), paying the bills that have piled up since Joyce's death, taking care of Dawn. She also has to deal with the peculiarly violent nature of her supernatural role as the Slayer; the savagery of the Hellmouth seems a harsh sentence

> O Earth, you're too wonderful for anyone to ever realize you! Do any human beings ever realize life while they live it? Every, every minute?
>
> —Emily in Thornton Wilder's *Our Town*

after the perfect peace she has experienced in paradise. She finds she cannot face life. In the brilliant musical episode "Once More, with Feeling" (6.7), she sings about sleepwalking through her life's endeavor, about wanting to feel alive but being numb to the world around her. Her friends, who think she has been in a hell dimension instead of a paradise, believe that Buffy is suffering from a sort of mystical version of posttraumatic stress syndrome: "She came from the grave much graver," Anya sings.

Buffy finds herself immune to the simple joys of life—"family and friends" and, most significantly, "knowing that it ends." Life *should* come to an end eventually. Buffy's depression arises at least in part because her friends didn't understand that her death should have been a permanent separation and that she was in a better place. Buffy was happier when she could rely on the fundamental truth that human beings both fear and cling to: death is final and therefore gives sweetness to life. Her resurrection subverts the natural, reassuring rhythm of life and death, because her friends—in a curious mixture of selfishness and altruism—refused to let her remain in the grave.

Buffy has previously confided in the one person in her circle of friends who is personally familiar with death—Spike. Now, ironically, it is Spike who coaxes her back into some measure of vitality: "You have to go on living," he sings to her, explaining that her pain will only diminish by engaging with life again, not by detaching herself. The episode closes with Buffy and Spike passionately kissing, beginning a sexual relationship that Buffy knows is destructive and degrading but seems powerless to stop. She just wants to feel *something*, and the emotional and physical pain of her relationship with Spike connects her, at least for a short time, with a capacity to feel.

Buffy's degeneration in the sixth season is painful to watch. Actress Sarah Michelle Gellar has said numerous times that she disliked the story arc that season and thought it was too dark. "It wasn't who Buffy was, or why people loved her," she told *Entertainment Weekly*. "You don't want to see that dark heroine; you don't want to see her punishing herself. . . . It didn't feel like the character that I loved." The season showed Buffy isolated from her friends and incapable of feeling genuine emotion. Writer and producer Marti Noxon has called the sixth season Buffy's "dark night of the soul"—and with good reason. The experience of death—and more significantly, what Buffy felt was an unnecessary rebirth—have rendered her incapable of feeling alive, and the ensuing episodes dissect her slow and painful rejuvenation.

But Buffy learns from this experience. After struggling with her return to this world for most of the season, she has an unexpected epiphany in the finale, "Grave" (6.22). When she crawled out of her grave some months earlier, Buffy now tells Giles, she left a part of herself behind. "I don't understand . . . why I'm back," she confides. She knows that she died at the right time, doing what she was called to do. So why is she back, enduring the pain of life? Giles has no answer to give her.

At the close of the episode, however, Buffy discovers that answer for herself. After the apocalypse has been averted (again), she finds herself crying tears of joy, rejoicing that she has enough life in her to want the world to continue. The visual continuity of the opening and concluding images of season six is startling: whereas in "Bargaining (Part Two)" (6.2), a confused and animal-like Buffy scratched her way out of her grave alone, now she and Dawn claw their way eagerly to life together. When Buffy emerges from the grave this time, she does so with a renewed understanding of her mission: "Things have really sucked lately, but it's all gonna change," she tells Dawn. "And I want to be there when it does. . . . I want to see you grow up. The woman you're going to become. Because she's going to be beautiful. And she's going to be powerful. I got it so wrong. I don't want to protect you from the world. I want to show it to you." Buffy has found her calling, the reason for her return to earth. It's not to be the Slayer or to rid the world of evil creatures, but to show her sister the beauty of life. Through death and rebirth, Buffy has come full circle and can once again embrace this world.

As with Buffy's eventual understanding, a realistic sense of death will give us insight into the meaning of life and our purpose for being here. (Hopefully, we will not have to endure even a fraction of the pain she went through before arriving at that conclusion.) As the Dalai Lama writes, "It is better to decide from the beginning that you will die and investigate what is worthwhile. If you keep in mind how quickly this life disappears, you will value your time and do what is valuable."

CHAPTER 4

"The Anger Gives You Fire"

Can Negative Emotions Be Constructive?

> You will not be punished for your anger; you will be punished by your anger.
> —The Buddha

"If we could live without passion, maybe we'd know some kind of peace," says a voice-over in *Buffy*'s second season, "but we would be hollow. Empty rooms, shuttered and dank. . . . Without passion, we'd be truly dead." The fact that the voice is that of the evil Angelus doesn't make the statement less true. Without passion our lives would be worth little—easy, safe, and predictably boring. *Buffy* never adopts the stoic position that passions, which we will refer to as strong emotions, are inherently harmful and to be avoided at all costs. Neither, however, does the series give license to Angelus's approach of giving full sway to unchecked emotions, especially negative and destructive ones. Rather, Buffy and her friends carefully negotiate those two extremes, searching for what the Buddha would have called the middle way. The show offers some insightful clues about a balanced approach to incorporating emotions—even negative ones—into a spiritual life. In this chapter we'll consider an emotion that crops up often in the series: anger. On *Buffy* anger can be a tool that provides much-needed strength for fighting, but it can easily lead to self-destruction if it is not governed by reason.

'My Emotions Give Me Power': Buffy and Kendra

Buffy's second season introduces a character who entirely refuses to give place to anger or any other emotion. In the two-part episode "What's My Line?" (2.9–2.10), a new Slayer shows up in Sunnydale. Kendra's sudden appearance makes Buffy question her own approach to slaying, because the two young women are so different. Giles in particular seems impressed by the dedicated newcomer, who studies meticulously, reads his kind of fusty ancient texts, and even obeys her Watcher. She adheres to everything in the Slayer handbook, whereas Buffy didn't even know that a handbook existed. Buffy is skeptical about her: "Get a load of the she-Giles," she quips.

The young women's different approach leads to an invigorating discussion about emotions and their role in a Slayer's life: Kendra views them as distractions and reveals that she has never been allowed to have proper friends. She was sent away from her Jamaican village early in life and can't even remember what her parents looked like. She thinks that this kind of detachment is the ideal for which all Slayers should strive: "Emotions are weakness, Buffy," she warns. "You shouldn't entertain them."

"Kendra, my emotions give me power," Buffy counters. "They're total assets." Buffy maintains that although Kendra's physical technique is flawless, Buffy would have defeated Kendra in the end, because Kendra has "no imagination." She's a human automaton, a textbook-taught Slayer functioning on a regimen of mindless obedience and removal from real human interaction. To prove her point, Buffy taunts Kendra and makes her angry—and then points out how much better Kendra would do if she permitted a little dose of fury to inform her fighting. "You feel it, right? How the anger gives you fire? A Slayer needs that." The implication is that anger can make a Slayer strong: used wisely, it can be a powerful tool in the service of good. In fact, Kendra learns this lesson well enough that she lets herself get incensed by a vampire skirmish at the end of the episode. When a vampire slashes Kendra's blouse, she is furious: "Dat's me favrit shirt! Dat's me *only* shirt!" she exclaims menacingly. Her fighting is improved by this sudden burst of passion, and she defeats her foe in no time.

Anger can, at least momentarily, make us feel strong and in command. In "Never Kill a Boy on the First Date" (1.5), Buffy is enraged when she thinks that a vampire has murdered Owen, the pensive poet with whom she's been trying to have a normal evening. "You killed my date!" she bellows at the vampire. Willow notices that Owen is in fact gaining consciousness and is about to tell Buffy this when Xander stops her. "Just give her a sec!" he implores, watching as Buffy furiously kicks, punches, and finally cremates the vampire she thought was responsible for Owen's death. Xander knows that in this situation, Buffy's anger is making her more effective and that she's a better warrior for it.

> The person who controls her anger, reining it in as though it were a runaway chariot, is a true charioteer, unlike those who loosely hold onto the reins.
>
> —The Dhammapada

In "The Freshman" (4.1), anger again helps Buffy defeat a formidable opponent. In this case the enemy is Sunday, who leads vampires in preying on college freshmen (after all, "No one can eat just one") and stealing their belongings. Having been humiliated by Sunday once before, Buffy finds her anger mounting when she discovers that her dorm room has been emptied of all her possessions. When she spies Sunday and the other vampires trying on her clothes and playing with her stuffed pig, Mr. Gordo, Buffy is incensed, but she has a tough time fighting Sunday, who injures Buffy and taunts her. The turning point comes when Sunday stomps on Buffy's Class Protector Award, the small umbrella she received for helping her high school class achieve the lowest mortality rate in Sunnydale High's history. Fueled by her anger at this low blow, Buffy begins fighting back—hard. "When you look back at this, in the three seconds it'll take you to turn to dust," she tells Sunday, "I think that you'll find the mistake was touching my stuff." Sunday is history.

'Anger Leads to Hate': The Danger of Rage

As Buffy's example shows, anger is not wrong in and of itself, and its very presence can be a sign that we've rightly perceived an injustice. It's fine to feel angry at others when they behave poorly or hurt us, and it's proper to use that anger as a catalyst for righting the wrong. As the spirituality writer Thomas Moore explains, anger "strengthens our resolve" and "can help us make important decisions." As Buffy puts it, emotions can give us power.

But anger can also be destructive; as the trite-but-true saying goes, anger is only one letter short of danger. Xander is mostly joking when he tells Buffy in "The Freshman" that "anger leads to hate" and "hate leads to anger." He's confused by his own circular logic, and Buffy chuckles that this is just a "dadaist pep talk." But Xander's also on to something: anger and hatred are inextricably connected. Anger that is out of control can spiral into a hate-filled rage that destroys everything it touches.

We see this clearly in *Buffy*'s third season, when Kendra's foil (and to a large extent, Buffy's) appears in Sunnydale in the form of Faith, another Slayer (3.3). Called into service after Kendra's death, Faith is Kendra's emotional opposite: she is entirely driven by her appetites and passions. The shooting script's stage directions describe her as "young, loose and fast, 18-ish, biker type meets trailer park." She's a wild high school dropout, and unlike Buffy, she actually loves slaying; she gets a heady rush from violence and enjoys feeling powerful. "When I'm fighting, the whole world goes away, and I only know one thing: I'm gonna win, and they're gonna lose," she tells Buffy's mom, Joyce. "I like that feeling." She says that she's always "hungry and horny" after killing vampires, suggesting that her chief appetites—for violence, food, and sex—are interrelated and always at the forefront of her mind. Her taste for violence is so strong that she continues to pummel vampires long after she could have staked them, to feel the full extent of her power and to work off some of the rage and unexpressed grief inside her. Faith's motivations for eventually moving over to "the dark side" are complex—she has never felt the love of a parent, and she revels in the avuncular affection that the Mayor lavishes upon her; she is jealous of Buffy and wants some of what Buffy has. But she also *enjoys* rage. Although she eventually undergoes a painful redemption and moral regeneration (which we'll explore in a later chapter), Faith is susceptible to evil in the first place because she has allowed anger and a lust for power to take a prominent hold on her life. She has never successfully balanced her emotions but is driven by pleasure only; anger is actually gratifying because it makes Faith feel powerful.

> Be angry but do not sin; do not let the sun go down on your anger.
>
> —Ephesians 4:26

Other major characters, including those fighting at Buffy's side, also sometimes struggle with anger and even rage. In "Passion" (2.17) Giles composedly tells Buffy that although Angelus is stalking and terrorizing her, she cannot lose emotional control: "Buffy, I understand your concern, but it's imperative that you keep a level head through all this," he lectures. "As the Slayer you don't have the luxury of being a slave to your passions. You mustn't let Angel get to you, no matter how provocative his behavior may become." Giles's advice is simply to ignore Angelus's actions, even if they are intended to cruelly intimidate.

But when Giles is on the receiving end of Angelus's reign of terror, he doesn't follow his own counsel. After discovering the body of his love interest, Jenny Calendar, he knows that Angelus is responsible for the murder. And Giles—that stuffy, bookish, scone-y Watcher—utterly loses control. Although his character is typically reserved and hyper-rational (Willow remarks in episode 3.3 that whenever Giles gets mad, he's too English to say anything and just makes a "cluck cluck" sound with his tongue), he now goes hunting for Angelus with his best weapons, endangering himself. The same man who earlier told Buffy that she did not have the luxury of being a slave to her passions has become his own cautionary tale. Now a servant of his fury and his desire for revenge, he has become very much like Angelus. This temporary loss of control almost costs Giles his life.

'That Would Be Anger You're Feeling': Acknowledging and Expressing Anger

Near the close of the fifth season, the magical barrier between Ben, a young hospital intern, and the well-shod hell god Glory begins to break down (5.21). As Glory is engulfed by "all the bile" of human emotion, she begins to buckle under its weight. People aren't even animals, she complains: "They're just these meatbaggy slaves to . . . to hormones and pheromones and . . . their feelings! Hate 'em!" She rages on that human beings are useless puppets, driven by their emotions. "Call me crazy, but as hard-core drugs go, human emotion is just useless! People are puppets! Everyone getting jerked around by what they're feeling. Am I wrong?"

She's not entirely wrong. As Giles's example shows, human emotions and passions can be so powerful that they transform us into someone we don't recognize. All of us are constantly struggling to balance our emotions, and anger is one of the most powerful feelings of all. As Thich Nhat Hanh warns in his book *Anger,* for example, "Anger is a living thing" and can easily overwhelm us if we allow it to. Too much anger can poison a spiritual life, and Hanh cautions that it can even kill us. In *Buffy* we see a visualization of the dangerous effects of anger every time a vampire gets ticked off: the vampire's face transforms from a human countenance to that of a monster. It's an apt image for the way rage sometimes manifests itself in our lives.

How are we to cope with our anger? The first task lies in admitting it, because the anger that we don't allow ourselves to acknowledge or understand is the anger that is most likely to become destructive. It's sometimes surprising how much dormant anger exists beneath our serene surfaces. The episode "Doppelgängland" (3.16) opens with Willow levitating a pencil as she and Buffy relax on the high school grounds. "It's all about emotional control," she tells Buffy, proud of her achievement. When their conversation turns to Faith, Buffy senses that Willow, who seems calm, doesn't want to talk about her. "No, it's OK," Willow insists. "It doesn't bother me." But the pencil goes whizzing out of control and stabs a nearby tree—reflecting Willow's withheld but deep-seated anger toward Faith.

Recognizing the presence of anger is a fine first step. We then have to find appropriate ways to express it, ideally by understanding its roots. Often this involves tactfully but firmly confronting the person who caused it. William Blake put this well in the poem "A Poison Tree":

> I was angry with my friend;
> I told my wrath, my wrath did end.
> I was angry with my foe;
> I told it not, my wrath did grow.

If anger is not communicated appropriately, it will fester and grow, finding ways to lash out surreptitiously.

Many times the characters on *Buffy* express their anger responsibly. In "Innocence" (2.14) Willow is hurt and angry after she's discovered Xander kissing Cordelia in the library. Despite the fact that Xander has always hated Cordelia (and is in fact treasurer of the We Hate Cordelia Club), he is sexually attracted to her, something Willow cannot understand. But Willow is able to put aside her own hurt for the time being in the interest of helping Buffy defeat the Judge. "Let's get this straight," she lectures Xander. "I don't understand it, I don't wanna understand it, you have gross emotional problems, and things are *not* OK with us. But what's happening right now is more important than that." Willow is honest and assertive without being vengeful or full of rage. She is able to put her feelings into perspective and do what needs doing—a sharp contrast to the Willow of the fifth season, who vengefully attacks Glory ("I owe you pain!") for hurting Tara (5.19) or the Willow of the sixth season, who allows rage to so consume her that she loses her humanity (6.20–6.22). In her struggles with anger, Willow goes from being a girl who suggests to Buffy that "it's a good idea to count to ten when you're angry" ("Phases," 2.15) to a young woman who is capable of flying into a fury and destroying the world.

> **Anger is a short madness.**
> —Horace, *Epistles*

Xander, too, sometimes struggles with the best way to appropriately express anger. In the first-season finale, "Prophecy Girl" (1.12), he conquers his own anger and feelings of rejection to help Buffy serve the greater good. After finally mustering the courage to ask Buffy out, Xander painfully discovers that his romantic feelings for her are not reciprocated. She says no to a dating relationship, and he thinks he knows why: she has fallen for Angel. "I guess a guy's gotta be undead to make time with you," he tells her. Rebuffed by Buffy, he goes home and listens to country music, "the music of pain."

But this is the episode in which Buffy—whose death at the Master's hands has been predicted in vampire prophecy—has to face up to her first-season nemesis. And when the chips are down, Xander usually comes through for his friends. He is the one who goes to get help from Angel, whom he doesn't really trust or like. Despite Xander's anger and hurt at being rejected, he seeks out the one person that he feels is the root cause of his suffering and builds a bridge with that person. And in the end Xander's action prevents the rise of the Master and the predicted end of the world. Xander succeeds because he expressed his feelings: he spoke about them to Buffy, Angel, and Willow; and he also allowed himself a little wallowing in the form of at least one pathetic Patsy Cline tune. But he didn't let his pain determine the course of his actions.

Buffy is generally very good at recognizing her own anger and channeling it constructively. But in the sixth season, after her friends have torn her out of heaven and brought her back to earth, Buffy doesn't tell them she's angry or depressed about returning (6.3). In fact, she lies outright, thanking Willow for casting the resurrection spell and allowing her friends to persist in believing that they saved her from a horrific hell dimension. "You guys gave me the world," she tells them. "I can't tell you what it means to me." But the truth is that Buffy feels she is now stranded in hell on earth. She is so numb and depressed that Willow even tries to make her angry so that she'll be more engaged with life: "Anger . . . is a big, powerful emotion you should feel," she tells Buffy in "Flooded" (6.4). But Willow backs away from really confronting Buffy about her hollow emotional state: "Forget I ever said anything."

Suppressed anger is often the origin of depression and is certainly a cause of Buffy's behavior in the sixth season. She turns her anger inward, shutting down emotionally, and also outward, as she physically abuses Spike (who, he says, is "really not complaining" about the abuse). Both responses are harmful. Because of unexpressed anger, Buffy sinks to becoming both victim and victimizer, incapable of giving and receiving love. Buffy, who has usually been able to confront her angry feelings and use them constructively, has changed from being a person who sometimes experiences anger to being an angry person. Coping with it takes her all of the sixth season and even some of the seventh. Clearly, anger is such a powerful emotion that harboring it inside ourselves can poison everything that is good about our lives.

As Angelus notes (2.17), passion "speaks to us, guides us. Passion rules us all, and we obey. What other choice do we have?" For the evil Angelus, there is no choice: his life (or rather, his undead existence) consists of simply satisfying his craving for blood and his passion for revenge. Unlike Angelus, we have a choice. It's certainly true that "without passion, we'd be truly dead," but the trick is to balance those powerful emotions with a determination to use their energy constructively. As Willow puts it, anger is a big, powerful emotion that we should feel; the key is learning to control it and express it in suitable ways.

CHAPTER 5

The "Monster Sarcasm Rally"

Humor as Power

"Sarcasm accomplishes nothing," Willow admonishes Giles in "Pangs" (4.8) as they try to figure out why Xander is manifesting symptoms of a mystical syphilis. Giles counters that sarcasm is actually "sort of an end in itself." But in terms of the Buffyverse,

> Against the assault of laughter nothing can stand.
> —Mark Twain, "Chronicle of Young Satan"

they're both wrong: sarcasm accomplishes something vital, and it's not just an end in itself. On *Buffy* humor is not merely an entertaining distraction but a powerful weapon for fighting the forces of darkness. The Scoobies' wisecracks contain great wisdom, and some of the gang's most interesting and powerful foes are those who know how to exchange verbal barbs as well as physical blows.

"See What Happens When You Roughhouse?": Humor and Control

Many fans of *Buffy* say that the show's ingenious use of comedy first hooked them on the series. Effectively blending horror and sarcasm, silliness and profundity, *Buffy* draws viewers in and inundates them with rapid-fire satire. The humor not only entertains fans but also signals which of the characters is in control. We don't worry much about Buffy when she has her game face on and cleverly derides her foes. In fact, this is when we love her the most—as suggested by the presence of an entire section called "Fightin' Quips" in the online Buffy dialogue database.

Humor is essential when Buffy is fighting monsters. Using her razor-sharp wit, she lectures them ("Don't play with your food," she instructs a pack of human hyenas; 1.6) and jeers at them ("Should I say 'undead American'?" she asks a vampire; 2.1). Before attacking, she cheerfully warns her victims about the fate that is going to befall them. "This is not going to be pretty," she informs Darla in the pilot episode. "We're talking violence, strong language, adult content. [She stakes an attacking vampire] See what happens when you rough-house?" Her verbal repartee is so much a part of her fighting style that one vampire has to ask her, "Uh, are we gonna fight? Or is there just gonna be a monster sarcasm rally?" (4.1). In the season-five finale (5.22), Buffy encounters a vampire who has never heard of the Slayer before. She interrupts him as he's about to bite a teenage boy and informs him that they shouldn't be fighting, because "fighting's *not* cool." The vampire snarls that he doesn't mind having Buffy as an appetizer. "You ever heard the expression 'biting off more than you can chew'?" she asks him. He gives her a blank stare. "OK, how about 'Oh God, my leg, my leg'?"

> **Nowadays I am suspicious of any spiritual teaching that lacks humor.**
>
> —Gerald May, foreword to *Zen for Christians*

She kicks him hard. "Oh God, my leg!" screams the vampire. "See?" she retorts, preparing to dust him. "*Now* we're communicating."

By outlining for her victims beforehand what to expect in their hand-to-hand engagements, Buffy shows that she is the one in control. Her ability to use humor in a crisis demonstrates command of the situation. Intuitively, Willow also understands this, as shown when she and Xander attempt to stand in for the absent Buffy at the beginning of the third season (3.1). Willow feigns pure confidence and brazenly taunts a vampire to "come and get it," a phrase that Xander ridicules after the vampire has easily fled the scene. Willow tries to explain: "The Slayer always says a pun or a witty play on words, and I think it throws vampires off and makes them frightened that I'm wisecracking." Although she's too nervous to carry it off herself in a dangerous confrontation, Willow is on to something here: humor is indeed a powerful weapon.

There's also something ineffable about it. Buffy's humor, which emerges from her confidence, power, and keen mind, is not an easy thing for the Scoobies to replace, either in the beginning of the third season or three years later, after Buffy's death. In her place the Buffybot gamely but inadequately attempts to emulate Buffy when she stakes vampires. "That'll put marzipan in your pie plate, bingo!" the robot announces proudly at the beginning of the sixth season (6.1). Willow explains that she tried to program some new puns into the machine but ended up with "word salad." The Buffybot can never be the real Buffy, and her pitiful puns and knock-knock jokes are painful reminders that the real Slayer is in the grave.

We see the importance of Buffy's humor most clearly when we witness how her strength seems to be depleted without it. While Willow is trying to fill Buffy's shoes and imitate her humor in "Anne" (3.1), the real Buffy is having a terrible time of it in Los Angeles. She's weary and alone, working as a waitress and eating pasta from a can. She's utterly devoid of her usual confidence and spark. When one of her customers insults her and then slaps her on the rear end, Buffy has no response: there's no witty comeback followed by the jerk's forcible expulsion from the diner. She simply sighs. Later in the episode, drawn into helping an acquaintance, Buffy is enslaved in a work camp where young runaways must surrender their names and identities and be worked literally to death. Finally, we see Buffy take back the night, a transformation that is evident when she announces her first name—which is not Anne, as she has been telling everyone; Anne is actually her middle name—and cops an attitude: "I'm Buffy the Vampire Slayer. And you are . . . ?" she demands of the demon guard. Not coincidentally, when Buffy gets her power back, she also regains her offbeat sense of humor. "Hey, Ken, wanna see my impression of Gandhi?" she quizzes her captor as she bashes his head in. "Gandhi?" her companion Lily asks, puzzled. "Well, you know, if he was really pissed off," Buffy replies. She has her mojo back.

But the episode "Anne" is not the only time that Buffy surrenders her powers, either by her own choice or by more nefarious means. In

"Helpless" (3.12) Buffy's Slayer strength is drained in preparation for a trial on her eighteenth birthday. As she feels her strength ebbing away, her powerful humor seems to disintegrate along with it; at the beginning of the episode, Buffy is cracking so many jokes that Giles scolds her to concentrate and try to be "glib-free." But after losing her strength, Buffy is severely shaken. She confides to Angel that she's not sure she can live without her powers, knowing what she does about

Buffy (Sarah Michelle Gellar) often uses her most powerful weapon: humor.

what really goes bump in the night. What if she spends the rest of her life hiding from danger, terrified and helpless? Wearing a red hooded jacket, Buffy goes walking alone at night through the cemetery and confronts a host of big bad wolves: a heckler asks her for a "lap dance," and she is almost killed by two attacking vampires. Unable to defend herself, Buffy feels weak and vulnerable as she screams for help and attempts to flee. She is relieved when Giles saves her but then horrified to discover his complicity in the scheme to drain her powers. Feeling betrayed by Giles and uncertain whether she can fight off vampires without the supernatural might she has taken for granted, Buffy appears defeated.

But when the time comes for her to face the vampire that the Watchers' Council has sent to test her, Buffy doesn't hesitate; she goes directly to the lair where her mother is being held captive. Although she's no match for the vampire's physical strength, Buffy shows tremendous ingenuity by leaving him a glass of holy water to drink with his medication. She looks on as he begins to smoke and then disintegrate. "If I was at full Slayer power, I'd be punning right about now," she says calmly. Buffy recognizes that her humor is a by-product of her power, and she knows that even in her weakened state, she possesses the internal qualities a Slayer needs: "cunning, imagination, [and] a confidence derived from self-reliance." She is livid about the Council's test but has regained enough of her self-assuredness to insult the head of the Watchers' Council when he congratulates her for passing it: "Bite me," she spits at him. She knows what she is made of, even without physical prowess, and she revels in her mordant humor.

In "Superstar" (4.17) we see another example of Buffy's humor being lost and found. It's not just her Slayer powers that take a hit when Jonathan becomes the numero uno star; it's also her keen wit. She tries to chide Spike (who doesn't even remember her correct name in this alternate reality) by saying he's a "big, bleached . . . *stupid guy!*" Tongue-tied, she can't manage a decent verbal assault. Throughout

Time spent laughing is time spent with the gods.
—Japanese proverb

the episode Buffy has a nagging suspicion that she's supposed to be more than she is and that it's odd that Jonathan is so much stronger than the Slayer. As she gradually gains confidence and recaptures an understanding of her unique abilities, she reacquires her cocky humor. The next time she confronts Spike, she surprises him by lunging at him, threatening to block his supply of butcher's blood; if he doesn't provide her with the information she needs, she tells him, he might find himself "getting kind of thirsty." Both Spike and Jonathan are surprised by her initiative. When she fights the demon (and Jonathan cowers behind a rock), she smiles and says she remembers that feeling of power—and likes it.

Because Buffy's humor comes from her confidence and belief in herself, it's not surprising that the sixth season is probably the series' most humorless. On the one hand, that season deals with dark themes—depression and anger, guilt and revenge, power and death—but on the other hand, *Buffy* has always dealt with those themes. So what is the difference? Buffy herself. Her misery, her profound despair, makes it impossible for her to crack jokes. Humor seems pointless; life itself seems pointless. What humor exists in the sixth season is mostly provided by Spike and the would-be villains the

Troika (also known as the Evil Trio). In the seventh season, we see some of the old Buffy returning, but until the end of the season she is more likely to issue generalissimo-type speeches to the Potential Slayers than she is to crack jokes. But Buffy shows occasional signs of her old self, even before what seems to be the worst Big Bad she's ever faced. When she confronts the über-vampire in "Showtime" (7.11), for example, she lectures it before fighting, showing her old power and control: "I'm the thing that monsters have nightmares about." By the series finale, "Chosen" (7.22), Buffy is able to make great jokes again; the Slayer Scythe, for example, "slices, dices, and makes julienne preacher." She hurls insults at the First Evil, who appears in the form of Caleb the priest: "Have you ever considered a cool name? I mean, since you're incorporeal and basically powerless. How about 'the Taunter'?" Not coincidentally, this exchange is the same conversation in which Buffy finally recognizes how to defeat the First Evil. "I just realized something," she tells Spike a moment later. "Something that really never occurred to me before. We're gonna win." Buffy's humor, which has been dormant for much of the season, reappears in precisely the same episode where she reclaims her power.

The Darkest Villains Know How to Lighten Up

If the ability to draw on humor demonstrates control of a situation, it should come as no surprise that some of Buffy's strongest and most memorable opponents are those with a funny bone. As Steve Wilson explains in an article about the show's multilayered use of humor, "Buffy's foes are menacing not because they're capable of destroying the world (what competent villain isn't?) but because they're able to get in the last word." In *Angel*'s first season, for example, there's a funny scene in which Angel and Wesley are trying to exorcise a demon from a small boy (A1.14). When the resident demon sarcastically spits out, "Your Latin sucks!" we know that this will be no easy task—this foe is authoritative and surprisingly self-aware.

Beginning with the Master in the first season, Buffy has had the privilege of confronting demons and vampires whose humor is sometimes as well developed and caustic as her own. When the Master revels in the long-awaited earthquake that he believes will restore his power, we see him shaking with depraved ecstasy and clenched fists as the earth shifts and buckles beneath him (1.12). "Yes! Yes!" he exults. "This is a sign. We are in the final days! My time has come. Glory! Glory!" What appears to be a moment of stereotypical villainy is broken, however, when he turns to the Anointed One and asks in a normal voice, "Whaddya think? Five point one?" The Master is capable of self-parody, which makes him not less but *more* frightening. He is a worthy opponent for the Slayer.

The Master's palpable sense of control makes it believable that he is able to hold Buffy in thrall when she attempts to confront him. He even ridicules her use of "feeble banter" before they fight, which throws her off guard. When he mesmerizes her, he taunts her for being the one who has inadvertently set him free. Then he bites her neck, draws strength from her blood, and abandons her to drown in a pool of water. After Buffy dies and is resuscitated by Xander, she comes back to life stronger than before. Not surprisingly,

> Laugh yourselves into stitches.
> —William Shakespeare, *Twelfth Night*,
> Act 3, Scene 2

she has also regained her humor with a vengeance: "I may be dead," she tells the Master, "but I'm still pretty, which is more than I can say for you." He is dazed by her sudden appearance: "You were destined to die! It was written." Buffy shrugs. "What can I say? I flunked the written." She pretends to be ensnarled by his power, only to turn the tables on him at the last moment. "You have fruit-punch mouth," she tells him saucily. "Save the hypnosis crap for the tourists." She is at the top of her game and bests him with ease.

Another miscreant who makes us laugh is the Mayor. His combination of folksy, earnest wisdom and pure evil is fascinating; as with the Master, the Mayor's ability to draw on humor demonstrates an alarming kind of authority. He is always in control, whether exhibited in his cleanliness fetish (even when he's impervious to physical harm, he still hates germs) or his humor. His to-do list tells him that he needs to get a haircut, call the temp agency, become invincible, and attend a PTA meeting. He jokes that he would sell his soul for a better golf game if only he hadn't sold his soul long ago; he gets a lift and turns his "frown upside down" by using the paper shredder (3.15). In "Graduation Day (Part One)" (3.21), the Mayor shows the Scoobies a bit of what they are up against when his chest instantly heals after Giles has thrust a sword through it: "Whoa! Well now, that was a little thoughtless," the Mayor admonishes. "Violent outbursts like that, in front of the children? You know, Mr. Giles, they look to you to see how to behave." The Mayor is calm, cool, and collected. As he ingests the spiders that will help him begin his ascension, the Mayor waxes rhapsodic about the power he feels suffusing his being. "Plus these babies are high in fiber," he adds. "And what's the fun in becoming an immortal demon if you're not regular, am I right?" His humor emanating from a well of self-assurance, the Mayor is clearly a villain to be reckoned with. But of course, Buffy finds she is more than a match for him, with the aid of the entire Sunnydale High School graduating class.

The special nature of humorous Big Bads like the Master and the Mayor comes into sharper relief when we compare them to other villains who simply don't have that same finesse. Many fans count Adam, the fourth season's Big Bad, as one of the show's least interesting adversaries. Despite his insatiable curiosity about the world, Adam has no sense of humor; his one real attempt at a joke is when he tells Spike that "parts of" him used to be a Boy Scout (4.19). He is pompous and ponderous; and although he boasts that no one has ever been as "awake" as he is, he is not self-aware enough to laugh at others or himself. But Adam isn't as dull as the amorphous First Evil, a force that in "Amends" (3.10) bores Buffy with its self-adulation: "I am the thing the darkness fears. You'll never see me, but I am everywhere. Every being, every thought, every drop of hate." Buffy is nonchalant. "All right! I get it! You're evil. Do we have to chat about it?" Buffy's words, as much as her fighting, help put evil creatures in their place.

Fighting Words: Language and Humor on the Spiritual Journey

"I've always been amazed with how Buffy fought," reflects Xander in "Anne" (3.1), "but in a way, I feel like we took her punning for granted." Xander counts humor and communication as tools that are possibly just as valuable as the Slayer's superstrength. The use of humor on *Buffy* is one extension of the show's love affair with language; as some scholars have pointed out, "mere" words are often powerful and effective weapons in the Buffyverse. When Cordelia wishes aloud that Buffy had never come to Sunnydale, it becomes literally true, and she finds herself in an alternate universe that is alarmingly vampire-ridden and Slayer-free. Her wish has become command. And when Xander and Willow try to explain magical spells to Riley in "Superstar" (4.17), Willow notes that making a spell work takes serious concentration. Xander agrees: "You can't just go *'Librum incendere!'* and "expect . . ." He is cut off when suddenly the book he is holding catches fire. "Xander, don't speak Latin in front of the books," Giles chastises him. Clearly, language is power.

Humor serves many different purposes on *Buffy* and in our own lives. On the spiritual path, it can actually function to underscore what is sacred. As the early-twentieth-century Christian writer G. K. Chesterton said, the only subjects worth joking about are serious ones, like "being married or being hanged." *Buffy*'s characters show humor in the face of the apocalypse ("If the apocalypse comes, beep me"; 1.5) and death, as when Buffy speculates about whether going to hell might mean she'd have to take final exams for all eternity (2.21). When it named Buffy its Theologian of the Year in 2002, *The Door* magazine lauded what it called the show's "sacramental sarcasm" and "lexicon of coolness." Whether characters use humor to clear the air—as Xander often does—or thwart a foe, it is a powerful weapon.

> **Humor is a prelude to faith and laughter is the beginning of prayer.**
> —Reinhold Niebuhr,
> *Discerning the Signs of the Times*

Buffy's humor takes the weight off the plot, which often addresses very serious topics, and allows the show to offer a moral perspective without excessive moralizing. "*Buffy* uses ironic humor to underscore the ongoing themes of the series without having to lecture or preach on the subjects," says *Buffy* fan Chelsea Quinn Yarbro. Without the humor, she adds, the series "would be heavy-handed and ponderous." In the same way, a healthy dose of humor can help us on the spiritual journey: it strengthens relationships, helps us deal with setbacks, demonstrates control, and provides a much-needed perspective. Buddhist nun Pema Chödrön writes that although practice and mindfulness are extremely important, lightening up is also essential: "The key to feeling at home with your body, mind, and emotions, to feeling worthy to live on this planet, comes from being able to lighten up," she observes. "This earnestness, this seriousness about everything in our lives—including practice—this goal-oriented, we're-going-to-do-it-or-else attitude, is the world's greatest killjoy."

Even when situations seem dire, we do well to retain our sense of humor: as Giles says in "The Zeppo" (3.13), "All we know is that the fate of the entire world rests on . . . Did you eat all the jellies?" The message is that even the end of the world looks a little brighter with a touch of buffoonery (and a few doughnuts). And when Buffy describes the sixth season's terrible events to Giles in "Grave" (6.22), catching him up on the twists and turns he's missed by being in England, they both find it wonderfully cathartic to see the hilarity in the situation. Their full-out, no-holds-barred laugh session in this otherwise very serious episode speaks volumes about the essential role of humor.

Companions on the Journey

CHAPTER 6

'What Can't We Face if We're Together?'

The Power of Friendship

In "Out of Mind, Out of Sight" (1.11), the adolescent nightmare of social invisibility becomes real when an unpopular Sunnydale High School student named Marcie actually becomes invisible and wreaks havoc on all those who once ignored her. That includes Willow and Xander, both of whom had signed her yearbook the previous year and had several classes with her but don't remember her at all. The episode gives the distinct impression that our perception shapes our reality—that Marcie became invisible because the world perceived her as such. It also points to the idea, central in the show, that friendship has vital significance for our very identity. On *Buffy* the need for friendship is so strong that those individuals without friends can literally disappear.

For those who dwell in the world and desire to embrace true virtue, it is necessary to unite themselves together by a holy and sacred friendship. By this means they encourage, assist, and conduct one another to good deeds.
—*Saint Francis de Sales*

The reverse is also true. In Buffy's world the most powerful individuals are those with a strong support system—friends and family members who share responsibility and heartache and who encourage one another to fight the good fight. The show doesn't preach about friendship, offering flat and colorless platitudes about relationships and human love. (As Henry David Thoreau put it, "Whatever we might say about friendship will sound like the science of botany compared to flowers.") Instead, *Buffy* shows us the power of friendship in action and prompts us to ask ourselves why friendship makes us so much stronger.

'We Stick Together and Everything Should Be Fine': The Power of Friendship

Buffy's emphasis on friendship stands in sharp contrast to some other depictions of superheroes in popular culture. At the end of the film version of *Spider-Man*, for example, Peter Parker learns that he does indeed have the affection of the girl he's always loved. But instead of allowing himself a happy ending, he walks away. Alone. No one knows his true identity, and he feels that other people's lives will be endangered if he fails to keep his lonely secret.

This is a scene that we've never witnessed on *Buffy the Vampire Slayer*, precisely because Buffy's friends would never let her pull that kind of macho stunt. It's instructive that Buffy *has* a circle of close friends. In the early seasons, she does occasionally try to snub their attempts to help her, worrying that they might get hurt. "There is no 'we,' OK? I'm the Slayer, and you're not," she informs Xander in "The Harvest" (1.2). But he and Willow insist on helping, which sets the pattern for the entire series. Giles continues to caution her about keeping a low profile: "Buffy," he warns in "Never Kill a Boy on the First Date" (1.5), "maintaining a normal social life as a Slayer is problematic at best." Although she retorts that she's hardly going to go around wearing a button inscribed "I'm the Slayer! Ask me how!" she does believe that it's possible to have a relatively normal life. With Buffy, as opposed to many other superheroes, we see strong tendencies toward integration, cooperation, and valuing of relationships. *Buffy* scholar Rhonda Wilcox notes that in this show "the choice to fight alone, while heroic, is also presented as wrong." The highest ideal is one of teamwork and collaboration, not lonely grit.

Buffy's friends do more than whittle stakes for her and help fight demons. They also keep her accountable to her mission. Particularly in the early seasons, Willow and Xander act as Buffy's collective moral compass, prodding her to embrace her calling and convincing her to take responsibility for her mistakes. In "Prophecy Girl" (1.12) Willow's terror at having discovered the dead bodies of classmates she knew galvanizes Buffy into resuming her role as the Slayer, which she had tried to renounce. And in "When She Was Bad" (2.1), Buffy snaps out of a particularly self-absorbed period only when she knows she has to save Willow from a nasty fate. She almost doesn't make it in time, a fact that later haunts her and fills her with remorse. Buffy finds herself considerably chastened when she realizes that her own self-indulgence almost got her friends killed.

Buffy is unique among Slayers because she has friends who support and even participate in her mission. Although Kendra and the Watchers' Council don't approve of the fact that Buffy's Slayer identity is something of an open secret, it's clear that her relationships make Buffy a formidable opponent for her vampire foes. "A Slayer with family and friends," says Spike in "School Hard" (2.3). "That sure as hell wasn't in the brochure." In that episode Spike hatches a plan to murder the Slayer but finds himself handicapped by the presence of her enterprising sidekicks: Giles discovers Spike's Slayer-thrashing history through

> Nothing among human things has such power to keep our gaze fixed ever more intensely upon God than friendship for the friends of God.
> —Simone Weil, *Waiting for God*

library research; Angel and Xander thwart Spike's plan to massacre students at the school; and Joyce, wielding an axe, derails the long-awaited moment of killing Buffy. It's clear that although Buffy is supposed to be the only Slayer in the world ("She *alone* will stand against the . . . vampires," explains the opening voice-over), she becomes a force to be reckoned with because of the Scooby gang.

By the third season, Buffy's inner circle opens a bit wider: Joyce is in on the secret, and Buffy also comes to command the grudging respect of her peers. "The Prom" (3.20) contains a touching moment when Buffy's classmates at Sunnydale High recognize her as their class protector. They may not understand her identity as the Slayer, but they are aware that they have achieved the dubious distinction of being the graduating class with the lowest death rate in the school's history—something they know is due in no small part to Buffy. That season ends with the whole senior class joining in to help Buffy defeat the Mayor, who wants to use his commencement address as an opportunity to turn into a giant demon-snake and devour the students (3.22). With the class helping her, Buffy is able to do what she could not do alone.

This sort of joint action is an ongoing theme of the series; as Joss Whedon says in the voice-over commentary on "Hush" (4.10), "Two people together can accomplish more than when they're alone." In that episode Willow and Tara discover that although neither can succeed alone in magically moving a soda machine to block a deadly attack, they are able to merge their power and realize their goal together. "It's a very empowering statement about love," says Whedon.

On *Buffy* that love is sometimes manifested in family ties, as individuals enjoy loving relationships within the fold of hearth and home. For example, Joyce and Buffy have a fairly healthy mother-daughter relationship, particularly after Joyce understands about Buffy's role as the Slayer. But far more often, the show makes the point that our real family consists of the loving relationships we forge with people who are not biological relations. Xander and Willow have parents who are primarily an offstage presence—a mostly neutral presence in Willow's case and a psychologically damaging one in Xander's. But both characters are able to create loving ties with the Scoobies, who function as an ad hoc family. This theme is paramount in the fifth season, which makes clear that our real kin are the "kindred spirits" we choose. In "No Place Like Home" (5.5) and "Blood Ties" (5.13), Buffy realizes that Dawn is just as much her sister as she would have been if her whole "history" as a Summers were true. Buffy loves Dawn, plain and simple, despite the fact that Dawn is not her biological sister. The act of loving *makes* Dawn family. In "Family" (5.6) Tara discovers that her controlling, cruel family of origin is not her true family of spirit and that it is the Scoobies who will truly love and protect her. And in "The Body" (5.16) we see that Joyce has been a mother to far more people than just Buffy and Dawn. She has become a surrogate mom to all of the Scoobies, even Spike, and her death devastates them all.

Friendship, whether with the characters' peers or in their own homes, is vital to their very survival. In the sixth-season finale, "Grave" (6.22), Xander's friendship with Willow is so deep and richly textured that it literally saves the world. As Thomas Hibbs points out, Willow's struggle here is between accepting evil, which is nihilistic and self-serving, or embracing good, which is predicated on relationship. Because the foundation of evil is pure selfishness, anyone on the dark path must necessarily reject friendship, which requires empathy, teamwork, and a dose of selflessness. "By contrast to goodness and in parasitic dependence on it, evil involves isolation from the rest of humanity, a closing off of the possibility of love, friendship, and communication; it is a will to raw, unconstrained power, a nihilistic drive to destroy all that is, including oneself," Hibbs explains. Willow chooses to take a chance on life and goodness by clinging to a friendship that has strengthened her since she was five years old.

Despite setbacks, divergent life paths, and occasional misunderstandings—which happen in every close friendship—Buffy, Willow, and Xander continue to cultivate and deepen their friendship as the series progresses. By the final season, they have seen the best and worst in one another and understand each other intimately. They have achieved the kind of steadfast friendship that Ralph Waldo Emerson suggested when he wrote that a friend was a person with whom he could think out loud. In fact, by the seventh-season episode "Showtime" (7.11), Buffy's friendship with Willow and Xander has developed so much that she is able to transcend the "out loud" part of Emerson's notion: when Buffy needs to secretly communicate a plan to Willow and Xander, she brainstorms with them telepathically, entering their minds. Their wordless communication is a symbolic example of the way they have grown to understand one another, blocking out the rest of the world so that they can concentrate on their mutual mission.

'In the End, You're Always by Yourself': Friendship Versus Self-Reliance

"In the end you're always by yourself," says the demon Whistler in the second-season finale (2.22). "You're all you got. That's the point." It's true that for all of the attention lavished on friendship and cooperation in *Buffy*, the series also retains a place for a certain rugged individualism. After Whistler's speech to Buffy, for example, she comes face-to-face with her lover-turned-nemesis, Angelus, who has her back literally against the wall. As he moves in for the kill, her death seems assured, and she cowers against the wall in fear. "That's everything, huh?" he taunts her. "No weapons, no friends. No hope. Take all that away and what's left?" Buffy seems defeated by his words, closing her eyes as she prepares for his final attack. But as he lunges forward, charging his sword directly into her face, she unexpectedly catches the blade between the palms of her hands. Stopping his assault just inches away from her, she opens her eyes with a new resolve: "Me," she tells him firmly, knocking the sword's hilt back into Angelus's face and kicking him in the chest.

Buffy knows that even when her friends are not able to help her, she can always rely on herself, and she finds an inner strength that enables her to defeat Angelus. Although the series clearly stresses mutual effort and group cooperation, independence and self-reliance are important values too. At times Buffy relies on others to see her through difficult circumstances, and at other times the buck stops with her. She accepts the full responsibility of Slayerhood and proves herself more than capable of fighting alone when she has to. Like Buffy, the other principal characters all have occasion to stand alone from time to time: Xander saves the school from zombies in "The Zeppo" (3.13), and Willow cleverly saves herself from the Mayor's henchman in "Choices" (3.19). And of course, the characters on *Buffy* sometimes fail each other and wind up going it alone because someone in the group has been irresponsible or thoughtless. When Riley fails to show up for patrol in "Listening to Fear" (5.9), for example, Xander, Giles, and Willow pick up the slack, although they nearly get killed because of the less-than-ideal situation. Still, they find an instinctive reserve that they wouldn't have suspected, and they are able to defeat the vampires. "I dusted two of them!" Willow gloats. "Yay on me!"

> Fate chooses our relatives, we choose our friends.
> —Jacques Delille, *Malheur et Pitié*

The series maintains a tension between braving it alone and working together. "Understand, we'll go hand in hand, but we'll walk alone in fear," the Scoobies sing in the musical episode "Once More, with Feeling" (6.7) as they clasp hands and then abruptly break formation. Their frankness points to a fundamental truth: people will fail us, friendships will sometimes disintegrate, and a certain amount of alienation is part of the human experience. Self-reliance is a crucial and sometimes life-saving value.

Taken too far, however, self-reliance at the expense of friendship can be suicide in the Buffyverse, where loners simply don't last. In "The Wish" (3.9), for example, we see what Buffy's life might have been like if she had no Watcher and no friends. She is a lone Slayer, cold and callous. In fact, she's very much like Faith, whom Buffy wisely said at the start of the episode might have been her under different circumstances. Had Buffy's life been different—had she been motherless and friendless—she believes she might have turned out very much like Faith. In the alternate reality that Cordelia's wish created, we see that Buffy's quite right. Significantly, Buffy also dies at the end of this episode. "In this reality, without them [her friends] to give her emotional strength and practical help, death seems more inevitable for Buffy," writes Kathleen Tracy. Although "The Wish" is one of many episodes that show us how Buffy would be compromised as the Slayer if she didn't have her friends, it also offers a glimpse of where her friends would be without Buffy: they'd be vampires.

As we've seen, Buffy's decision to have good friends and allow them to help her flies in the face of conventional wisdom about what it means to be the Slayer. In the dream episode "Restless" (4.22), we learn that this notion of the Chosen One standing alone stretches all the way back to the First Slayer. "No friends . . . just the kill," she tells Buffy. But Buffy responds that she is not alone, and this insistence on relationship is nothing less than the foundation of Buffy's spirit. "The key to her psyche is that she is not alone, that she has friends. . . . The side of her that is Buffy is as important as the side of her that is the Slayer," says Joss Whedon in the episode's voice-over commentary. "That is what, in fact, makes her the greatest Slayer that has ever been."

Buffy still struggles with the inherent loneliness of being the Slayer, particularly in the seventh season, when the Potential Slayers and Scoobies question her authority and begin to follow Faith. As Buffy knows and as Faith discovers, the Slayer can feel alone even in the best and most supportive of circumstances. But Buffy realizes in the final episode, "Chosen" (7.22), that she doesn't have to walk alone. Self-reliance is not all she has. By using the Slayer Scythe to empower every Potential Slayer around the world, Buffy changes the rules, choosing cooperation and shared power over pure individualism. "It flies in the face of everything . . . every generation has ever done in the fight against evil," Giles says about Buffy's plan. "I think it's bloody brilliant." She effectively rewrites the Slayer handbook, granting power to girls everywhere so that the Slayers can rise up as a collective force to defeat the First Evil. In the end Buffy—who has always acknowledged the important role that others have played in helping her fulfill her calling as the Slayer—wins by sharing power.

Friendship on the Spiritual Journey

"In human relationship, filled with its shortcomings and trouble, what can console us if not the faithfulness and mutual affection of true friends?" This sentiment by Augustine of Hippo resonates just as deeply today as it did sixteen hundred years ago. *Buffy* is always honest, often painfully so, about the ups and downs of human relationships and the many ways that people disappoint one another. But the series also depicts the consolation and hope that derive from those same flawed relationships. As *Buffy* writer and producer Marti Noxon says, the show is about "the relationships you build with people while you struggle." Although the final destination of our journey may be elusive, "the quest and the questors, and the people that you find, who are not necessarily your family, are the only thing that lends the journey meaning."

As fellow questors we can teach each other quite a bit about the spiritual journey, beginning with the act of friendship itself, which serves as a potent reminder of the interconnectedness of all life. When we extend ourselves to another person, we lower the barrier between ourselves and every human being, not just the one we are befriending. In friendship we gain a taste of the infinite worth of each person and, ironically enough, the relative insignificance of each person—in essence, we begin to understand the interdependence of the cosmos. This prepares the way for spiritual awareness. "In Zen literature the word *intimacy* is often used as a synonym for enlightenment," writes Zen priest Norman Fischer. "In the classical Zen enlightenment stories, a monk or a nun is reduced simultaneously to tears and laughter as he or she suddenly recognizes that nothing in this world is separate, that each and every thing, including one's own self, is nothing but the whole, and that the whole is nothing but the self." If intimacy is enlightenment, then friendship is a door to greater spiritual understanding.

The series offers much wisdom about how to be a friend, beginning with the fundamental premise that human beings are to treat one another with respect. The show rejects the idea that using another person is permissible. In the fourth season, when Faith, in Buffy's body, declines to allow Riley to risk his life to help her thwart a vampire attack, she tells him emphatically, "I can't use you" (4.16). It's a double entendre, because she's communicating more than a simple refusal to allow him to help. She's also subtly confessing the lesson that she has only recently learned: people cannot, should not, use one another for selfish reasons. It's a lesson that Buffy also learns (or relearns) in the sixth season, when she finally ends her violent and demeaning sexual relationship with Spike (6.15). Using him is killing her, she says. To cement this truth, she calls him by his given name, William, for the first time. It's a recognition of his innate humanity, which she has violated.

Friendship on *Buffy* is a laboratory for another value that the show consistently emphasizes: forgiveness. Despite their courage and wisdom, all of the series' main characters are deeply flawed. Although he has a loving heart, Xander can be plagued by jealousy and slow to forgive. Willow, too, is sometimes beset by insecurity, and her stunning descent into darkness in the sixth season is a culmination of many of the fears we saw in earlier episodes such as "Nightmares" (1.10) and "Restless" (4.22). Giles sometimes allows his head to rule his heart to such an extent that Buffy finds his suggestions repulsive—such as advising that she sacrifice Dawn's life in the fifth season to serve the greater interest of averting the apocalypse (5.21). Finally, Buffy, in her turn, is not always a good friend. Too self-absorbed at times to even recognize the pain her loved ones might be experiencing, she can get so wrapped up in her own Slayer duties and personal crises that she takes her friends entirely for granted.

It is precisely the characters' faults and blemishes that make the show interesting, however, and their continuing saga allows us to draw parallels with our own spiritual journeys. Although many of us labor under the romantic illusion that true spirituality is something that only solitary monks sitting lotus-legged in a desert chanting "Om" can cultivate, the fact is that the vast majority of us don't have the luxury of solitary contemplation. We walk our spiritual paths in the company of others—partners, friends, children, parents. We learn our most enduring lessons about God and human nature from them, because we offer our most unguarded, raw selves to our friends and family. It is also from them that we must learn the importance of forgiveness, because hurts between strangers simply don't have the lasting significance—or the potential for pain—as the betrayals of our own Judases. We'll take up this issue of forgiveness, on *Buffy* and in our spiritual lives, in a later chapter, but for now suffice it to say that some of our most meaningful spiritual growth happens in the company of friends. And to learn those lessons, we have to be willing to forgive each other. As the nineteenth-century Protestant minister Henry Ward Beecher said, we would all be wise to keep "a fair-sized cemetery, in which to bury the faults" of our friends.

> Two are better than one, because they have a good reward for their toil. . . . And though one might prevail against another, two will withstand one. A threefold cord is not quickly broken.
>
> —Ecclesiastes 4:9, 12

That's a lesson that the characters put to good use in the last few episodes of the fourth season, a story arc that offers superb examples of the power of friendship on *Buffy*. Adam, that season's superdemon Big Bad, strikes a deal with Spike (4.20): if Spike can bring the Slayer to Adam—alone—then Adam will deactivate the chip in Spike's head that prevents him from killing humans. Spike sets out sowing seeds of enmity among the Scoobies. This episode (called "The Yoko Factor" to allude to the Beatles' final separation from internal divisions) shows how the insecurities and personal differences that have been festering all season come to full, destructive fruition for Buffy and her friends. Spike suggests to Xander that his friends really think he's useless and that he should go off and join the army to do something with his life. He tells Willow, who has kept her growing relationship with Tara a secret from most of her friends, that Buffy and Xander have been gossiping about her forays into witchcraft and a lesbian relationship. He insinuates that they think Willow is "being trendy" and going through "a phase." Spike makes Giles feel as though Buffy doesn't need or want him in her life anymore. Although the Scoobies should realize immediately that Spike is playing them off each other by preying on their weaknesses and insecurities, they have drifted so far from one another that they immediately believe what he says. Their hurt feelings erupt in a terrible fight at Giles's house, and Buffy summarizes just how severe things have gotten when she remarks that she is "starting to understand why there is no ancient prophecy about the Chosen One . . . and her friends."

The next day, after a conversation with Spike, Buffy realizes the truth of his involvement in planting discord. She calls a meeting with Giles, Xander, and Willow, who sheepishly come to understand that Spike has "made with the head games" (4.21). The Scoobies also acknowledge that defeating Adam is going to take all of their combined skills. "Hey, no problem!" jokes Xander. "All we need is combo Buffy. Her with Slayer strength, Giles's multilingual know-how, and Willow's witchy power." Although he makes this suggestion in jest, the others realize that he's on to something; and Willow crafts a complicated enjoining spell that will merge those qualities (along with Xander's stout heart) into a single Buffy warrior. When the über-Buffy spell kicks in, Buffy is already fighting Adam and getting the worst of it. Things change immediately when she is endowed with her friends' powers; she engages their abilities as well as her own and proves more than a match for Adam.

Friendship saves the day. "You could never hope to grasp the source of our power," the über-Buffy tells him. Of course he won't; he can't. Adam has been created to be a mighty and solitary demon, almost a reversal of the biblical Adam. In the book of Genesis, God creates the world, saving humankind for last, and regards it all as good. God realizes that no human being should be alone and creates Eve to be a helpmeet—the Hebrew actually means "an equal helper"— to Adam. Her name is derived from the Hebrew word for *life*, and the text explains that she is to be "the mother of all living."

In *Buffy*, by contrast, the psychologist Maggie Walsh has created her hybrid Adam out of demon and human parts; and her creature actually murders her immediately upon gaining consciousness (4.13). Just before slaughtering her, he calls her "Mommy," demonstrating a subversion of the biblical order: she is the mother of her own destruction. This Adam will always be alone, because his goal is annihilation. Although he calls Riley his "brother," he seeks to dominate and control Riley—not exactly a recipe for friendship. And so he has no experience to draw on when faced with the über-Buffy's enjoined power. Her friendships have made her stronger than he could ever be.

As in most mythological sagas, Buffy is a heroine who both does and does not walk alone. She faces the lonely destiny of a Slayer, but she faces it with a stalwart gang of fiercely loyal companions. Our friendships enrich our lives immeasurably; we play off one another's strengths and compensate for each other's weaknesses. As we progress in our spiritual development, we have to determine our levels of independence or interdependence and understand that the sum of our friendships is almost always greater than its parts. Buffy's friends give her strength and courage, saving her life on numerous occasions and—even more than that—offering the kind of love that makes life worth living. As Buffy and the Scoobies sing in the sixth-season musical episode (6.7), "What can't we face if we're together?"

CHAPTER 7

Obey Your Teacher, Except When He's Wrong

Spiritual Mentors on the Path to Maturity

"I'm tired of being mature," Buffy declares, downing a drink at a frat party in "Reptile Boy" (2.5). Weary of her constant training and the burden of Slayerhood, she has lied to Giles and feigned the flu, cutting training in order to attend the party. It turns out to be a rotten idea—and doesn't every rotten idea have life-threatening consequences on Buffy? She and Cordelia are drugged and chained in the basement, soon to be fed as offerings to the demon that lives below the fraternity house. It's a good thing that Giles, Angel, and the gang show up to save her (even though she was already doing a fine job of saving herself). After conquering the demon, Buffy is still in denial about her childish decision: "I told one lie. I had one drink," she insists to Giles. He is extremely angry with her: "Yes. And you were very nearly devoured by a giant demon-snake," he counters. "The words 'Let that be a lesson' are a tad redundant at this juncture." Then he softens a bit. As her Watcher he knows the terrible danger she faces, which is why

> The ideal condition
> Would be, I admit,
> that men should be
> right by instinct;
> But since we are all
> likely to go astray,
> The reasonable
> thing is to learn
> from those who
> can teach.
> —*Sophocles*, Antigone

he has pushed her so hard—too hard, he now realizes. He promises to stop driving her so relentlessly. "Just . . . an inordinate amount of nudging," he says. As they leave the fraternity basement, Giles holds Buffy's arm in a fatherly way, his physical gesture a symbol of the role he has come to play in her life, as trusted protector and guide.

The road to spiritual maturity is long and sometimes painful, and we all stand to benefit from such gentle shepherding. On *Buffy* it's clear that unquestioning, blind obedience is not the path to full development, but neither are we expected to simply go it alone. As we saw in Chapter Six, companionship brings great strength; and the guidance of a friend is particularly welcome when that friend is farther along the path than we are. Spiritual mentors and teachers have much to offer us if we are humble enough to listen and learn.

The Watcher Who Doesn't Just Watch: Giles

When Buffy meets Giles for the first time in the high school library, she's dismayed to learn that he already knows about her past role as the Slayer (1.1). There's tension in their relationship right from the beginning, as Buffy says she has "both been there and done that" and is moving on with her goal to have a normal, slay-free life. "Hey, I know!" she says. "Why don't *you* kill them?" Giles stutters that he's a Watcher and hasn't the skill—a Watcher's job is to train and prepare the Slayer. And in the early episodes, this is primarily what Giles does: he helps Buffy behind the scenes, doing research, casting defensive spells, and training her. He critiques her fighting methods ("execution was adequate, but a bit too bloody for my taste") and pushes her to improve. But until "Never Kill a Boy on the First Date" (1.5), Giles sees Buffy as a Slayer first and a person second; in that episode he begins really fighting by her side. He confesses that he understands some of her ambivalence about being the Slayer, because he was hardly thrilled himself when he learned at age ten of his destiny as a Watcher. "My father gave me a very tiresome speech about responsibility and sacrifice," he tells Buffy. He also very touchingly reveals that although he has "volumes of lore, of prophecies, of predictions," he doesn't have an instruction manual for how to train Buffy as the Slayer. "We feel our way as we go along. And I must say, as a Slayer you're doing . . . pretty well."

This scene sets the stage for the evolving relationship between Buffy and Giles over the seasons to come. Giles jokes about being just a Watcher; in the episode "Family" (5.6), for example, he tries to avoid taking an active part in moving Buffy's things from her dorm room by saying that he saw his role as "more patriarchal . . . lots of pointing and scowling." But he's just blustering, and they both know it. When Buffy needs him, Giles is there—a dedication we see in the astounding number of times he suffers head trauma or is rendered unconscious while he fights at her side. (As Cordelia says, "How many times have you been knocked out, anyway?"; 3.11.)

Giles doesn't just risk his life physically to help Buffy; he is also there for her when things get rough emotionally, offering support but not blame. When Angel turns evil in the second season, Giles says that Buffy could not have expected it and that it's not her fault. "If it's guilt you're looking for, Buffy, I'm not your man. All you will get from me is my support. And my respect" (2.14). However, Giles is not above sharply criticizing Buffy when he believes that she's compromised her mission. When in "Revelations" (3.7) he learns that she's been secretly harboring Angel, recently returned from hell, Giles waits until he and Buffy are alone before giving her a stern and impassioned lecture ("You have no respect for me or the job I perform").

> Your teacher can open the door, but you must enter by yourself.
> —Chinese proverb

He is deeply disappointed in her and says as much. It's not for nothing that when Giles is temporarily transformed into a demon in "A New Man" (4.12), Buffy recognizes him solely by the disappointment she sees in his eyes: "You're the only person in the world that can look *that* annoyed with me," she tells him. When circumstances require it, Giles is capable of a serious rebuke.

Fundamentally, though, Giles believes in Buffy and is willing to acknowledge when she is right and he is wrong. In "The Pack" (1.6), for example, when she knows something strange and supernatural has happened to Xander, Giles just thinks that Xander's viciousness means that he's behaving like a normal teenage boy. Buffy is right; Xander has in fact been possessed by a hyena.

Buffy also believes in Giles, even when—perhaps especially when—he reveals his feet of clay. In "The Dark Age" (2.8), Giles admits his past life as Ripper, a dark side of himself that he had hoped Buffy would never have to see. "I'm not gonna lie to you," she tells him. "It was scary. I'm so used to you being a grown-up, and then I find out that you're a person. . . . Who would've thought?" She concedes that although seeing him as a full person is "a little weird," it's also "kind of OK."

Buffy sometimes finds herself in situations in which she can benefit from Giles's cool head and cautious approach. In "Fear, Itself" (4.4), for example, Giles translates aloud from one of his books about how to prevent a fear demon from manifesting. Giles says that there are two ways to effectively defeat the demon and goes on to describe destroying its "mark." But before Giles can finish this sentence, Buffy pulverizes the demon's mark, or icon, thinking that Giles was about to say that destroying the mark was a way to destroy the demon itself. In fact, Buffy's impatience means that she has actually summoned the demon rather than destroyed it. She should have listened more patiently to her Watcher. (Happily, the book's illustration of the demon turns out to be the demon's actual size, so Buffy has no trouble squashing it like a beetle.)

Giles's superb mentoring is especially impressive in contrast to two other characters who try to assume his role as Buffy's guide: Wesley Wyndam-Pryce and Maggie Walsh. In the third season, the Watchers' Council fires Giles and replaces him with Wesley, a stiff and initially inept British Watcher who has only encountered vampires in "controlled settings" and is almost entirely ineffectual when faced with the real thing (3.14). (A great joy of watching the spin-off *Angel* is seeing Wesley's character develop into one of the strongest and most passionate individuals in the Buffyverse.) Whereas Giles treats Buffy with respect and consults her on all major decisions, Wesley simply attempts to give orders. Buffy teases Wesley by telling him, "Whenever Giles sends me on a mission, he always says 'Please.' And afterwards I get a cookie" (3.14). Buffy and Giles essentially ignore Wesley's orders and even his presence, neglecting to inform him of their plan to discover Faith's true allegiances in "Enemies" (3.17) and generally doing an end run around him. Because he doesn't treat them with respect, he's not worthy of their respect.

In the fourth season, a far more nefarious influence enters Buffy's life in the form of Professor Maggie Walsh, who temporarily impresses

Buffy with her intelligence and apparent commitment to fighting demons. Interestingly, Professor Walsh and Giles have a heated discussion about Buffy and the best way to direct her path (4.12); Giles advocates a more freewheeling approach to mentoring, while Walsh prefers a tight leash. She wants discipline, order, and hierarchy; Giles favors individual freedom and egalitarianism. Because Walsh turns out to be a fairly unscrupulous character and Giles shows us through seven seasons that he's a caring and responsible one, it's fairly clear which values the Buffyverse honors most.

The debate between Giles and Professor Walsh demonstrates what media expert Lynn Schofield Clark calls "the program's irreverent approach to authority"; the show posits a relationship of near-equals as the ideal, whereas staid hierarchies can lead to abuses of power. Mere position is no reason for automatic respect. As science fiction novelist David Brin observes, "In *Buffy*, an expert or authority figure is judged good or evil by a simple set of standards that have nothing to do with their status or class or birth. . . . The sole criterion that matters is whether you treat others decently." By this measurement Giles emerges with flying colors.

Fundamentally, Buffy recognizes that Giles is her supporter, her cheerleader, and the involved father she rarely had. In "Who Are You?" (4.16), when Faith has switched bodies with Buffy and the real Buffy finds herself captured by the Watchers' Council, Giles is the first person she seeks out for help after she breaks free. And when she finds her mother's dead body (5.16), Giles is the first friend Buffy calls: "You need to come," she says with controlled emotion. And she knows that he will. As Buffy tells him in the fifth season, Giles means the world to her: "You're like my fairy godmother, and Santa Claus, and Q all rolled up into one. . . . Q from Bond, not *Star Trek*" (5.4). Giles is a mentor worthy of Buffy's respect.

Thinking for Ourselves: The Danger of Blind Obedience

Although effective, strong mentoring is an important component of an authentic spiritual path, it is most emphatically *not* the same as blind obedience. In *Buffy* we see numerous examples of how unthinking obedience can lead to disastrous consequences. The series is rife with characters who become prey for strong, evil individuals because they have not learned to think for themselves. In the second season, for example, Kendra learns from Buffy about what it means to be a Slayer (2.9–2.10). She is beginning to emerge from her cage of by-the-book slaying by the end of that season—but

Giles (Anthony Stewart Head), Buffy's Watcher, mentors all the Scoobies.

not before a newly powerful Drusilla finds her (2.21). Kendra does not die because her fighting method is flawed or her enemy is too physically overpowering. Instead, Kendra, who has not had much experience as an independent thinker, is easy fodder for Drusilla's mind tricks. Zoe-Jane Playden puts it this way: "Kendra is trained; Kendra is mesmerized and killed. Buffy is educated; Buffy survives." Kendra fights valiantly and with great technique, but Drusilla can disable her in a moment by simple hypnosis. Kendra is killed because she has always obeyed without question and has not strengthened her mind and spirit by discovering her own unique path.

Another character whose story serves as a cautionary tale is Andrew, the weakest of the Evil Trio, the three geeky villains of season six. In contrast to Warren's growing fascination with evil and Jonathan's increasing urge to do the right thing and take responsibility for his actions, Andrew is just along for the ride. He is looking for someone to tell him what to do, and he begs Jonathan to take charge after Warren's death: "I *like* taking orders. Just tell me what to do" (6.21). Jonathan's response to this pathetic plea is to pin Andrew against the wall and tell him to grow up. It's interesting foreshadowing, because in the final season, Andrew's deep-seated need to follow someone and his refusal to become his own moral agent cause Jonathan's death (7.7). Andrew is easy prey for the First Evil when it appears to him in the form of the deceased Warren and demands that Andrew kill Jonathan, his only remaining friend. Andrew does so with little hesitation and spends the rest of the season coming to terms with his terrible act.

Evil creatures on *Buffy* often manifest an unquestioning obedience to authority. In the first and second seasons, for example, we see powerful vampires defer to the Anointed One, a chosen individual who has been foretold in prophecy but who, in his child's body, appears relatively powerless. Only when Spike roars into Sunnydale do we see the first hints of any real discord in the ranks: Spike calls him "the Annoying One" and doesn't understand why the other vampires obey him. At the end of "School Hard" (2.3), Spike suddenly hoists the Anointed-Annoying One up into the bright sunlight—a nasty, sizzling death for a vampire. "From now on," he rails, "we will have a little less ritual and a little more fun around here!" But Spike, who thrives on the chaos created by the subversion of hierarchy, is an iconoclastic anomaly among evil beings (which is what makes him such an interesting character). More typical is Ted, Buffy's would-be stepfather who turns out to be a cruel robot (2.11). Programmed to elicit absolute obedience from women, Ted becomes violent when a strong woman questions his authority: "I don't take orders from women!" he barks. "I'm not wired that way!"

On *Buffy* authority figures are often up to no good. The major Big Bad of season three is the Mayor of Sunnydale, the highest political authority in the town. Even Faith's new Watcher, Gwendolyn Post, turns out to be evil—a turning point for Faith, who has been betrayed yet again by an adult she trusted. Faith is therefore very susceptible to the solicitous attentions of the Mayor, who showers her with fatherly affection, presents, and folksy aphorisms while she works as his assassin. He's the mentor she's been craving, and when he tells her to do something, she doesn't challenge him. When one of her victims asks why the Mayor has sent Faith to kill him, she gives this offhand reply: "You know, I never thought to ask." Faith does what she's told (3.21).

By far, however, the theme of the dangers of unquestioning obedience plays out most thoroughly in season four, when Agent Riley Finn begins to grow up. Riley, Buffy's psychology teaching assistant at UC Sunnydale, is a clean-cut all-American boy. He has what he calls "an honest face," spends each Thanksgiving in Iowa with his family, and seems to be what Buffy has longed for since the first season: a "nice, normal" boyfriend. But he's also part of Professor Walsh's top-secret government agency, the Initiative (located right under Riley's house), and like Buffy, he has a clandestine identity as a demon hunter. Riley and Buffy don't learn the truth about each other until midway through season four, when they realize they are fighting on the same side. For a time they try working as a team, bringing Buffy into the Initiative and providing her with a pager so that she can assist with curbing any demonic activity. But it isn't long before they realize their strategies are entirely different. Riley never questions an order or even grumbles about Professor Walsh's strategies. He takes his "vitamins" (which are really souped-up steroidlike drugs to make him more powerful) and tells Buffy, "In the military you learn to follow orders, not ask questions" (4.13). This is a sharp contrast to Buffy, who never stops asking questions—even interrupting four times when Professor Walsh leads an Initiative briefing about a demon.

Professor Walsh finds Buffy a menace because she declines to follow orders without discussion. Walsh is also threatened by Buffy's romantic relationship with Riley, who is Walsh's protégé and like a son. (In "The I in Team," 4.13, Riley refers to Professor Walsh as "Mother.") Walsh even plays the voyeur when Buffy and Riley first make love, watching their consummation via a hidden surveillance camera in Riley's bedroom (4.13). Things come to a head when Walsh arranges Buffy's death: she sends Buffy out on a staged reconnaissance mission, equipping her with a faulty weapon and trapping her in a sewer with two dangerous demons. Of course, Buffy survives. "If you think that's enough to kill me, then you really don't know what a Slayer is," she informs Walsh. "Trust me when I say you're gonna find out." Riley, horrified by his superior's murderous duplicity, walks away, leaving Professor Walsh alone.

Maggie Walsh is a villain not because she intends to do outright evil in the world but because she abuses her authority and answers to no one. She is the show's chief example of what mentoring is not supposed to be. As we saw in Chapter Six, Walsh's ego naively refuses to accept the notion that she will not be able to control her demonic creation, Adam, whom she designed to be the ultimate warrior. As Madeline Muntersbjorn puts it in an article about science in Buffy, "The scientist's faith that she alone knows what's in the best interest of the greater good places *everyone* in danger." That includes Walsh herself: as we saw in Chapter Six, Adam kills her first when he is awakened.

Riley's evolution suggests an important spiritual truth: sometimes people reach heightened maturity more by questioning authority than by obeying it. Early in their relationship, Riley asks Buffy whether she ever obeyed the Watchers' Council's orders, and she admits that she only obeyed the ones she was planning to follow anyway (4.15). Her self-awareness is precisely the point: she is her own moral agent, generally clear about right and wrong and willing to follow authority when it does not conflict with the demands of her own conscience. Riley is just learning this lesson. It's interesting that he becomes his own moral agent only when he abandons the official title of *agent*: he begins growing up when he leaves the military and starts to think for himself. In the fifth and sixth seasons, we see him reintegrate his old military job with his new self-understanding but on his own terms.

'Buffy Does as She Will': Growing Through Disobedience

As Buffy suggests to Riley, she sometimes defies direct orders because she feels pulled by obedience to a higher mandate—to save others. In "Prophecy Girl" (1.12), for example, Giles has second thoughts about sending Buffy to face down the Master, and he ultimately orders her not to go. Buffy goes anyway. Later, when Xander reproaches Giles for allowing Buffy to do this, Giles protests, "As the soon-to-be purple area on my jaw will indicate, I did not *let* her go. Buffy does as she will." Giles understands that Buffy is her own moral agent, and he appreciates the fact that she wants to carry out her duty even when her Watcher's affection threatens to stand in her way. Sometimes, though, Giles finds Buffy's stubbornness irritating: "I appreciate your thoughts on the matter," he tells her in "I Only Have Eyes for You" (2.19), when he alone is convinced that the poltergeist haunting the school is Jenny Calendar. "In fact, I—well, I encourage you to always challenge me when you feel it's appropriate. You should never be cowed by authority . . . except of course in this instance, when I am *clearly* right and you are *clearly* wrong." But near the end of the episode, Giles reluctantly agrees that the poltergeist couldn't be Jenny, because she would never want to hurt them the way the poltergeist is doing.

Buffy's understanding of right and wrong sometimes leads her to key and intentional acts of disobedience, particularly as regards the Watchers' Council. In "Helpless" (3.12), for example, Giles undermines Buffy's trust when he confesses to her that he has participated in a Council test to temporarily remove her supernatural abilities on her eighteenth birthday. She feels betrayed when she discovers his complicity in this rite-of-passage scheme, which (of course, because it's Sunnydale) goes awry and almost costs her life. It was Giles's blind obedience to authority that put Buffy in this dangerous situation in the first place; against his better judgment, he signed on with a Council plan that he did not support. Giles loses his job, because even though he grudgingly participated in the test, the Council feels that his affection for the Slayer is clouding his judgment. But more important, he also loses Buffy's trust for a while; she has a hard time forgiving him. By poisoning her body with drugs to destroy her powers, he has also poisoned their relationship.

> The true teacher defends his pupils against his own personal influence. He inspires self-trust. He guides their eyes from himself to the spirit that quickens him.
>
> —Bronson Alcott, *The Dial*

After this debacle Buffy regards the Watchers' Council with a healthy dose of skepticism. And as we've seen, when Wesley shows up to replace Giles, Buffy doesn't exactly rush to salute him. In fact, at the end of the third season, when the Council refuses to provide help to a dying Angel, Buffy declines to obey their orders anymore (3.21). "This is mutiny," complains Wesley. "I like to think of it as graduation," Buffy replies confidently. And so it is.

An explicit echo of this disobedience sounds in the fifth-season episode "Checkpoint" (5.12). The Watchers' Council descends on Sunnydale, presumably to provide Buffy with some vital information about Glory, the powerful new threat that has arisen in town. But first they want to assess Buffy and Giles to determine whether they are to be trusted with the information. In an insufferably arrogant gesture, they interview Buffy's friends, critique her fighting skills, and threaten to deport Giles and put the Magic Box out of business if Buffy doesn't cooperate. So she valiantly tries to submit to their demands, knowing that the "poncy sods" could take away Giles's green card. (As Xander puts it, they'd not only be destroying Giles's livelihood but condemning him "to a lifetime diet of blood sausage, bangers, and mash.") But after enduring a horrible day—a mock blindfolded attack with instructions given in Japanese, a surprise visit from Glory, and a full-fledged onslaught from some knights in medieval armor—Buffy's patience is shot. She arrives at the Magic Box and tells Quentin Travers, the chief Watcher, that she isn't going to cooperate with their scheduled Slayer review. She has figured out that she has something the Council needs: power. She tells the Council members that they are going to reinstate Giles as her Watcher, reopen his store, give her the information she needs, and then leave her to do her job. She exerts her innate authority. And to the Council's credit, the Watchers treat her act of disobedience as an exhibition of maturity and celebrate it with a round of single-malt scotch. Without Buffy the Watchers' Council is "pretty much just watching *Masterpiece Theater*"; they can't stop Glory by themselves, and they know it. However, working together, with Buffy's strength and the Council's extensive knowledge, they have a fighting chance.

The Changing Need for Mentoring

Buffy's display of authority and self-actualization does not mean she has reached the stage at which she no longer needs a mentor. In fact, the series amply demonstrates that people require different things at various times in their lives. In the fourth season, for example, Giles struggles with feeling obsolete; he experiences what writer David Fury once called an "empty-nest syndrome" period. In "The Freshman" (4.1) Giles urges Buffy to figure things out for herself, telling her she's more than capable of handling the new situations she's facing in college. Giles wants Buffy to move on, to take charge, to be complete without him. Interestingly, though, he feels utterly conflicted about this decision, wrestling with it all night and finally chasing Buffy down at the end of the episode. "I know I'm supposed to teach you self-reliance, but I can't leave you out there to fight alone. To hell with what's right; I'm ready to back you up. Let's find the evil and fight it together." It's actually too late for him to be of any assistance, because Buffy and her friends have already dusted the vampires, but she appreciates his affection just the same. Throughout the fourth season, we see hints of Buffy's affection for Giles. In the extremely witty episode "Something Blue" (4.9), for example, Buffy and Spike succumb to the effect of a spell and plan their wedding. When Buffy asks Giles to give her away, he is momentarily delighted before he remembers how ludicrous it is that Buffy is engaged to Spike. Despite such poignant moments, however, Giles struggles with feeling out of place throughout the season, thinking that Buffy doesn't really need him anymore. In fact, he's about to return to England at the beginning of the fifth season when Buffy asks him to act as her Watcher again (5.1). When she needs to understand the darkness she has found within herself, she craves his guidance.

This push-pull cycle—Buffy standing on her own, then finding she needs Giles's direction—repeats itself again at the start of the sixth season, when Buffy returns from the dead and feels entirely adrift. Although Giles aids her financially and steps in to help her take care of Dawn, he sees how Buffy has shut down emotionally and knows that she needs to regain her independence. His attempts to help her are actually preventing her from growing up and facing her responsibilities. In the musical episode "Once More, with Feeling" (6.7), Giles pushes Buffy toward reclaiming her duties as the Slayer, telling the other Scoobies not to help her save Dawn from the demon du jour—although, as in "The Freshman" (4.1), he later changes his mind. Giles feels that he is standing in Buffy's way, and he is resolved to return to England. "As long as I stay, you'll always turn to me if something comes up that you feel you can't handle, and I'll step in because . . . because . . . I can't bear to see you suffer." He has taught her all he can about being the Slayer, and her mother, Joyce, taught her all she needed to know about life. "You're not going to trust that until you're forced to stand alone," Giles concludes. His departure is devastating for Buffy, and she and the other Scoobies make some disastrous choices on their own. These decisions—and

> I do not call you servants any longer, because the servant does not know what the master is doing; but I have called you friends, because I have made known to you everything that I have heard from my Father.
>
> —John 15:15

their consequences—force the gang further along in the painful process of growing up. When Giles returns in the last episode of that season (6.22), things have really come full circle, and he acknowledges to Buffy that growing up sometimes involves asking for help.

Giles and Buffy's mentoring relationship does not follow a strict linear path; it winds circuitously and occasionally seems to repeat itself. This is because people's needs change as they grow and face new situations. In the latter seasons, Buffy is generally comfortable fulfilling her normal duties as the Slayer, but when unusual circumstances arise (say, dying and coming back to life), she still needs Giles's help. Like a parent, Giles struggles with the balance between wanting her to grow up, which involves facing tough realities, and wishing to spare her pain.

Why Do We Need a Spiritual Mentor?

Buffy's rocky road to maturity may sound familiar to many of us. Although we often take the idea of maturity for granted, becoming an adult and being a bona fide grown-up are not the same thing at all. As Norman Fischer points out in *Taking Our Places*, becoming "mature individuals in this world is not work we can do alone. We need others to help us, and we need to help others." Although we, like Buffy, sometimes chafe at the idea that we need guidance from those who are more experienced and discerning than we are, our path will be enriched by such mentors. We need role models and protectors. And when we screw up—which we will inevitably do—we need individuals around us who are wise enough to criticize our mistakes and help us to use them as catalysts for growth.

Submitting ourselves to mentoring and direction is, at its foundation, an act of humility: we are acknowledging that we still have important lessons to learn. We relinquish a certain amount of control in exchange for wisdom and, we hope, greater maturity. We also receive what Quaker writer Richard Foster calls a freedom, a sense of release from our own "stubborn self-will."

Our own mentors may be senior figures in formal relationships: teachers, rabbis, priests, Zen masters, parents. But mentoring alliances can also arise informally, through a wise neighbor or a friend.

Foster explains that for spiritual formation, the ideal form of the mentoring relationship is less a disciplined, conventional master-guru interaction and more that of "an adviser to a friend." Sometimes relationships that begin in a formal way grow naturally into the adviser-friend scenario. This is certainly true for Buffy and Giles, who begin with strict channels of authority but allow their interaction to evolve into something much richer and more rewarding for both of them.

Perhaps the greatest compliment that Buffy can pay to Giles is to grow up enough that she can eventually pass on some of the wisdom she's learned. In the show's final season, Buffy emerges in the new role of mentor. From semirebellious teenager, she has become a trainer of Potential Slayers and a guidance counselor at Sunnydale High. Buffy has slowly evolved into these roles, drawing on her knowledge of what it means to be the Slayer and her memories of being a quasi-outcast in high school. She also embraces the role of big sister and guardian to Dawn—a role she mostly resisted when Dawn initially appeared. As Buffy steps forward into adulthood, Giles (who returns from England in the seventh season) is often by her side. His guidance is not perfect, and they sometimes disagree—as when he stalls and distracts her while another character tries to assassinate Spike (7.17), whom Giles feels is expendable, or when Giles sides with the Potential Slayers in a mutiny that temporarily ousts Buffy as the group leader. That mutiny, in fact, is caused in part because Buffy has forgotten how awful it is to be inexperienced and under the thumb of someone who barks orders and tries to maintain a rigid hierarchy. Buffy feels she has to protect the Potentials at all costs, and so she is unnecessarily demanding—shades of Giles in "Reptile Boy" (2.5). As a leader, Buffy has to relearn some of the same lessons that she learned when she was young and relatively new to slaying.

As Buffy grows into this new stage in her life, she and Giles understand that they are in the war together, training the next generation and (as usual) staving off the end of the world. His advice to her rings true for us as well: "As adept as you are as the Slayer, there are always new things to learn" (7.17).

CHAPTER 8

The Higher Way

Choosing Forgiveness over Revenge

In the second season, the night before the Sadie Hawkins dance, strange things begin happening at Sunnydale High (2.19). A janitor shoots a teacher for no apparent reason; snakes wreak havoc on the school cafeteria; Xander is nearly choked to death by a monster in his locker. It's a bizarre turn of events, even for a school whose official motto, Xander says, should be "Something weird is going on." The Scoobies determine that the source of the trouble is an unhappy poltergeist plagued by some traumatic event from the past. Giles says that the key to banishing the poltergeist lies in understanding its unresolved pain and helping it achieve some form of closure. "Fabulous," Buffy remarks. "Now we're Dr. Laura for the deceased." They learn that a student named James murdered a teacher in 1955 on the night of the Sadie Hawkins dance, when she tried to break off their clandestine affair. He followed the tragedy by killing himself. Willow and Xander both feel a bit sorry for the victims, but Buffy is adamant that the student was a psychopath and deserves no compassion: "He's a murderer, and he should pay for it. He should be doing sixty years in a prison breaking rocks and making special friends with Rosco

> For someone who is noble, not needing to retaliate is a great gift.
> —The Dhammapada

the weightlifter." Arms folded over her chest, face resolute, Buffy is determined that the student did wrong and should pay. "Yikes!" says Xander. "The quality of mercy is not Buffy."

Buffy gradually begins to understand that the spirit of James wants forgiveness, but she still believes he's not entitled to it. She's glad that he is doomed to repeat the murder again and again and that forgiveness seems impossible for him. Giles gently corrects her perspective: "To forgive is an act of compassion, Buffy. It's not done because people deserve it; it's done because they *need* it." Buffy rejects this and is clearly equating James's murderous act with Angel's betrayal and transformation into a monster (2.14), an act she cannot forgive. ("OK," says Cordelia, looking on. "Overidentify much?")

James's spirit, needing help, calls Buffy to the school—where she meets Angelus. The two of them reenact the same heartbreaking tête-à-tête that has always resulted in the teacher's death. Buffy, playing James's part, shoots Angelus and then retreats to the music room to reenact the subsequent suicide. But because bullets cannot kill vampires, Angelus is able to return as the teacher and offer the healing words of forgiveness and love that James has needed to hear for more than forty years. After a dramatic kiss, the poltergeist departs in peace, and Buffy and Angelus "awaken" to find each other in a tender, confusing embrace. Revolted, he flees immediately, and Buffy is left to piece together why James picked her for help. "Part of me just doesn't understand why she would forgive him," Buffy later confesses to Giles. The twin story lines point to Buffy's own need to receive forgiveness for herself—she has come to identify with James, who felt abandoned and betrayed by a lover. She feels guilty that she "killed" Angel by causing him to lose his soul, even though Willow and others have assured her this wasn't her fault. As Joss Whedon observes, "She . . . learns that she's done something others have done, that she can be forgiven, that she can move on, [and] that there is redemption out there for her."

To err is human and to forgive divine. Through seven seasons of *Buffy*, we repeatedly hear the message that vengeance is not ours to seek. This does not mean that evil goes unpunished—Buffy is, after all, a Slayer, whose job is to wage an all-out war on evil—but it does mean that the route to peace usually lies in sowing seeds of reconciliation whenever possible. *Buffy*'s characters deeply love one another but fail each other often and in devastating ways: Xander abandons Anya at the altar (6.16); Spike, rejected by Buffy in the sixth season, tries to rape her (6.19); Willow commits two murders and then tries to end the world (6.20–6.22). But their friendships survive these atrocities, and the Scoobies are able to move on together, battling evil side by side. Their choice to forgive one another—and themselves—makes them stronger individually and as a group. Ultimately, forgiveness is an expression not of weakness but of spiritual power; as Gandhi put it, "The weak can never forgive. Forgiveness is an attribute of the strong."

'Vengeance Is What I Am': Anya and Revenge

A Chinese proverb states that whoever opts for revenge should dig two graves. It's a wise observation about an important truth: vengeance does not satisfy and can in fact destroy us. As Giles tells the Scoobies in "Pangs" (4.8), "Vengeance is never sated. . . . Hatred is a cycle." Choosing the higher road of forgiveness may be the most difficult decision in the world, as Anya learns in the sixth and seventh seasons. But it is the only path to lasting peace.

Anya first enters the show as the demon Anyanka in the "The Wish" (3.9), when she grants Cordelia's vengeance wish for a Buffy-free Sunnydale. (Note that this craving for vengeance actually strikes back at Cordelia herself, as she is killed in the alternate reality that her own angry wish created.) As a vengeance demon, Anyanka has granted the wishes of scorned women for more than a thousand years. She has turned men into trolls, made at least one man cannibalize himself, and was even "somewhat responsible" for the chaos and destruction of the 1905 Russian Revolution (7.5). But after Giles breaks Anyanka's talisman in "The Wish," she reverts to a human state, complete with heartaches such as not being of legal drinking age ("I'm eleven hundred and twenty years old! Just gimme a friggin' beer!") and learning how to be tactful around people. When she falls in love with Xander, it is with a wide-eyed and almost childlike naiveté, and she is utterly bereft when he suddenly leaves her at the altar on their wedding day (6.16). Humiliated in front of all their friends and devastated by Xander's betrayal of her trust, Anya's first instinct is to retaliate.

Two episodes later in "Entropy" (6.18), Xander apologizes to Anya, but he admits he's not ready to get married. She feels desolate and lashes out at him, her face contorting into its former vengeance countenance: "I wish you were never born," she spits out. But nothing happens. "I wish you felt the pain of a thousand searing pokers boiling your heart in its own juices," she curses him. There is a beat while she waits for her wish to come true, then a moment of dismay when nothing happens. "I wish you had testicles where your beady eyes should be!" Still nothing. "I wish your intestines were tied in knots and ripped apart inside your lousy gut!" There is a bit of hopefulness on her face when a chagrined Xander admits that this is exactly how he feels about hurting her so badly. But this is not what she is looking for. "Those are *metaphor* intestines," she fumes. "You're not in any real pain!"

Unable to curse him, she storms out of the apartment and seeks comfort from her old demon friend, Halfrek, who reminds Anya that a vengeance demon can't curse someone on her own behalf, only someone else's. Halfrek suggests that Anya try to find someone to state the wish *for* her. Dressed in blood red, the color of revenge, Anya first approaches

Anya (Emma Caulfield) and Willow (Alyson Hannigan) both struggle with forgiveness.

Willow and Tara, because she assumes that lesbians must hate all men and would be delighted to curse Xander for her. When they gently refuse, she also takes her case separately to Dawn and Buffy. "I don't think he could feel any worse," Buffy tells her. "Let's test that theory," Anya responds eagerly. But all of the friends refuse to help, and Anya does not know where to turn. "It's just . . . it hurts!" she cries. "He hurt me so much!" She seeks comfort in the bottle and in a disastrous one-night stand with Spike, who is also suffering from rejection and abandonment. Although she didn't sleep with Spike for the express purpose of hurting Xander, that's the effect it has: when Xander discovers it, he is shattered. Once Anya realizes the power she has to wound Xander, whom she still loves, she does not feel triumphant but chastened, and she actually stops Spike when he is about to wish a curse on her ex-fiancé. Anya is learning that one hurt should not always necessitate another and that there are better ways of dealing with her agony.

Because *Buffy* is an emotionally sophisticated show, Anya doesn't learn this lesson overnight. She says, for example, that she will support Willow in her quest for vengeance against Warren, demonstrating that she hasn't fully learned that retribution is not the answer (6.20). The seventh season finds her still struggling with her desire to wreak vengeance on mankind. In "Beneath You" (7.2) she turns a woman's nasty ex-boyfriend into a worm, though she reluctantly reverses the spell at Xander's request (despite the fact that doing so causes her to lose her teleportation privileges). Anya has become more human than she likes to admit. When Willow says tactfully, "I got the impression that you enjoyed . . . you know, *inflicting*," Anya sighs. "Well, causing pain sounds really cool, I know, but it turns out it's really upsetting," she explains. "Didn't used to be, but now it is." She's only halfheartedly into the vengeance game again, which is why Halfrek accuses her of being "Miss Soft Serve": when Anya was supposed to turn a man into a frog, for example, she merely transformed him into a Frenchman. Anya is in a quandary and doesn't seem to know what she wants.

She comes to a crossroads in "Selfless" (7.5), when she loses all sense of control and murders a dozen men at a fraternity party. The brothers had invited a young woman to the party, only to watch and laugh as her boyfriend broke up with her in front of everyone. The young woman's situation so parallels Anya's own humiliation that it pushes her over the edge and she lashes out. But her first words after the massacre—"What have I done?"—reveal just how much Anya has changed. While Halfrek gleefully exults over the mayhem, Anya is horrified by the screaming and bloodshed she has caused. She welcomes the chance to end her own pain through death, thinking first that Buffy will slay her and then that the demon overseer D'Hoffryn will allow her to undo the spell by taking her own life as a substitute for those of the fraternity boys. But D'Hoffryn, who once taught Anyanka never to go for the kill when she could go for the pain, kills Halfrek instead in order to punish Anya, who actually wants to die. D'Hoffryn forces her to persist in her miserable and lonely life. At the end of the episode, Xander tries to comfort the teary Anya, who rejects his offer to accompany her home but appreciates the fact that he still cares about her.

Although retaliation and vigilante justice at first appear to be attractive, even necessary, options, pure vengeance is simply not the answer. Anya learns that a mature human response is to express her pain verbally to the one who inflicted it but then to eschew vengeance for the higher road of forgiveness. She and Xander are able to reconcile toward the end of the seventh season, a peace made possible by the fact that she didn't have his heart boiled in its own juices.

There is no lasting solace in revenge, only in forgiveness. As the Dhammapada, a collection of core Buddhist teachings, states, "Hatred can never put an end to hatred. Love alone can. This is an unalterable law." In other words, simply meeting injustice with hatred will never conquer the situation; it will only prolong the bitter conflict. Or as Buffy tells Giles, "You can't beat evil by doing evil. I know that" (7.14).

But arguments about why we should forgive for the sake of forgiveness often seem pointless to someone who has been grievously wronged. Moreover, it's doubly hard at such times to conceive of forgiving someone because *they* need it; securing the offending party's peace and happiness is usually not the top priority of someone who has felt the sting of injustice. But there's another compelling, admittedly selfish reason: we need to forgive because our own peace and happiness utterly depend on not clinging to bitterness and old resentments. It's remarkable how such wounds will fester if we allow them to and how they can eventually consume our spirits.

According to early vampire lore in eastern Europe, people became vampires because they were seized by a need to exact revenge on someone who had wronged them. In such legends those who had endured a particularly violent death could become vampires and avenge their own murders. (Of course, this is not the way it plays out on *Buffy*, where anyone can be a vampire's victim; there is a sense of randomness to sirings in the Buffyverse. As Buffy puts it, we are all "there but for the grace of getting bit"; 3.16.) Though fanciful, these early vampire stories provide a perfect metaphor for the way an old hurt can metastasize into an obsession that drives us single-mindedly toward exacting our idea of justice. The basic human problem, in the early vampire stories and in our own spiritual lives, is that this headlong pursuit of revenge against one person winds up literally sucking the lifeblood out of ourselves and everyone around us. And it never ends: in the legends the vampire remains a vampire long after avenging the original wrong. The punishment against the first evildoer isn't the end of the story; it's only the beginning of centuries of soulless bloodletting.

> **The only thing harder than forgiveness is the alternative.**
>
> —Philip Yancey,
> *What's So Amazing About Grace?*

The price of vengeance is seen in "Innocence" (2.14), interestingly enough in the ongoing story of a Romanian gypsy tribe. A man named Enyos comes to Sunnydale to try to persuade his niece Janna (also known as Jenny Calendar) that she must help him ensure that Angel suffers terribly under his curse. It's a curse born of revenge: their clan inflicted it on Angel to avenge the death of one of their own a century before, and Enyos is determined that it remain in place. "You know what it is, this thing vengeance?" he asks her. "Vengeance is a living thing. It passes through generations. It commands. It kills." She tells him that his way is "insanity," to which he replies that it is not justice he serves—it is vengeance. But vengeance is a hard master: at the end of the episode, Enyos is killed by Angelus, who goes on to murder Jenny Calendar. Like the vampires in the early Romanian legends, these characters are consumed by their desire for revenge, and it is their ultimate undoing.

The old Romanian folktales point to a deeper truth: too much bitterness can destroy our lives. Our nature is to seek justice in the form of an eye for an eye and a tooth for a tooth. But as the New Testament says, we should move beyond this quid pro quo mentality and embrace forgiveness, seventy times seven if necessary. Gandhi was surely right when he pointed out that the attitude of an eye for an eye only ensures that the whole world will become blind. Forgiveness is the only path to peace.

'I Was a Moron': Truth Telling and Forgiveness

We hear many platitudes about forgiveness, including the ridiculous adage that "forgiving is forgetting." What people often mean when they say this is that a wrong has been swept under the rug, never to be referred to openly. But such buried hurts tend to fester and strike out in other ways, poisoning relationships. Also, forgetting inexcusable behavior does nothing to change people's hearts. Simply forgetting an injustice is the most direct path to ensuring that the injustice happens again. "In forgiving, people are not being asked to forget," says South African Archbishop Desmond Tutu. "On the contrary, it is important to remember, so that we should not let such atrocities happen again. Forgiveness does not mean condoning what has been done. It means taking what happened seriously . . . drawing out the sting in the memory that threatens our entire existence."

True forgiveness requires acknowledgment of wrong as the very first step. There doesn't have to be a "guiltapalooza," as Xander would say, but there does need to be a conscious choice to acknowledge wrongdoing and try to make amends. "Punishing yourself like this is pointless," Giles tells Buffy after she feels she has endangered Xander and Willow in "When She Was Bad" (2.1). "It's entirely pointy," Buffy insists. "I was a moron." She is willing to admit she was in the wrong and to take the consequences (although she'd rather hide from everyone by crawling into a cave, especially if it had cable TV).

Forgiveness is also not about making excuses for others when they wrong us or for ourselves when we wrong others. When it's real, forgiveness has to be based in the truth, spoken openly, without minimizing the wrong. This is a lesson that Andrew learns in "Storyteller" (7.16), when Buffy leads him to the Seal of Danzalthar (the cover to the

Hellmouth, located under Sunnydale High School), which he opened by spilling Jonathan's blood. A trembling Andrew is afraid that he is about to be sacrificed, because Buffy has told him that the blood of the one who opened the seal is needed to close it. She interrogates him about what really happened when he killed Jonathan. He keeps coming up with alternate versions of that event, casting himself as tragic hero and victim—in one story Jonathan charged him in anger, and the murder was self-defense; in another Jonathan was possessed by evil forces. Finally, Andrew admits the truth and bursts into tears, horrified by the fact that he murdered his best friend. He tells Buffy he does not feel redeemed, "because I killed him. . . . And now you're gonna kill me. And I'm scared, and I'm gonna die. And this—this is how Jonathan felt." He feels genuine remorse and compassion for his victim. When one of Andrew's tears falls on the seal, it stops glowing and closes; what was required to stop its evil was not more bloodshed but honest repentance and contrition. Andrew's process of redemption is well under way, and the seal's fastening provides a visual metaphor for the peace that we all seek: a literal, palpable sense of closure.

> **Forgive yourself for your faults and mistakes and move on.**
> —Confucius

Another character who finds forgiveness and transformation is Spike. After he tries to rape Buffy near the end of the sixth season, he is tortured by what he has done (6.19). (Interestingly, his words are the same as Anya's—"What have I done?"—immediately followed by the demonic corollary question "Why didn't I do it?" Spike is still a soulless vampire who doesn't fully understand his warring nature and motivations.) The season ends with Spike going to Africa to regain his soul (6.22). It's a gift that feels more like a curse, however, because his reensoulment effectively gives Spike a conscience. Like Angel, he becomes tormented with the memories of his past victims, so much so that he even tries to cut the soul right out of his chest. Hiding out in the basement of the rebuilt Sunnydale High School, he's easy prey for the First Evil, who appears to him in his confused and weakened state (7.1).

In the midst of all this, Spike and Buffy's relationship needs healing. In their first real conversation after the assault, Buffy, still justly angry about Spike's descent to would-be rapist, heads off any attempt at apology and forgiveness: "Do *not* start by saying you're sorry" (7.2). Spike says he hasn't come to atone but to help her fight the evil force he knows is coming. She confronts him with the blunt truth of what he did: "You tried to rape me." She is so revolted by the memory that she hardly knows what other words to speak. Unable merely to apologize to Buffy, he is able to tell her that he's changed, and she accepts this.

Not until the end of the episode, when Buffy follows Spike into a church, does she learn just how he has changed: he has a soul, a "spark" as he calls it. He got it for her, so that he could become the kind of man who would never hurt her. "She shall look on him with forgiveness, and everybody will forgive and love," Spike mutters wearily. "He will be loved." He then drapes himself over the crucifix, his body sizzling and hissing from touching the cross. Although the episode does not offer a clear-cut spoken expression of forgiveness, the visual image of the cross hints that such forgiveness is possible, and Buffy's tears make it complete. Throughout the rest of the season, Buffy extends the hand of cautious friendship and eventually love to Spike, who ultimately proves to be a tremendously valuable asset in the war against the First Evil. His act of draping himself over the cross is a fascinating foreshadowing of his ultimate sacrifice in the series finale (7.22), when he will achieve a measure of redemption by pouring out his life for others.

> Though justice be thy plea, consider this:
> That in the course of justice none of us
> Should see salvation. We do pray for mercy . . . .
>
> —William Shakespeare, *The Merchant of Venice*, Act 4, Scene 1

The Hardest Task of All: Forgiving Ourselves

Forgiving others is one of the most difficult choices we can make, overcoming our very human desire for retaliation in favor of the more nebulous prospect of reconciliation. But for many people, the most terrifying notion is not in granting forgiveness but in receiving it. Charles Williams, a mid-twentieth-century British novelist and friend of Christian theologian C. S. Lewis, captured this well when he remarked, "Many promising reconciliations have broken down because while both parties come prepared to forgive, neither party comes prepared to be forgiven." People who don't in their hearts believe they are worthy of forgiveness have a difficult time accepting forgiveness from others. Willow, for example, feels so repulsed by her own sixth-season foray into darkness that she has trouble believing that her friends would ever want to love her again. She has embraced rage and vengeance, and although those forces were not strong enough to defeat Giles with his "true essence of magic" and Xander with his declarations of unconditional love ("I saved the world with talking from my mouth!" he later exults, after telling the story for the umpteenth time; 7.3), they have left a permanent mark on her. She is afraid of herself and her own power, and she faces a long, slow road of rehabilitation and self-forgiveness.

As the seventh season opens, Willow is deep into her recovery, training with Giles in England (7.1). Although she has gone abroad expecting imprisonment or punishment, Giles has turned "all Dumbledore" on her, gently teaching her to meditate and control her power. Willow is terrified that she'll go "all veiny and homicidal again" and that she'll lose the self-control she has worked so hard to achieve (7.2). She is also secretly petrified that her friends will not be able to forgive her. Giles doesn't offer platitudes; he admits that there's no way to tell how her friends feel unless she returns home, where they are facing a new evil force rising up in Sunnydale. "You may not be wanted, but you will be needed," Giles tells her, so she gets on a plane.

Although the Scoobies want to welcome her back—and are in fact waiting at the airport with a "Welcome Back Willow" sign scribbled in yellow crayon—Willow can't see them, and they can't see her (7.3). Because of her deep-seated fear that her closest friends won't forgive her, she secretly wishes to become invisible to them, and her power is substantial enough that this unvoiced desire becomes a reality. Anya, however, can see her, and is not exactly the most charitable person Willow could have encountered on her first day back. "Here's something you should know about vengeance demons," Anya scolds when Willow tries to apologize for trashing the Magic Box. "We don't groove with the 'sorry.' We prefer, 'Oh God, please stop hitting me with my own rib bones.'"

Trying to hook up with her other friends, Willow goes to the new high school, only to find a human body on the construction site. It has been skinned alive, and in the Willow-less reality her friends are inhabiting, they suspect that Willow, who has proved in the past that she knows how to "make with the flaying," might be responsible. Actually, though, it's the work of Gnarl, a flesh-eating spider demon, who flays his victims alive in much the same way Willow once killed Warren. Willow is almost the creature's next victim, ironically suffering a slower and even more painful version of the torture she once committed when she murdered Warren. She worries that her friends might have intentionally sealed her into Gnarl's cave to suffer this fate; and at some deep level, she wonders if this isn't the best way to pay for what she has done. But there is some forgiveness at the end of this episode, as her friends save her from the monster and take her home, where Buffy and Willow have a powerful scene of reconciliation. "It's nice to be forgiven," Willow says. "Too bad I need so much of it." Buffy takes Willow's hands in her own and offers her best friend some Slayer strength as she heals from the physical trauma of almost being eaten alive.

Although Willow hasn't forgotten "one second" of the horror she caused in flaying Warren, the seventh season sees her embarking on a slow path of self-forgiveness. Buoyed by the knowledge that her friends are ready to move beyond what she did—and are in fact willing to trust her to do magic much sooner than she would choose to herself—Willow realizes that what Giles told her is correct. She is needed. Although she struggles with forgiving herself and with believing that anyone else should forgive her, she finds she is able to move on. Her friends' forgiveness frees her to forgive herself and others, including Andrew, a former enemy who comes into the fold to fight the First Evil by Willow's side.

For Willow, and also for us, the experience of having been forgiven is the best reminder of why we forgive: Giles's comment to Buffy bears repeating. We don't forgive because people deserve it but because they need it. And so do we. Forgiveness is a reminder of our own human frailty and imperfections; it helps us to cultivate compassion for each other, because we recognize that all of us hurt one another in seemingly unforgivable ways. As Jesus told the crowd that had gathered around the adulterous woman in the New Testament, only the person who is without sin has the right to cast the first stone.

Forgiveness offers healing and release and is the glue that enables relationships to continue. "Without being forgiven, released from the consequences of what we have done, our capacity to act would, as it were, be confined to a single deed from which we would never recover," observed the political theorist Hannah Arendt. "We would remain the victims of its consequences forever, not unlike the sorcerer's apprentice who lacked the magic formula to break the spell."

Saving the World

CHAPTER 9

What Goes Around Comes Around

Consequences

In "Buffy vs. Dracula" (5.1), the Scoobies enjoy a lovely outing at the beach—one of the only times we ever see these Southern Californians reveling in their native sun and sand. When Willow casts what seems to be a simple spell to ignite the fire to cook their burgers, Xander is suitably impressed: "Willow, check you out! Witch fu." She is pleased with the attention but tries to be modest. "It's no big," she insists. "You just have to balance the elements so when you affect one, you don't wind up causing . . ." Just then, the perfect cloudless day is ruined by a sudden squall, as dark clouds and driving rain appear out of nowhere. "I didn't do it! I didn't do it!" Willow cries, as her friends hastily gather up their beach gear. Clearly, the spell has backfired, one of many instances in which Willow's use of magic to save time or heartache has unforeseen consequences. This very comic scene is also troubling, as

> Freud tells us to blame our parents for all the shortcomings of our life, and Marx tells us to blame the upper class of our society. But the only one to blame is oneself. That's the helpful thing about the Indian idea of karma. Your life is the fruit of your own doing. You have no one to blame but yourself.
> —Joseph Campbell,
> The Power of Myth

it foreshadows some of Willow's more serious abuse of magic later in the series.

In other television shows, characters flit from relationship to relationship with little continuity or emotional attachment (*Friends*, anyone?). In other television shows, key characters die or are written off and their absence seems to have little lingering effect on those left behind. Characters get away with evil deeds and seem none the worse for wear. *Buffy*, however, has always forced its champions to face the consequences of their actions. When Buffy loses her virginity, her boyfriend quite literally turns into a monster the very next day. When Spike and Angel are ensouled, they are tormented by the memories of all of the people they murdered in their decades as vampires. When Buffy gets drunk (presumably for the first time), she turns into a cavewoman who is capable of only monosyllabic grunts. In the series as in life, growing up involves learning to accept the consequences of our actions and acknowledging responsibility for them. When Willow issues her funny disclaimer after accidentally conjuring the storm, she ignores this basic element of the show's premise: actions have consequences, and it's our task to face up to them.

Karma and the Law of Return

All religions teach some notion of consequences in their overall ethic. Christians believe in sin and judgment, whether that judgment takes place in this life or the next. Buddhists and Hindus adhere to the notion of karma, which is essentially the law of cause and effect. Traditionally, particularly in Hinduism, the law of karma meant that an individual's actions in this life would result in reincarnation in a lower or higher caste in the next life. However, the idea has roots even for those of us who don't believe in reincarnation, because it stresses the importance of ethical behavior now. On *Buffy* we sometimes see "eternal" consequences for people's actions—Angelus is condemned to a hell dimension; Buffy dies and dwells in paradise—but we are far more likely to witness the natural consequences of people's decisions as they play out in this life, not the next.

Wicca is another religion that informs the show's understanding of consequences. The first law of Wicca is nonharming, often rendered in Wiccan literature as "An it harm none, do what thou wilt." In other words, Wiccans believe that people can follow their hearts and their own desires only insofar as their actions do not damage anyone else. Many practitioners hold to the *threefold law,* a moral code that states that any good that is wished upon another person in a spell will rebound threefold on the person who cast it. By the same token, any spell that seeks to harm another will also rebound threefold—a phenomenon we witness, for example, in the first-season episode "The Witch" (1.3). When Amy's mom, Catherine, viciously casts a hex on Buffy ("the dark place will have her soul!"), the quick-thinking Slayer deflects it with a mirror so that the spell will curse Catherine herself. Catherine is ever after trapped, mute, inside one of her own cheerleading statues, a dark and dusty tribute to her halcyon days. There she is condemned to live out another curse she tried to put on her daughter, Amy: Catherine will never be able to make trouble again.

The threefold law, also called the law of return, is implicit throughout the Buffyverse, where magic is used as a metaphor for power, and every spell has consequences. We see this most clearly when magic is abused for selfish reasons. In the hilarious episode "Bewitched, Bothered, and Bewildered" (2.16), Xander spies Amy handing in "invisible homework" and charming her teachers into believing that she has fulfilled all of her assignments, when in fact she's not producing anything. (You'd think that Amy might have learned from her mother's treacherous example in "The Witch" that abusing her powers for selfish ends was not such a terrific idea.) Xander threatens to spill the beans, blackmailing Amy unless she casts a love spell for him that will reensnare Cordelia. The trouble is that the spell works on every woman in Sunnydale *except* Cordelia, and Xander is left to flee the amorous advances of not only his friends Buffy and Willow but also adults like Joyce and Jenny Calendar. The women become murderous as they fight each other over the hapless Xander.

We see a similar abuse of magic in the fourth-season episode "Superstar" (4.17), when Jonathan uses an augmentation spell to make himself famous, handsome, popular, and brainy. The writers clearly had fun with this one; even the credits were edited to make it appear that Jonathan, not Buffy, was the star of the series. Jonathan's spell rewrites history, making him responsible for inventing the Internet (sorry, Al Gore). He's also a chess whiz, playboy, self-help guru, relationship expert, military strategist, recording artist, and World Cup soccer coach. The local movie theater in Sunnydale is showing *Being Jonathan Levenson,* and he even has his own swimsuit calendar (which Giles keeps concealed under his desk blotter). The spell Jonathan cast has made him a paragon, an example of what everyone would like to be. "If you really want it," he says at one point, "you can make anything happen."

But of course, the spell that Jonathan cast to aggrandize his own powers has a drawback. ("That happens a lot," Xander remarks.) It has created a demon, an apelike monster that attacks young women in Sunnydale. Jonathan is inexplicably tied to the demon; both show the same triangular mark on their bodies, and Jonathan needs the demon to exist in order for his alternate reality to continue. When a vampire suggests to Adam that Jonathan could be killed, thereby putting an end to the substitute reality

> What is hateful to thyself do not do to another. This is the whole Law; the rest is commentary.
>
> —Rabbi Hillel

that only Adam realizes is counterfeit, Adam does not believe this is necessary: "I don't need to do anything," he replies. "These magicks are unstable, corrosive. They will inevitably lead to chaos."

Adam speaks with some perception. The consequence of Jonathan's augmentation spell has been to create what physicists might call an equal and opposite reaction—his spell calls forth the best, while the corresponding demon brings out the worst. The demon is created so that the forces of good and evil can remain in balance. In his self-seeking desire to be popular, Jonathan has created a monster; and as Buffy comes to embrace her powers and trust her intuition (which, in this reality, happens for the first time), Jonathan realizes that what he did was dangerous.

Sometimes even spells that are cast for altruistic reasons can have adverse consequences on *Buffy.* (As Oscar Wilde once quipped, "It is always with the best intentions that the worst work is done.") In "Primeval" (4.21), as we've seen, Willow, Xander, and Giles join their skills to imbue Buffy with extra emotional power, knowledge, and magical ability to enhance her own superhuman strength. The über-Buffy they create defeats Adam with *Matrix*-like maneuvers and witchcraft. But in the next episode, the dream-based finale "Restless" (4.22), we see that the enjoining spell has enraged the spirit of the First Slayer, who insists that Buffy must always fight alone. In the episode wrap-up, Giles notes that "somehow, our joining with Buffy and invoking the essence of the Slayer's power was an affront to the source of that power." Buffy is a little put out: "You know, you could've brought that up to us *before* we did it." Giles insists that he *did* warn them that there could be dire consequences from the spell. "Yeah," says Buffy, "but you say that about chewing too fast."

Even Giles could not have foreseen how this particular spell would invoke very specific consequences for the four individuals who participated in it. In their dream-realities, the characters are individually deprived of the precise skills (Willow's spirit, Xander's heart, Giles's intellect, and Buffy's strength) that they contributed in the enjoining spell. Willow's dream, for example, shows her returning to high school and to the powerlessness she once felt before gaining confidence with magic. Willow is utterly defenseless when the First Slayer attacks her and drains her very essence—symbolic of the fact that Willow had given her spirit, the source of her magical power, in the enjoining spell. In Xander's dream his abusive father tells him he doesn't have the "heart" to ever leave home and move on with his life, and then the First Slayer viciously stabs Xander through the heart. Giles bravely informs the First Slayer that he can defeat her with his intellect and cripple her with his thoughts, but then she scalps him—a clear reference to the role his brain had in creating the über-Buffy. Buffy's dream shows her reaching a hand into her weapons bag and coming up with just the primal mud that represents the First Slayer, which Buffy spreads on her own face. Her dream also includes Tara handing her a manus (hand) tarot card, symbolic of her physical power.

The action in this episode takes place the very same night that the enjoining spell has been cast, and it's clear to Giles what caused the First Slayer's anger. Sometimes, however, the consequences of characters' actions aren't immediately apparent, and it can take months or even years for them to be made manifest. In 1977, for example, Spike killed a Slayer named Nikki in a Manhattan subway car, but it's not until 2003 that her son, Principal Wood, realizes who Spike is and seeks revenge. Giles dabbled in dark magic as a teen and was responsible for a person's death, but the crime doesn't come back to haunt him until adulthood. When Willow casts the spell to raise

Buffy from the dead, there are both short-term and long-term consequences: in the episode "After Life" (6.3), we see that her spell (which involved spilling the blood of an innocent fawn) has actually created a deadly demon. As Willow tells the Scoobies, "The world doesn't like you getting something for free, and we asked for this huge gift." The world demanded something in return. But the full consequences of Willow's spell don't surface for an entire year; the rise of the First Evil in the seventh season was precipitated by Willow's raising Buffy from the dead in the sixth. It disturbed the natural order and created a new vulnerability in the Slayer line. As Anya says, Willow's determination to resurrect Buffy placed them all into the clutches of the First Evil. Clearly, consequences can sometimes be a long time in coming, but the fissures and cracks created by our actions will rupture eventually.

It's important to remember, though, that not every negative incident that happens on the series is payback for some past act. Even in the Buffyverse, bad things happen to otherwise good people; and not every tragedy is a karmic recompense for selfish or wrong behavior. In the fifth season, Joyce simply dies of natural causes (5.16). This is no one's fault, Willow suggests, and is just one of those things that happens. In the sixth season (6.20) Tara is killed only because she happens to be in the wrong place at the wrong time (not that this is remotely comforting to Willow, who casts aside the stoic acceptance she manifested after Joyce's death in favor of vengeance). In our own lives as well, many painful events happen with apparent randomness, and cannot—should not—be traced to wrongdoing. In the New Testament, for example, the Pharisees ask Jesus about a certain blind man, assuming that either he or his parents committed some great sin and that God punished the family by making him blind from birth. Jesus responds that no one sinned; the man was simply born blind, and God has reasons that are not apparent to us. Such things happen. Not all painful circumstances can be traced to a karmic cause.

It's Not All About You: Taming Selfish Behavior

Although we must accept that there is a randomness to some of the pain in the world, we also know that much of it is the direct result of people's actions. Tara was not the intended victim of Warren's shooting spree, for example, but the spree itself is the consequence of Warren's established pattern of self-involved behavior and disregard for the feelings of others. As early as the fifth season, his intense self-absorption is reflected in the creation of April, a female robot built to do his bidding and be his sex slave (5.15). What Warren wants is not an autonomous girlfriend but an extension of himself, demonstrating his self-centered nature. In designing April, a sexbot who is programmed never to question him, never to cry, and to be content knitting him sweater after sweater, Warren has abused power (in this case, a technical proficiency rather than magical power) for selfish reasons.

Throughout the season Warren is impervious to other people's pain. He doesn't even understand why his real girlfriend, Katrina, is angry with him after she discovers the robot. By the sixth season, Warren has concocted a plan to take over Sunnydale, with Andrew and Jonathan as his henchmen and comic sidekicks. Warren's once-amusing forays into darkness grow far more serious as he gives way to

> We are the heirs of our own actions.
> —The Buddha

his egotistical desire to shape the world according to his needs. Although Jonathan tries to rein him in, Warren's fury is unchecked, and he cannot be stopped. In fact, he has such a rage inside him that when Katrina refuses to simply bow to his wishes, she becomes his first murder victim. From that point, killing becomes quite easy for him. One thing leads to another, and Warren becomes the supervillain he has admired in comic books. He never gets the opportunity for redemption, because Willow flays him at the height of his power (more on that in a moment). What pop culture master Andrew might call Warren's "turn to the dark side of the Force" comes to a screeching halt at the end of season six.

In contrast to Warren, Faith is another character who once refused to identify with the feelings and the pain of others. Although her character became far more developed and complex than Warren's, and she ultimately found healing and redemption, the third season shows Faith with an apparently cavalier attitude about death and killing. When she and Buffy are slaying in an alley in "Bad Girls" (3.14), Faith mistakes a human for a vampire and winds up accidentally staking a bystander. (This turns out to be a bystander of the not-so-innocent variety, but that doesn't mitigate the enormity of what Faith has done in taking a life.) Although Buffy is sick and horrified, Faith insists that she simply doesn't care: What is one casualty compared to all of the evil creatures she has dusted? She has saved thousands of lives, so what could it matter to take just one? Although we privately see that Faith is more rattled by this murder than she lets on, she appears callous and indifferent when she speaks of it to Buffy. She even jokingly suggests that she did the world a favor by ridding it of a boring individual who "was about as interesting as watching paint dry." Slayers, she tells Buffy, are warriors, and they are therefore special; in fact, they are better than any other humans. Buffy counters that no one is above the law, not even the Slayer, but Faith's course is set: "I see. I want. I take," she explains. The taking can be stealing weapons needed for slaying, as in "Bad Girls," or it can be taking human life, as we see in the aptly named episode "Consequences" (3.15). Once a person has crossed the line by murdering a human being, Angel explains to Buffy, it "changes everything."

Several story lines come to a head in "Consequences," and it's not just the bystander's death that has karmic reverberations. Xander's hasty decision to sleep with Faith comes to roost here too, as his friends discover the liaison and are troubled by it. Willow, in particular, is deeply hurt. Faith makes it perfectly clear that she simply used Xander as a "boy toy for a night" and wants nothing more to do with him—in fact, she almost kills him. Buffy, who joined Faith in bad-girl activities in the previous episode, recommits herself to working on the side of good, having seen what Faith is capable of. Also, Buffy learns that her decision to spend more time with Faith than with her loyal best friend, Willow, has made Willow feel lonely and rejected. Interestingly, Willow's first act after this rejection is to try to reclaim Amy from rat-hood, foreshadowing the dangerous reason Willow reawakens Amy in the sixth season: Willow is lonely and doesn't have anyone around her who understands magic. Buffy, trapped in her own self-destructive patterns and emotional pain, simply doesn't see Willow's despair, a neglect that becomes critical as the sixth season progresses.

'I Just Wanna Learn Stuff':
Willow and Dark Magic

One theme that ties Warren's and Faith's descents into darkness is their self-centeredness. Warren imagines that the world revolves around him; Faith is incapable of understanding that being the Slayer does not give her license to do anything she wants. But the series' most interesting downfall by far is that of Willow, who is *not* an inherently selfish character. Lovable, sweet, brilliant Willow, who loves Buffy but resents being a sidekick, comes to be a powerful witch as the seasons progress. She uses her evolving powers to help Buffy slay monsters and avert the apocalypse several times. But even toward the beginning of the series, there are hints that she's sometimes more interested in acquiring knowledge and power, and avoiding emotional pain, than she is in doing the right thing. For instance, after she's helped save Buffy's mother, Joyce, from Ted, the evil robot patriarch, in the second season (2.11), Willow speaks wistfully about what a genius Ted must have been. "There were design features in that robot that predate . . ." Buffy interrupts her. "Willow, tell me you didn't keep any parts." Willow says she didn't keep "any big ones." "Oh, Will, you're supposed to use your powers for good!" Buffy reminds her. Willow is slightly sheepish. "I just wanna learn stuff," she replies.

And learn she does. By the third season, she knows enough magic to save her own life, levitating a wooden pencil up behind an attacking vampire and plunging it into his heart from the back (3.19). But in the third season, we also see a hint of Willow's vampire alter ego in the outstanding alternate reality episodes, "The Wish" (3.9) and "Doppelgängland" (3.16), foreshadowing the evil person she will become in the sixth season.

Willow begins college in the fourth season very confidently, relishing the collegiate atmosphere and the additional challenge of her classes. The fact that she's attending UC Sunnydale at all is a tribute to her dedication to the forces of good, because she was accepted at more prestigious colleges but realized that fighting evil was her vocation. But somehow the first year of college does not turn out as she had hoped. After Oz's abrupt departure, a crushed Willow turns to beer and magic to deaden her pain. In "Something Blue" (4.9) Spike notices that Willow is "hanging by a thread." She's desperate to make her pain disappear—as she says, to "go poof." When Buffy suggests that it takes time for such deep pain to heal, Willow protests that this maxim is simply not good enough; she doesn't want to wait. So she casts a spell to do her "will"—an interesting pun on her own nickname—which has comic repercussions. She intended for her loneliness to vanish, but instead her words exact a literal reality: she accuses Giles of not really seeing, and he turns blind; she says that Buffy is spending so much time with Spike that she might as well marry him, and suddenly they are engaged. Most amusingly, she turns Xander into a "demon magnet" by pointing out all of his doomed relationships with women like Insect Lady, Inca Mummy Girl, and Anya. Xander has to run for his life as various demons break into his basement to attack him. At the end of the episode, Willow feels terribly guilty and atones for the havoc she wreaked, baking cookies for the Scoobies and detailing Giles's car. (Willow: "Did I mention about the sorry part?")

She hasn't really learned not to abuse magic, however. When the going gets tough, Willow begins to turn to magic immediately, rather than as a last resort, and starts using it more frequently to mold the world to her own wishes. This tendency is brought into sharp relief when Joyce dies and Dawn is in emotional agony. Dawn wants Tara and Willow to help her cast a resurrection spell, and they refuse—but for different reasons. "Magic can't be used to alter the natural order of things," a patient Tara explains in "Forever" (5.17). "We don't mess with life and death." Willow misses the point, talking about whether it's theoretically possible, while Tara is elucidating why it's wrong. Tara brings the discussion back to an ethical focus, saying, "Witches can't be allowed to alter the fabric of life for selfish reasons. Wiccans took an oath a long time ago to honor that." Willow says they can't perform the spell because it's too dangerous. Tara says that they can't because it would be morally wrong. Unbeknownst to Tara, Willow facilitates Dawn's quest for information about resurrection spells by magically pulling out the very book Dawn would need to attempt such a spell and leaving it for her to find. Willow has entirely ignored Tara's argument about not using magic for selfish reasons and not playing with life and death. She wants her will to be done, and she convinces herself it's for a good cause.

In the sixth season, Willow becomes addicted to magic (again, a metaphor for power and sometimes for sensuality or drugs), and magic becomes her first solution to any problem. In the Halloween episode "All the Way" (6.6), Willow wants to use a spell to search for Dawn in the Bronze (Sunnydale's only bona fide nightclub), casting everyone who is not a fifteen-year-old girl into an alternate dimension for a few moments so she can spot Dawn more easily. Tara is horrified by this, considering the possibly irreversible effects if the spell were to go wrong (as Willow's spells often had—and would again in "Tabula Rasa"; 6.8). Although Willow chooses to perform a less dangerous spell instead (silencing the room for a moment), the two lovers have an awful row, and Tara accuses Willow of using too much magic. At the end of the episode, Willow, not wanting to face the consequences of her misuse

> **You reap whatever you sow.**
> —Galatians 6:7

of magic and Tara's wrath, causes Tara to forget that they ever had an argument at all. When in the next episode, the incomparable musical delight "Once More, with Feeling" (6.7), Tara discovers that Willow has violated her memory in order to make Tara forget the quarrel, it's the last straw. Tara knows she has to leave; from this point, Willow descends into a terribly dark period assisted by Amy and her warlock friend, Rack.

After a promising but temporary period of recovery, Willow goes off the proverbial deep end at the end of the season (6.20–6.22), so enraged by Tara's sudden death that she is bent on destroying the world. ("Not a terrific notion," quips Xander.) Buffy knows that Willow has overstepped the boundaries of right and wrong: "We can't change the universe," Buffy cautions. "If we could, magic wouldn't be changing Willow the way it is. There are limits to what we can do. Willow ignored that, and now the powers want to hurt her . . . to hurt all of us."

There are limits to what we can do—to what we *should* do. Buffy has learned this lesson, and Willow likewise comes to understand that her actions have consequences that she must face. Like her, we can't take shortcuts through emotional pain or grief. Pain and consequences are instructors and have much to teach us if we have the patience to trust in the process. Karma, it turns out, is not so much a punishment as a natural law. As Spike says near the beginning of the sixth season, "There's always consequences" (6.3).

CHAPTER 10

The Monster Inside

Taming the Darkness Within Ourselves

One may defeat a thousand obstacles and adversaries, yet he who defeats the enemies within is the noblest victor.

—*The Buddha*

In "Primeval" (4.21) the über-Buffy tells Adam that he could never understand the source of her power. She is partially correct—as we saw in the chapter on friendship, Adam has no concept of the deep power that resides in Buffy's close relationships with her core group of friends. But this isn't the entire story of her strength. In the following episode, the dream montage "Restless" (4.22), Buffy dreams that Adam, now in human form, says that although aggression is a natural human tendency, he and Buffy come by their aggression in another way. "We're not demons," Buffy answers flatly. "Is that a fact?" Adam responds. It's a fascinating hint of the seasons to come, which will divulge the other source of Buffy's power: darkness. Ironically, it is the villain Adam who accurately voices Buffy's worst fear: that she, like him, is a hybrid of both human and demon.

Buffy has never shied away from exploring themes of darkness and ambiguity. Even the premise of the show—which rests on the delicate balance of power between good and evil, vampires and the Slayer who hunts them—points to the pervasive nature of darkness. One of the series' most compelling messages is that this darkness is not simply an external force to be easily staked, dusted, or otherwise conquered. It is an ongoing inner reality for every person. "Particularly today, the vampire serves as our reflection," argues literary critic William Patrick Day in *Vampire Legends in Contemporary American Culture*. "After all, when one stands next to Dracula and looks in the mirror one sees only one-self." It's an astute observation; on *Buffy* the vampire serves as a stand-in or a metaphor for some of the darkest impulses and animalistic tendencies of human nature. Particularly in the last three seasons of the show, *Buffy*'s focus on evil moves from the monster without to the monster within.

How do we deal with the darkness inside ourselves? What happens when we become our own worst enemies, as the Scoobies do in the deeply *noir* sixth season? How can we acknowledge and respect our own darkness without plunging ourselves into its abyss? In this final section, we've been exploring how *Buffy* can teach us lessons about saving the world. But unless we acknowledge our ability—and often, our hidden desire—to do harm, we are unlikely to do much good. We will not save the world unless we know fundamentally that we are saving it not only from external threats but also from the monsters inside ourselves.

'How Do You Like My Darkness Now?': Buffy

"All those years fighting us," Dracula coaxes Buffy in the fifth-season opener (5.1). "Your power so near to our own . . . and you've never once wanted to know what it is that we fight for? Never even a taste?" Slitting his arm with a fingernail, Dracula offers his own blood for Buffy to sample, urging her to "find it. The darkness. Find your true nature." She glimpses that darkness in her own memories, as her mind fills with abrupt images of herself fighting monsters, of the First Slayer, of a vein with blood coursing through it. In this episode Buffy is able to resist the call of the darkness within her, even while she yearns to know more about it. Casting off Dracula's mesmeric thrall, she stakes him (not once but twice, because she's watched all of his movies and knows that he always comes back) and pronounces him "eurotrashed." But the darkness remains, an unsettling presence within the Slayer. It's interesting to reflect on the old adage that the darkness is always most evident in the hour before dawn: in this episode that aphorism turns out to be literally true, as Buffy discovers the depths of her own darkness just moments before the character of Dawn appears for the first time.

Dracula's insinuations, and her intuition about her own darkness, lead Buffy to reenlist Giles as her Watcher and begin a strenuous program of physical and spiritual training. She wants to know more about the source of her power and about the other Slayers. Buffy realizes that Dracula actually understood her power better than she does, and she knows she needs a greater self-awareness. Although Buffy began the series as a teenager repulsed by the gore of her life—dead kids falling out of lockers, blood stains constantly on her clothes—she has begun to struggle with an evolving tendency to enjoy her power. Near the end of the third season, for example, she is ready to break the Slayer code by killing Faith, a human, to save Angel, a vampire (3.21). Xander tells Buffy that he's worried about losing her, but it seems that he means "losing" her in a moral sense if she murders Faith. Faith, as many viewers and scholars have pointed out, "represents the darker side of Buffy herself: the power of the Slayer ungoverned by caution and unguided by morality." It's a fine line to walk. Buffy's life is violent by nature, and this reality changes her enough that Spike is not far wrong when he taunts good-boy Riley that Buffy is the type who prefers her men dangerous and dark (5.8). By that point in the series, Buffy is going out patrolling more often—every night, in fact. But she really knows that this "patrolling" is closer to what Dracula calls it: hunting. There is darkness inside of her.

More than two years later, we find out why. When Principal Wood gives Buffy a keepsake belonging to his mother, a former Slayer, Buffy wonders if the box will hold some of the answers she's been seeking (7.15). The box contains shadow-casters, which tell a story when put in motion. First, the story goes, the earth was created and was populated by demons and men. To fight the demons, the men enslaved a girl by chaining her to the earth. "And then—and I—I can't read this," says Dawn, who is translating the ancient document from Sumerian. "Something about darkness." The shadow-casting mechanism begins to spin of its own accord. "What about darkness?" asks Buffy.

Her curiosity piqued, Buffy enters a portal into another dimension, where three men shackle her wrists and chain her to the ground. Her power, they inform her, descends from the way they created the First Slayer: by mating a girl with the essence of a demon. They offer to do the same for Buffy, increasing her power to equip her to fight the First Evil. In fact, they attempt to force this upon her, telling her that becoming one with the demon is the only way: "This will make you ready for the fight," says one of the shamans. "By making me less human?" Buffy responds, refusing to cooperate.

Just as she did with Dracula, Buffy resists the allure of acquiring more power through darkness because she rejects its accompanying loss of humanity. Screaming, she insists that this isn't the way. "You think I came all this way to get knocked up by some demon dust?" she demands. Even if she is not powerful enough to defeat the First Evil— and the apocalyptic vision that one of the shamans gives her just before her return to her own world is enough to convince her that she's not—she knows that power forged in darkness is too dangerous. Buffy is grateful for the knowledge she's gained from the Shadow Men and Dracula, whom she admits "opened [her] eyes a little." But instead of propelling her on a path toward deeper engagement with evil, this knowledge makes Buffy more wary of her own darkness and more conscious about choosing the light.

'The Wolf Is Inside Me All the Time': Oz

Buffy isn't the only character who has to confront inner darkness. One morning in the second season, Oz awakens to a lovely day and is surrounded by trees and chirping birds (2.15). The trouble is that he is naked and has no memory of how he lost his clothes or wound up in the forest. "Huh," he says in his usual noncommittal tone. It's the beginning of a new phase of life for Oz and of a struggle between his loving human heart and the beast that seethes just below the surface.

When he learns that a werewolf has ravaged Sunnydale the night before, Oz phones his aunt (in one of the show's all-time most comical scenes) and manages to work a difficult question into their polite conversation: "Aunt Maureen. Hey, it's me. Um, what? Oh! It's, uh . . . actually it's healing OK. That's pretty much the reason I called. Um, I wanted to ask you something. Is Jordy a werewolf? Uh-huh. And how long has that been going on? Uh-huh. What? No, no reason. Um . . . Thanks. Yeah, love to Uncle Ken." Despite his understated approach, Oz knows that the bite he received from his toddler cousin has effectively cursed him for life: he is a werewolf, a condition for which there is no cure.

Giles reveals that a werewolf is "a potent, extreme representation of our inborn animalistic traits" and "acts on pure instinct" with no conscience. When Oz first realizes that he must be the vicious Sunnydale werewolf, his first response is to withdraw from Willow and try to hide his secret from the Scoobies; he is terrified and ashamed. But after Willow discovers his secret, she indicates that she'd still like to have a relationship with him (and concedes that there are several days of the month when she's not exactly pleasant to be around, either). For the next two years, Oz settles into a comfortable routine of allowing himself to be caged three nights a month, so that he doesn't hurt anyone. And apart from an isolated episode in which he breaks out of the cage and kills a zombie in "The Zeppo" (3.13), the situation seems to work well for everyone.

> Self-reverence, self-knowledge, self-control,
> These three alone lead life to sovereign power.
>
> —Alfred, Lord Tennyson, "Oenone"

But Oz has never really come to terms with what it means to be a werewolf, to have an animal raging inside him. In the fourth season, he experiences a mysterious attraction to a woman named Veruca, a fascination that lures him from confinement one night when he is in wolf form (4.6). He is bewildered when he once again wakes up in the woods with no memory of what transpired the previous night. Only this time, Veruca is lying next to him, and he comes to discover that she too is a werewolf. Veruca is Oz's character foil; she revels in being a werewolf, regardless of the destruction it causes for others, and she has given herself over fully to her dark side. Oz is both repulsed and enthralled by her, drawn to the darkness, freedom, and danger that Veruca represents but guilty and acutely conscious that he's betrayed Willow. For Oz—taciturn, stoic, gentle Oz—there's an intoxicating liberation in the uncaged life Veruca leads, even though he knows it's wrong and he doesn't want to hurt people. "The animal, it's powerful, inside me all the time," Veruca coaxes him. "Soon you'll start to feel sorry for everybody else because they don't know what it's like to be as alive as we are. As free." However, Oz knows that the freedom that Veruca extols comes at the terrible price of the lives of others and that such callous depravity is unconscionable. At the end of the episode, Oz kills Veruca in werewolf form in order to save Willow's life but then packs his bags and leaves Sunnydale. "Veruca was right about something," he tells the brokenhearted Willow. "The wolf is inside me all the time, and I don't know where that line is anymore between me and it. And until I figure out what that means, I shouldn't be around you . . . or anybody."

Oz's struggles with the wolf inside him are a dramatic representation of the difficulties many people have in controlling unhealthy passions or living inside constraints. Writer and producer Marti Noxon, who wrote "Wild at Heart" (4.6), says that the wolf "is the part that both men and women have, that you can destroy relationships even when people love each other." Oz longs to do what's right, but the darkness inside him—symbolized by the werewolf—demands to be seen. His struggle comes to fruition in "New Moon Rising" (4.19), when he returns to Sunnydale and seems to have gained control of his werewolf tendencies. He has gone to Tibet, Romania, and other places to learn meditation and how to keep his "inner cool," even when there's a full moon. He tells Willow that he's a different person than when he left and can now be what she needs.

But Oz discovers that he can consistently control his wolfish impulses only when Willow is not around, because his love for her calls forth both the best and worst in him. When he learns that she is involved with Tara, Oz transforms once again into a werewolf, his bodily metamorphosis a metaphor for the confusion and jealousy inside of him. Even though it's daylight, his strong negative emotions are enough to make him lose all his hard-won control. At the end of the episode, he leaves Sunnydale, realizing that even if Tara hadn't come into Willow's life, being around Willow makes his wolf surface more readily; and this danger means that they should not be together. For Oz the best way to live with the darkness is to remove himself from what provokes it, even if this is emotionally heart-wrenching.

'The Battle's Done, and We Kind of Won': Coping with Ambiguity

Good and evil, Giles tells Buffy, are actually "terribly simple. The good guys are always the stalwart and true; the bad buys are easily distinguished by their pointy horns or black hats. We always defeat them and save the day. No one ever dies, and everybody lives happily ever after." Given that the episode in which this dialogue occurs is called "Lie to Me" (2.7), we would be right to suspect that Giles is being satirical. "Liar," Buffy responds. They both know it's never that simple.

Just as there is darkness within every person—symbolized by the "demon" in Buffy and the "wolf" inside Oz—*Buffy* assumes a densely nuanced moral universe. Some vampires are good, and some humans are evil; choices are not depicted as being purely and obviously right or wrong but fraught with complexity; answers are never absolute but conditional and often in flux. Is it any wonder that the close of the musical episode (6.7) has Giles qualifying his joy at defeating yet another demon with the line "The battle's done, and we kind of won"?

One of the most intriguing aspects of this show is that its writers allow their characters to wrestle with such ambiguities and to be monumentally flawed. Buffy can be selfish and sometimes shallow; Willow's insecurities threaten to destroy her and others; Xander's fear of the future cripples his growth into a mature adult, and he winds up breaking Anya's heart. In the Buffyverse, as in life, most good people have elements of darkness in them, and some "evil" characters turn out to be good. Or at the very least, they often speak the truth: the Mayor is the first person to make Buffy and Angel think seriously about whether a future together is realistic, and Spike intuitively understands (and exploits) some of the tensions the Scoobies are experiencing in their relationships in the fourth season. In the seventh season, one of the things that makes the First Evil so pernicious is that it's not reliably unreliable. When it appears to several characters on the same night in "Conversations with Dead People" (7.7), the First Evil does not always lie. There are some truths mixed in with its noxious fictions, and it knew all about special times Willow had shared with Tara. How can people tell the difference between the First Evil's lies and its truths? Clearly, on *Buffy* villains can actually be more honest than the characters allow themselves to be, so dealing with them is always a tangled and messy enterprise.

Ambiguity is a difficult reality to live with. As we've already seen, the fourth season is a time for Riley to begin to learn to think for himself rather than simply obeying orders from his "superiors." He gainfully attempts to navigate a world that, for him, is newly complicated, because he has long depended on the military to direct, guide, and instruct him. Through his interactions with Buffy and her friends, Riley also comes to understand the more subtle entanglements of the war between good and evil. He has always compartmentalized good and evil the way Professor Walsh and the Initiative taught him: humans are good; demons are bad. But one of Buffy's gang is the vampire Riley knows as Hostile Number 17 (Spike), who sometimes works with the Scoobies to kill demons; Riley also learns that Buffy once had a vampire as a boyfriend. In "New Moon Rising" (4.19), Riley is about to kill a werewolf when he realizes that the monster is actually Willow's ex-boyfriend, Oz. Whereas moments before, he had been poised to kill the werewolf and was utterly sure that it was simply a "thing" and a "killer," now Riley realizes that reality is more complex than he has ever imagined. Knowing that his simple rubric doesn't work anymore, Riley comes to accept Buffy's explanation that "besides the wolf thing, Oz is a great guy." The black-and-white paradigm of "demons bad, people good" no longer serves to explain the realities that Riley's now observing in the world—not the least of which is that Professor Walsh, his trusted human mentor, turned out to be so deadly.

> This thing of darkness I Acknowledge mine.
>
> —William Shakespeare,
> *The Tempest*, Act 5, Scene 1

Riley's moral evolution in encountering ambiguity suggests how uncomfortable living with shades of gray can be. Like him, Buffy sometimes wishes that the world were more clear-cut and that her decisions would be easier. "I like my evil like I like my men," she complains in "Pangs" (4.8). "Evil. Straight up, black hat, tie-you-to-the-traintracks, soon-my-electro-ray-will-destroy-Metropolis *bad*." She rarely gets it, though, because absolute moral certainty remains distressingly elusive on *Buffy*. In fact, when Buffy returns from the dead in the sixth season, she sings that her heavenly sojourn was characterized by "no fear, no doubt" (6.7). In other words, paradise for her was an absence of ambiguity. But in the Buffyverse, such clarity cannot be achieved on earth, where good and evil mingle freely, and determining the most ethical course of action is often difficult.

Living with Our Shadow Selves

Ambiguity finds its most disturbing expression when we poke around inside ourselves, exploring the maze of contradictions within. We are spiritual and carnal, altruistic and selfish, magnanimous and narrow-minded, good and evil. What twentieth-century psychoanalyst Carl Jung called the "shadow self"—our darker double—is always with us. Jung told a relevant story about an upstanding family he once knew: the father, a Quaker, "could not imagine that he had ever done anything wrong in his life," Jung said, and he "would not take on his shadow." The man's denial of his shadow self played out in his children succumbing wholly to darkness, Jung believed; one of them became a thief and the other a prostitute. "Because the father would not take on his shadow, his share in the imperfection of human nature, his children were compelled to live out the dark side which he had ignored," Jung claimed. Although we may not agree with Jung's conclusion that this man's children took on their father's shadow in destructive ways, Jung's overall idea—that denial of our shadow selves is destructive to everyone around us—speaks a very real truth. As Joss Whedon notes in the voice-over commentary on the episode "Wild at Heart" (4.6), the most dangerous people are often those who are totally unaware of their dark sides. "Nobody thinks that they're a bad guy," Whedon says. "Nobody thinks that they're not righteous. I've dealt with people that are truly villainous, I mean *villainous* . . . people who have done appalling things to other people on purpose. And they think that they're righteous."

For Jung, and for us as well, the key is a greater self-awareness, with the goal of full identity integration. As Xander discovers in the very funny fifth-season episode "The Replacement" (5.3), the human psyche is composed of deeply intricate components that are delicately balanced. When Xander is accidentally hit by a demon's ray gun, it splits his identity so that one Xander seems poised and forceful but humorless; the other is unkempt and unconfident but funny.

(And he can do the all-important "Snoopy dance.") They are two sides of the same coin—represented by the shiny nickel that the suave Xander keeps twirling in his fingers throughout the episode. Neither can exist without the other, and both come to realize that they are integral halves of the same whole. When the two are magically reintegrated at the end of the episode, Xander knows that he has both aspects inside him and can draw on them both. The next day, he and the Scoobies move his things to the lovely new apartment that the forceful, confident Xander rented. His integrated identity is the principal factor in his long-deserved exodus from his parents' basement and his increased ability to move forward with his life.

Xander's example suggests the importance of integrating the many conflicting aspects of what we call the self. But what about integrating darkness into our personalities? On *Buffy* it's not just the "monster" characters who need to learn to tame their own darkness; all of the principals routinely grapple with their dark sides. Giles, for example, hardly seems the type to have an inner ogre, but in the second season we learn that in his youth, he had a renegade and troublesome life as Ripper (2.8). Giles spends much of his adult life trying to forget his Ripper period or at least to stem the tide of the damage he did then. But we see a shade of Ripper in Giles now and again, such as when he uses his demon status in "A

Angel (David Boreanaz) and Xander (Nicholas Brendon) confront their darkness.

New Man" (4.12) to terrorize Professor Walsh, who ridiculed and sneered at him once before. The Ripper part of him takes a certain perverse pleasure in seeing Professor Walsh run for her life. But Ripper is also an aspect of Giles that he can enlist to help in his fight for good, so Giles sometimes employs his dark side to stanch the power of evil. In "The Gift" (5.22), for example, Buffy has the chance to kill Ben, ending Glory's reign of power once and for all, but she cannot do so because Ben is a human being. Although the Slayer cannot end Ben's life, Giles remarks that he is bound by no such heroic code, and he calmly smothers Ben. Ironically, it's because Giles can tap into his darkness that he is able to do some good, defeating Glory forever. It's a morally ambiguous act—like many such acts on *Buffy*—but a necessary one.

Willow is another character who struggles with the darkness within her but learns to control it. In the alternate realities of the third-season episodes "The Wish" (3.9) and "Doppelgängland" (3.16), we get a glimpse of Willow as her alter ego: still clever and "kinda gay," as she puts it, but also purely evil and without conscience. When we see her evil side come to fruition late in the sixth season (6.20–6.22), it's almost as if the prophecy of these episodes has been fulfilled: Willow becomes her evil twin down to the last detail. Even the words that she utters before killing Warren—"Bored now"—echo those spoken by her villainous counterpart in the third season. Dark Willow is determined to erase all evidence of the mousy, sweet Willow of old ("Willow doesn't live here anymore," she jeers) and nearly ends the world with her rage.

By season seven, after being rescued by Xander and rehabilitated by Giles, Willow has learned to be very, very cautious of her own dark side, refusing to do magic at all even when it would help the Scoobies. She is, Buffy says, the "Wicca who won't-a" (7.15), anxious that using magic will bring back dark, veiny, scary Willow. After she is temporarily possessed by the First Evil in "Bring on the Night" (7.10), Willow is terrified, as she collapses on the floor crying: "It's still in me," she wails. "I feel it!" But by season's end, Willow casts the spell that saves the world, using the essence of the Slayer Scythe to empower all of the potential Slayers with superstrength. In doing so, she becomes transfigured, her hair a glowing white in contrast to the raven black hair and eyes she sported when she surrendered to dark magic a year before. This Willow is transformed by goodness and light, looking toward heaven as she reaches within herself to strike a powerful blow against evil.

Finally, Angel is another character who obviously struggles with the darkness inside him. His journey is taken up in the next chapter, but for our purposes here it's worthwhile to note that Angel offers an example of the best and worst that we are all capable of. In her essay "The Good, the Bad, and the Ambivalent," Laura Resnick reminds us that even *good* Angel experiences ongoing temptation and a desire to kill:

> Angel's inner darkness may be supernatural and demonic, but it's a rare person—and a rare *Buffy* fan—who has never once wanted to seize something he has no right to take; never once wanted to give free rein to instinct and desire with no thought for social mores; never once wanted to act out of anger without consideration for the consequences; and never once wanted to break a strict and unsatisfying diet (even in context, cold pig's blood sounds pretty unappetizing). . . . Though we may feel repelled by or wary of the demonic urges living so close to his surface, Angel's struggles are nevertheless *our* struggles—taken to dramatically heightened extremes by the supernatural qualities of the Buffyverse.

What makes Angel such a remarkable character is that against all odds, his desire to do good so often conquers the evil he carries all the time.

Buffy is all about confronting our dark sides and learning to live comfortably—or at least to coexist nonviolently—with our monster selves. Many people would rather deny their dark shadow, pretend it isn't there. But ignoring it entirely, according to the show, is as dangerous as allowing it to rule our lives. We have to find ways to acknowledge it and recognize its power without allowing it to take over. Ironically enough, the show's message seems to be that we are more likely to act on our evil intentions if we remain unaware of them; like Faith in the third season, we will easily surrender to the glorious darkness of our shadow selves if we aren't continually questioning our own motivations.

In the end Buffy's greatest battle is not with demons or vampires but with herself, with the inner darkness she cannot completely slay. It will always be with her, just as our own demons will continue to pursue us. What we will do is our choice: either give the darkness license to damage ourselves and others or respect and control the shadow's power. As Willow learns in the seventh season, she doesn't need to "be a bigger, badder badass than the source of all badness" (7.2). She needs to learn to control her darkness so that it does not control her. In the end she discovers that it's enough just to be Willow, with all of her complexities, all of her darkness, and her much stronger goodness.

CHAPTER 11

"Redemption Is Hard"

Personal Deliverance in the Buffyverse

> Our greatest glory
> is not in never
> failing, but in rising
> every time we fall.
> —Confucius

"Redemption is hard," sighs Andrew in "First Date" (7.14) as he is being stripped of a wire taped to his chest. Andrew has allowed the Scoobies to put the wire under his shirt in order to tape a conversation with the First Evil. It's his first heroic act and the only time he has ever put his own life in jeopardy to help others. The reason? Atonement. Andrew has much to regret, including his involvement with Warren and his complicity in the murders of Katrina and Tara. He also has blood on his own hands: under the influence of the First appearing to him as Warren, Andrew murdered his best friend, Jonathan (7.7). Andrew is aware of a deep guilt inside himself and desires to make things right. This is the beginning of his redemption.

On *Buffy* the redemption process starts—and ends—with the individual, an approach that has more in common with Buddhism than Christianity. The Buffyverse contains no external savior whose act wipes the slate clean for all humanity. Buffy is a Christ figure, but only insofar as she is constantly averting the apocalypse through her self-sacrifice. Preventing the apocalypse is not the same as redeeming humanity, which is what Christians believe Christ did once and for all time: Christ atoned for people's sin; on *Buffy* people must atone for their own. When Buffy or another character prevents the end of the world (yet again), people's hearts don't necessarily change. The demons will keep coming, the vampires will continue siring more vampires, and some humans will still make evil choices. Others, like Andrew, will make terrible mistakes and then atone for them by working on the side of good. The series has a great deal to say about individual responsibility, and although redemption is consistently one of *Buffy*'s most important themes, the message is clear: redemption is hard work, and it is up to us.

At one time or another, almost all of the characters on *Buffy* need redemption. As we've seen, Willow becomes addicted to dark magic, kills Warren to avenge the death of Tara, and does hateful things to hurt her friends (6.20–6.22). Anya, after being jilted at the altar, gets back into business as a vengeance demon and wreaks havoc on a college fraternity, murdering all of the men at a party (7.5). There's also Darla, who improbably attains a redemption of sorts on the spin-off *Angel*, when she gives her own life so that her son can live (A3.9). All three of these characters, like Andrew, spend significant amounts of time and energy on the bumpy road to healing and wholeness. But three other characters on *Buffy* are utterly defined by the quest for redemption, from their first appearances in the early seasons to the series finale in the seventh. Angel, Faith, and Spike have lost much and murdered many, and each of them must come to terms with forging a new future.

Angel: 'Am I a Thing Worth Saving?'

On *Buffy*, as in life, redemption begins with a change of heart. In the case of Angel, the "vampire with a soul," that change of heart came about quite unwillingly when he was reensouled by a gypsy curse. The reensouled Angel is tormented by remembering more than 140 years of his victims' fear, of hearing children's screams. "Funny," he tells Darla, the vampire who sired him, "you would think with all the people I've maimed and killed that I wouldn't be able to remember *every single one*." Each memory is a nightmare to him.

Angel spends a full century tortured by the reality of what he has done. Although he occasionally sticks his neck out to help someone (as in his doomed attempt to assist an acquaintance in the 1950s Hyperion Hotel), he mostly keeps to himself, buying pints of human blood and connecting with no one (A2.2). His process of redemption and healing really begins in earnest only when he risks his own life to save others. On *Buffy* and *Angel*, redemption is a process requiring action; words are not enough. The message of both shows is not simply "Go then, and sin no more" but "Go then, and devote your life to actively fighting evil in the world." *Buffy* is less about the cycle of one's own sin and salvation than it is about saving others; it is always outwardly, and not inwardly, focused. There's no salvation by grace in the Buffyverse; Angel and other characters find salvation only in work, self-sacrifice, and courageous choices. As Buffy scholar Thomas Hibbs points out, one of the flashbacks to Angel's more recent past (1996 Manhattan) demonstrates that the path of redemption is proposed to him in terms of specific duties and responsibilities. Whistler, the demon who wants to help Angel, says that he should assist the Slayer and shows him Buffy from a distance (2.21). Angel will achieve redemption by fighting demons and vampires at Buffy's side. "The big moments are gonna come," Whistler tells Angel. "You can't help that. It's what you do afterwards that counts. That's when you find out who you are."

> To do so no more is the truest repentance.
> —Martin Luther

Angel finds out that he is a "noble vampire," ready to work out his own redemption and atone for his past. In the pilot episode of *Buffy*, he gives the Slayer information about the Harvest that is coming, and their friendship deepens into something more as he aids her in battle. After Angel loses his soul, she is forced to kill Angelus, the monster he has become (2.22). After he returns to earth from hell in the third season (being dead on *Buffy* is really no obstacle to personal growth!), he has a terrible time readjusting to his life and worries that he will once again revert to being the evil Angelus. In "Amends" (3.10), an episode that is a clear homage to Charles Dickens's *A Christmas Carol* (Dickens is Joss Whedon's favorite novelist), the spirits of some of Angel's past victims visit him. He is deeply troubled about his former life and wonders why he's back on earth at all: "I should be in a demon dimension or suffering an eternity of torture," he tells Giles, who doesn't rush to disagree.

By the end of the episode, Angel is ready to commit suicide, just waiting for the Christmas morning sunrise to roast himself to death. He wants his repentance to be a literal version of the biblical Job's: it will take effect through dust and ashes. Angel prefers death to continuing the fight against his nature. "I can't do it again, Buffy," he says. "I can't become a killer." She pleads with him, but he says that the struggle is simply too hard. He thinks that the strong thing to do is to die so that he won't be a threat anymore. "Strong is fighting!" she protests. "It's hard, and it's painful, and it's every day. It's what we have to do. And we can do it together." Just as the sun is about to rise and incinerate Angel, an unthinkable act of grace occurs in Sunnydale: it snows. The white Christmas saves Angel's life, because the sky becomes too gray for the sun to scorch him. The absence of sun in Sunnydale grants Angel the remarkable and unexpected Christmas gift of a second chance. And second chances, fundamentally, are what redemption is all about.

For Angel, the road to happiness lies in helping others. In 1996, when Angel was feeding off the occasional sewer rat and trying to avoid contact with people, Whistler told him he had reached a crossroads. The vampire could go either way: "You can become an even more useless rodent than you already are, or you can become someone. A person. Someone to be counted" (2.21). Angel chooses the heroic path of a champion, shaping his redemption with good deeds.

Faith: 'How Does This Work?'

Angel's reensoulment was a curse, something that he never sought and that destroyed the "clarity" of his life as a vampire. Suddenly, he was forced to see victims as individuals, humans like he had once been, with fears and loves as he had once had. In one sense Angel's murders were understandable in the same way that the food chain is understandable: wolves eat sheep, and vampires feed off humans. Until Angel had a soul, he never had much of a choice about whether to kill, though he was renowned for taking a twisted pleasure in it. He lived off instinct and had no reason to question his actions.

Faith's story is very different. When she arrives in Sunnydale, Faith is full of bluster and bravado, although secretly in pain from witnessing the murder of her Watcher and feeling powerless to stop it (3.3). She comes into the show as a character whose iconoclastic brazenness fuses with a childlike vulnerability, a volatile mix. After enduring other betrayals in the third season—including the treachery of Gwendolyn Post, the new Watcher she has just started to trust—Faith snaps. As recounted elsewhere, Faith commits a murder, allies with the Mayor, tries to kill her former friends, and winds up in a coma for eight months. When she awakens, it's a different world: the Mayor is dead, the school is destroyed, and the Scoobies have mostly moved on to college. At first, Faith experiences a sense of pleasure in her new *raison d'être:* to exact revenge on Buffy. And she has the ultimate weapon to do so, because the Mayor has left her a device that enables her to switch bodies with her enemy. Faith gets to watch Buffy be arrested for Faith's own crimes, and she sets out to enjoy Buffy's life, which she has long envied.

> Deep, unspeakable suffering may well be called a baptism, a regeneration, the initiation into a new state.
>
> —George Eliot, *Adam Bede*

However, something odd happens to Faith, who begins to *become* Buffy as she inhabits her body. In "Who Are You?" (4.16) Faith slays a vampire who is attacking a young woman, mostly because she is posing as Buffy and knows that people would become suspicious if she didn't do her job. But when the young woman thanks her profusely, something clicks in Faith; she has done a good deed and saved a life. It's not a trivial thing. She sleeps with Buffy's boyfriend, Riley, expecting that this will be a marvelous payback, but the experience affects her deeply. Riley really *loves* Buffy; and Faith, who has always used men and been used by them, is confounded by this. She tries to insist that what they shared is "meaningless," but she's disturbed and frightened by what it feels like to be loved.

Throughout the episode Faith has mocked Buffy's sense of morality by repeating the phrase "because it's wrong" in a jeering tone. She comes on to Spike in the Bronze, for example, making explicitly sexual promises of what she could do to him but won't—"because it's wrong." But by the end of the episode, when Faith-disguised-as-Buffy is about to skip town and never have to face her past, she hears a television report about vampires holding hostages in a Sunnydale church, and she drops everything to save them. "You're *not* gonna kill these people," she tells the hungry vampires. "Why not?" one asks. And Faith repeats the mantra she's been mocking during the entire episode: "Because it's wrong." Only this time she knows it to be true. She has become so much like Buffy that when she fights the real Buffy (disguised as Faith), she is repulsed. Faith pummels her own body. "You're nothing!" she screams at herself. "Disgusting, murderous bitch. You're *nothing.*" She is revolted by the killer she has become, an awareness that spurs the first step on her road to repentance.

> O villain! Thou wilt be condemn'd into everlasting redemption for this.
> —William Shakespeare, *Much Ado About Nothing,* Act 4, Scene 2

After they switch back and reinhabit their own bodies, Faith flees Sunnydale for Los Angeles, and her story is taken up on the *Buffy* spin-off *Angel.* In "Five by Five" (A1.18) Faith sets out on a crime spree, trying to drown her own uncertainty in more violence. She accepts a job with Wolfram & Hart to assassinate Angel, and she enjoys viciously torturing Wesley, one of her former Watchers. But in the climactic fight with Angel, we see that what Faith really wants is not to assassinate her target but to have him kill *her.* She aches for her misery to end and repeats over and over that she's bad, she's evil. Angel refuses to kill her, to let her take the easy road of death and oblivion, as he had once tried to do: "Nice try, Faith," he says. "I know what you want. And I'm not gonna do it. I'm not gonna make it easy for you." Instead, he offers the harder path of repentance, the same road he has trod for more than a century. She is going to have to face up to all that she has done.

In the next episode, "Sanctuary" (A1.19), Angel offers Faith a place to stay while she hides out from the police. She is riddled by flashbacks of her crimes and tries to run again. Angel understands that Faith can no longer control her evil impulses. "You thought that you could just touch it [evil], that you'd be OK," he says. "Five by five, right Faith? But it swallowed you whole. So tell me, how'd you like it?" Angel doesn't make any simple promises about the journey of repentance, but he does tell her that it's the only way she'll ever have real peace. "The truth is, no matter how much you suffer, no matter how many good deeds you do to try to make up for the past, you may never balance out the cosmic scale," he cautions. "The only thing I can promise you is that you'll probably be haunted—and maybe for the rest of your life." Faith doesn't see how she can possibly get through the pain: "God, it hurts. I hate it that it hurts like this!" She is terrified of apologizing to Buffy, whom she has tortured emotionally, and to Wesley, whom she has tortured physically. How can a simple apology cover those kind of wrongs? But she is also determined to make a go of her new life, and at the end of the episode, she does what would have been unthinkable for the old Faith: she turns herself in to the police. Faith makes a courageous choice to confront her past and carve out a new future. When she emerges from prison three years later, she is a different person. (As one *Buffy* commentator points out, Faith is "probably the only person to ever come out of the California penal system better than when she went in.") She is in control of herself for the first time and is ready to lay down her life if necessary to save Angel and help Buffy defeat the First Evil.

'I Wanna See How It Ends': Spike

Spike's character is certainly the most morally ambiguous of this trio of powerful reformed killers. It's interesting that the show's lack of resolution about Spike has inspired perhaps more Web sites and fan fiction than any other character besides Buffy herself. Almost everyone wants to believe that Spike can be fully redeemed, and many new viewers have tuned in to *Angel* to see whether it will happen.

The implantation of the nonharming chip (4.7), like the restoration of Angel's soul, was certainly not Spike's choice, and he spends most of the fourth season scheming for ways to get the chip removed so he can return to the business of feeding off humans. Instead, the chip slowly becomes the vehicle for his redemption, as he forms friendships with the Scoobies and eventually falls in love with the Slayer. Toward the end of the fifth season, we see him begin to undertake the kinds of heroic acts that are the stuff of redemption on *Buffy*: he suffers Glory's terrible torture so as not to reveal that Dawn is the Key (5.18), and he risks his life to save Dawn despite the fact that Buffy has told him she could never love him (5.22).

From a religious standpoint, Spike's transformation would seem to be the ultimate nail in the coffin of the predestination-free will debates that have occupied religions for centuries. Spike, like Angel, is a vampire—and at the beginning of the series, he is a soulless killer who sees human beings as merely "Happy Meals with legs" (2.22). Yet as we saw in the chapter on change, even before he regained his soul, Spike was capable of love, could be emotionally hurt, and fought to improve himself rather than remain stagnant. During the fourth through sixth seasons, Spike changed so much that he actually had to keep reminding people that he was, technically, still evil ("Hello! Vampire!" he exclaims at one point; 6.9). In other words, *Buffy* makes the case that even the most unlikely individual is still capable of redemption. Everyone has choices. Being an undead bloodsucker doesn't mean that Spike isn't capable of profound change.

But he's not a harmless puppy, either. Writer David Fury notes that Spike's evolution has never been a case of pure heroism, though he can certainly be counted among "anti-heroes that rise to the occasion." Even with a soul, Spike is still full of moral ambiguity and is, in Fury's words, "ultimately not a good guy." He's not like Angel, who "makes that complete journey" from vampirehood to full humanity. Spike's is a redemption in process. Still, like Faith and Angel, he has always had a choice: even after getting the chip, he could have continued to aid and abet the forces of darkness, as he tried to do in the fourth season when he allied with Adam. But Spike abandons this road out of love for Buffy. All of his subsequent actions, including his determination to have his soul restored in order to make himself worthy of Buffy, arise from that love and from an increasing desire to do good for its own sake. This is demonstrated beautifully in the series finale, when Spike sacrifices his life to save the world. He does not do this to win Buffy's love; in fact, when she finally confesses that she does love him, he refuses to believe it but thanks her for saying so all the same (7.22). Spike's self-immolation has a kind of purity about it. His road to redemption has required the ultimate sacrifice, and his life goes up in the refining flames of the explosion that saves the world.

Interestingly, the show does a beautiful thing to subtly comment on the way Spike's life in Sunnydale has come full circle. When Buffy explains to Giles that Spike was the one who saved the town, the "Welcome to Sunnydale" sign wavers slightly and then pitches forward into the crater created by the explosion. This scene reminds viewers of the sign that Spike demolished in the second season when he first thundered into town (2.3) and another in the third season when he drunkenly returned to the Hellmouth after Drusilla dumped him (3.8). In contrast to those destructive acts, the Sunnydale sign falls again at the series' end as a testimony to Spike's heroism and willingness to die for others. His redemption, though not complete, has certainly been remarkable.

On *Buffy* redemption is never a sure thing, and it's not a onetime act that guarantees a happily-ever-after future. When Andrew complains that redemption is hard, he might add that, in the Buffyverse at least, it is also never-ending: characters sometimes regress, and they never really reach a point where they can be certain of their own hearts. (Christians would call this backsliding, an excellent term to describe the ease with which people can slip back into old patterns by simply ceasing to struggle against their worst selves.) Angel, for example, succumbs once to temptation and feeds off a dying human in a doughnut shop (A4.15). As the show's writers have said, he is like a recovering alcoholic who is always one drink away from a total reversion to his addiction. In the Buffyverse, in other words, redemption is never something that individuals can take for granted.

> He who repents of a sin is like someone who has committed no sin.
>
> —Muhammad, Hadith 754

Although the process of redemption is fraught with uncertainty, it is the route to inner peace. "The road to redemption is a rocky path," the incarcerated Faith remarks to Angel at the start of *Angel*'s second season (A2.1). He should know: in order to save someone's life, he's just been forced to croon a Barry Manilow ballad onstage in a demon karaoke bar—a humiliation that ranks high on the list of the worst things he's ever had to do in the service of good. "Think we might make it?" Faith asks Angel. "We might," he says, with emphasis on the conditional. And for now, that is enough. There are no guarantees that Faith and Angel will always remain on the redemptive path they have chosen, but they both understand that the journey itself is worth everything.

Epilogue

"Where Do We Go from Here?"

In the classic American musical, the final number offers an opportunity for the entire cast to reassemble and essentially congratulate themselves through song: the lovers have reunited; the foe is vanquished. There seems to be a whole lot to sing about. The tone is triumphant and the victory secure as the cast belts out this finale, which is usually a reprise of the show's most hopeful, optimistic song. After the cast reassures the audience members that they'll never walk alone, for example (*Carousel*), everyone departs the theater with renewed hope.

> Sir, you have wrestled well, and overthrown More than your enemies.
>
> —*William Shakespeare*, As You Like It, *Act 1, Scene 2*

In the finale of *Buffy*'s musical episode (6.7), by contrast, the cast laments that they'll "walk alone in fear" and that they're not at all certain about what's next. Everything ends with a poignant question: "Where do we go from here?" This kind of honesty sums up what I love most about *Buffy*. It doesn't tell me what I want to hear; the show gives it to me straight. *Buffy* gives me hope precisely because giving hope is not its goal. It carefully examines how tough life can be and how very flawed we are. I also appreciate the fact that the evil on *Buffy* just keeps coming. William Patrick Day points out that Buffy occasionally gets dejected about this reality: "On *Buffy the Vampire Slayer*, to be happy, to be good, to be truly human are difficult, endless pursuits. In one episode, depressed about how the vampires always come back, Buffy thinks to herself that because she will never win, her work is fruitless. 'No fruit for Buffy,' she says sadly. But she accepts that although Good will never actually triumph it is worth continuing to fight even for small and temporary victories against cruelty, violence and fear." Despite the seeming impossibility of a satisfyingly complete conquest of evil, Buffy continues to do what good she can. And so must we.

I resonate with the fact that the characters on *Buffy* often screw up in precisely the same ways they did several seasons ago and that they wonder aloud about which path to choose. My own spiritual journey is sometimes very much like that—far more like a spiral than a straight line, marching forward. (Is it any wonder that even in *Pilgrim's Progress*, that foundational book about the spiritual journey, the main character, Christian, seems always to be going in circles?)

In a spiral, though, we typically have the advantage. Walking in a straight line, undeterred by any activity to the left or right, we are always having to forge a fresh path. We are constantly navigating *terra incognita*, trying to understand the best strategy for strange terrain and new situations. But in the ascending spiral of a spiritual journey, we have the familiar sense of having been there before; the difference is that we cycle around again bringing all of our experiences to bear on a situation that is at once new and recognizable. We have grown since the last time we were here.

> So let us not grow weary in doing what is right, for we will reap at harvest-time, if we do not give up.
>
> —Galatians 6:9

So even though, as the musical finale suggests, the end seems distant and the path is unclear, we will rise up to meet that path—again and again, if we have to. Like Buffy, we can be strong. With the loving support of friends and companions, we can choose to change and to forgive, to be morally courageous even in the midst of darkness and doubt. We can be heroes. And that, as Buffy would say, is certainly "something to sing about."

A Guide to Buffy's Seven Seasons

This appendix will guide your exploration of the spiritual issues in this book and in the series on a season-by-season basis. If you would like more detailed plot summaries, please turn to the official *Watcher's Guides*.

Season One
Number of Episodes: 12

Primary Villain: The Master

Scoobies: Buffy, Giles, Willow, and Xander

Picking up where the movie leaves off, the first season introduces new characters and sets up some of the moral dilemmas that drive the whole series: choice and personal accountability; friendship as a source of strength; the balance of good versus evil; the long road to maturity. Throughout the first season, Buffy comes to terms with her calling as the Slayer and negotiates that with her desire to have a normal life.

When Buffy arrives in Sunnydale in "Welcome to the Hellmouth" (1.1), she's looking for a new start. We learn that she and her mother had to leave Los Angeles, where Buffy was expelled from school after burning down the gymnasium (a reference to what had happened in the film). Clearly, Buffy wants nothing more to do with vampires and is hoping to have a normal teenager's life. Soon enough, however, she is confronted not only with a Sunnydale High School student obviously killed by vampires but also with Rupert Giles, the school librarian who explains that he is her Watcher and that being a Vampire Slayer is Buffy's sacred duty. Giles also breaks the news that Sunnydale is situated over the Hellmouth, a portal to hell and a center for demonic activity.

Initially, Buffy looks for a way out of her role in the fight against all the dark forces that congregate in Sunnydale—she has come there, after all, to flee from the trouble her new identity caused her in Los Angeles. She focuses on her social life and studies, and meets Cordelia Chase, the most popular girl in the school; Willow, a nerdy genius; and Willow's geeky friends, Xander and Jesse.

Giles continues to pursue Buffy, however, and she does jump into action, killing a vampire to save Willow. However, she's not able to save their friend Jesse. In "The Harvest" (1.2), Jesse's transformation from geeky teen to self-confident sired vampire (so cool that even Cordelia will dance with him) gives viewers information about how vampires are created in the Buffyverse: when vampires kill, they have the option of siring their victim by allowing the victim to drink the vampire's blood. If the victim agrees, he or she also becomes a vampire. Vampires have two faces—the one they had when sired and a demonic face that emerges when they feed or become angry. Also, they feel newly empowered and are supernaturally strong.

Soon Buffy and Giles learn that vampires in the Hellmouth are plotting to help their Master regain his power and destroy the world in an apocalyptic Harvest. Buffy and Giles reluctantly share their identities as well as the truth about the Hellmouth with Willow and Xander, who begin to help them by using Giles's impressive library of ancient books to research the Master and his evil plan.

Revealing their identities is not a choice Buffy and Giles make lightly; Buffy is bound to secrecy regarding her identity, and the prophecy about her says that she alone will fight. Traditionally, Slayers have been lone wolves; but by bringing Xander and Willow into her confidence, Buffy breaks this tradition. At several crucial points throughout the series, she realizes that her connectedness to the Scoobies is what keeps her alive and the world from ending.

Nonetheless, Buffy keeps her identity a secret whenever she can, which creates several ethical dilemmas for her as she attempts to live within the bounds of acceptable teenage behavior and her duties as the Slayer. She has problems at school, where she is perceived as a violent troublemaker, and also at home, where her mother is frustrated by Buffy's reputation at school and by the distance in their relationship.

Once Buffy realizes that she cannot turn her back on her Slayer identity, she seeks to keep her calling from ruining her life. In "The Witch" (1.3) she tries out for the cheerleading squad to disastrous effect; and in "Never Kill a Boy on the First Date" (1.5) she dates a supposedly normal boy, only to discover that he is attracted to her largely because of his obsession with danger and death.

To complicate matters, Buffy finds herself drawn to Angel, a mysterious stranger who shows up to help her at key moments and then disappears. When they share a passionate first kiss in "Angel" (1.7), she is horrified to see him turn into a vampire. She soon learns that he is a 240-year-old vampire with a soul who stopped killing one hundred years ago.

Angel joins forces with Giles, Xander, Willow, and Buffy. Not only do they face the external threat of the Master and the Harvest, but they also struggle with unrequited love: Willow has loved Xander since childhood, and Xander has fallen for Buffy, whose feelings for Angel are mutual but doomed. In the wake of all this emotional turmoil, Giles discovers a disturbing prophecy in the season's final episode, "Prophecy Girl" (1.12): the Master will kill the Slayer, on Spring Fling night no less, and there's nothing they can do about it. Buffy initially attempts to flee from this horrifying reality but finally chooses to face it after a deadly vampire attack at the school. After the Master drowns her, he is empowered to break out of the Hellmouth and begin harvesting humankind. Before he gets very far, though, Xander and Angel find Buffy, and Xander resuscitates her. She hunts and kills the Master. The season ends with Buffy, in her soiled but beautiful formal dress, heading off with her friends to party.

In addition to introducing Buffy's achingly impossible dilemmas, season one portrays the moral universe in which Buffy must fight her battles and begins to explore the sticky issue of individual moral accountability. In the Buffyverse people exercise only limited agency in their pursuit of good and evil. Although the episodes that explore Buffy's development are central to the larger story arc, stand-alone episodes such as "The Pack" (1.6) and "Out of Mind, Out of Sight" (1.11) flesh out a world in which good and evil happen to relatively innocent people, whose only agency lies in their response to their misfortune. The series repeatedly depicts a reality in which evil is only partially chosen but always decisively punished. The degree to which the characters are held accountable for their misdeeds tends to be proportional to the level of free will they exercised when they committed them. Characters get some sympathy for mitigating circumstances (such as past traumas) but never have complete forgiveness until they have begun the hard work of redemption.

Season Two
Number of Episodes: 22

Primary Villains: Spike, Drusilla, and Angelus

Scoobies: Buffy, Giles, Willow, Xander, Angel, Cordelia, Jenny, and Kendra

Buffy begins the season having enjoyed a slay-free summer in Los Angeles, but her erratic (and erotic) behavior in "When She Was Bad" (2.1) reveals that she has not yet recovered from her experience with the Master. After destroying his bones at the end of this episode, she seems to experience some closure. This prepares her to deal with the bad elements in the season's many stand-alone episodes as well as those that further the larger story of the Scoobies' fight against Spike, Drusilla, and Angelus.

Stand-alone episodes such as "Inca Mummy Girl" (2.4) and "Lie to Me" (2.7) are ostensibly about other characters but reveal truths about Buffy's situation. In "Inca Mummy Girl," Buffy meets another teenage girl who was robbed of her youth—Ampata, an Inca princess who was ritually sacrificed five hundred years ago. Unlike the reawakened Ampata, who sucks the life out of others so that she might live, Buffy has made selfless, noble choices in response to her fate. And in "Lie to Me," Buffy is reunited with her old friend Ford, who is also dealing with cruel fate in the form of cancer. Ford, like Ampata, is willing to exploit and sacrifice others to achieve his goal of being sired by a vampire and living forever. When he tells Buffy that his terminal illness justifies his actions, Buffy says, "You have a choice. . . . You're opting for mass murder here, and nothing you say is gonna make that OK!"

Even Giles, in "The Dark Age" (2.8), reveals that he once responded badly to the fact that he had no choice in life but to be a Watcher. His flight from duty twenty years before led him to occult practices that come back to haunt him, leading to the deaths of most of his old friends from that time and to the temporary demonic possession of his love interest, Jenny Calendar. Each of these cautionary tales provides commentary on Buffy's situation: regardless of how bad her situation is—having to forgo normal life in order to accept a calling that will probably lead to her early death—she doesn't have an appealing alternative. If she flees from her calling, innocent people will die.

In "Halloween" (2.6), however, she learns to value her unique calling and abilities. On Halloween Buffy temporarily loses her powers when she becomes the stereotypically helpless eighteenth-century girl whose costume she wears. After regaining her true identity, Buffy begins to appreciate her calling and the agency it affords, quipping, "You know what? It's good to be me."

The season-two arc focuses on the introduction of Spike, a Slayer-killing vampire, and Drusilla, his insane, clairvoyant girlfriend. They come to Sunnydale to pursue a cure for Drusilla's unspecified mental and physical illness. They almost immediately become the town's alpha vampires when they kill Colin, the Master's Anointed One, by exposing him to the sun. Soon Spike and Drusilla have assembled everything they need to achieve her cure—including Angel, the vampire who sired Drusilla, who must be sacrificed as part of the healing ritual. To dispose of Buffy, Spike and Drusilla hire a trio of demonic assassins known as the Order of Taraka.

In the two-part episode "What's My Line?" (2.9–2.10), the Scoobies meet a new Slayer named Kendra who rose when Buffy briefly died at the end of season one. Kendra helps the Scoobies kill the bounty hunters, and she also learns a few lessons from Buffy about how to live a balanced life. Unlike Buffy, Kendra has experienced no ambivalence about her identity as Slayer. Her parents sent her to live with her Watcher when she was a little girl, and he trained her to be the perfect Slayer. Much to Giles's delight, this perfection involves being an avid reader, which Buffy is not. It also involves avoiding friendships (especially with boys) and taking an emotionless, by-the-book approach to battle. As she instructs Kendra about the value of relationships and emotions, Buffy realizes that compared to Kendra, she has achieved some balance in her life after all.

Meanwhile, the other Scoobies develop relationships of their own. Giles and Jenny Calendar begin dating; Xander and Cordelia begin an unlikely and initially secret affair; and Willow, who has continued to pine for Xander, is pleasantly surprised when Oz, the guitarist in a local band, begins to pursue her. (Considering the Scoobies' luck in relationships, it comes as little surprise that Jenny is actually a descendant of the gypsy tribe that cursed Angel with a soul and that Oz is a werewolf.)

Although the Scoobies manage to kill the bounty hunters and save Angel from being ritually sacrificed, the ritual goes far enough to cure Drusilla, who is now significantly more powerful and still clairvoyant. She and Spike set out to rebuild the Judge, a world-destroying demon that cannot be hurt by any weapon forged. In the midst of trying to stop them from rebuilding it, Buffy and Angel consummate their relationship.

Perhaps the most stunning and heartrending plot development in the second season is Angel's transformation back into a soulless demon. His sexual encounter with Buffy, which leads him to true happiness, lifts the gypsy curse that gave him back his soul one hundred years earlier. Once Angel becomes the soulless Angelus again, he returns to killing people, including Giles's love interest, Jenny Calendar. A devastated Buffy becomes both Angelus's hunter and his prey.

Episodes such as "Surprise" (2.13) use other characters to explore Buffy's fate as well as her ambivalence about Angel. "Surprise" points to a number of parallels between Buffy and Drusilla. In this episode both Buffy and Drusilla have prophetic dreams, one of which shows Buffy wearing Drusilla's dress, portending that Buffy may now be as vulnerable to Angelus as Drusilla once was. And viewers learn that just as Buffy has been dreaming of Drusilla, Drusilla has been dreaming of her. When Buffy leaves her own birthday party to crash a much more diabolical party being given for Drusilla, Drusilla exclaims, "I only dreamed you'd come." By portraying Drusilla as both victim and villain, and the formerly heroic Angel as the sadistic Angelus, this episode sets the stage for the series' many reversals—one season's villain can easily be another season's hero.

Injured in a fire during Drusilla's curing ritual, Spike watches resentfully from a wheelchair as Angelus moves in on her. When Angelus and Drusilla procure the Acathla demon and plan to use it to open the portal to hell, Spike decides to help the Scoobies stop them. As the final battle ensues, Drusilla kills Kendra, and the police think Buffy did it. Joyce finally learns that Buffy is the Slayer and does not initially take it well. Buffy discovers that she must kill Angelus at the portal as it opens in order to shut it again. As she does, Willow, who is recovering from her battle wounds in the hospital, performs a spell that restores Angel's soul. Buffy realizes that Angel has been reensouled just at the moment when she also realizes that the portal has opened and that she has no choice but to kill him. Grief-stricken at the loss of Angel and Kendra, estranged from her mother, expelled from school, and wanted by the police, Buffy runs away at the end of the season.

Season Three
Number of Episodes: 22
Primary Villain: The Mayor

Scoobies: Giles, Buffy, Willow, Xander, Oz, Cordelia, Angel, and Faith

In season three Buffy learns about herself by observing parallels between her own life and those of friends and acquaintances. In "Anne" (3.1) Buffy has run away from home and moved to Los Angeles, where she works as a waitress and goes by her middle name, Anne. Buffy meets Lily, an old schoolmate from Sunnydale, whom she saves from a hellish slave-labor camp. After this experience, Buffy is ready to go home.

When Buffy comes home, all who had been worried by her absence are relieved, but they also resent the fact that she deserted them. She is no longer a suspect in Kendra's murder, but her principal (and personal nightmare), Mr. Snyder, initially refuses to let her come back to school for her senior year. As Buffy attempts to make amends, she and the Scoobies meet Faith, the Slayer who rose up to replace Kendra. Faith's life and choices lead Buffy to ask questions about her own. Although Kendra's

Spock-like approach to slaying made Buffy wonder if she was slacking off, Faith's candor about her appetite for slaying (as well as for sex) makes Buffy wonder if she is a prude. At first the Scoobies and Joyce seem smitten with Faith; at the end of "Faith, Hope, and Trick" (3.3), however, Buffy and viewers learn that Faith helplessly watched an ancient vampire called Kakistos brutally murder her Watcher and that Faith's bravado masks a deep well of terror and vulnerability.

Faith achieves closure by killing Kakistos but continues to relish the power and violence involved in her job. In "Bad Girls" (3.14) Buffy, who initially felt "single-white-femaled" by Faith, comes to admire her and eventually tries to emulate her. This turns out to be a bad choice, because beneath Faith's swagger is a dangerously amoral approach to life. As she and Buffy rob a weapons store, Faith reveals that her motto in life is "Want. Take. Have." After being apprehended for theft, the two Slayers escape, only to encounter the evil, yet human, Deputy Mayor, whom Faith accidentally kills. Although Faith could now make amends for this mistake and move on, she instead insists that she is above the law and feels no remorse. Even though this is also a facade, Faith soon finds that killing has changed her.

As Buffy witnesses Faith's transformation from Slayer to stone-cold killer, her first response is to try to rehabilitate her former friend. But when the Scoobies discover that Faith has secretly begun working for Sunnydale's evil Mayor, most of them accept that Faith is morally a lost cause. Only when Faith falls into a coma and appears to Buffy in a dream in "Graduation Day (Part Two)" (3.22) does Buffy's faith in Faith seem to be validated and rewarded. In this dream Faith tells Buffy how to defeat the Mayor and offers Buffy unlimited access to her mind.

Oz and Willow continue their romance, as do Xander and Cordelia in the first half of the season. Buffy's love life is complicated by a new boyfriend named Scott, as well as Angel's unexpected return from hell. For several episodes Buffy hides Angel from the Scoobies, remembering that he tortured Giles after murdering his girlfriend, Jenny. Xander discovers Buffy with Angel, and Buffy again finds herself seeking the forgiveness of her friends, who are hurt and confused that she is harboring a person they believe to be a mass murderer.

While Angel slowly wins back the Scoobies' trust, he faces the First Evil—an incorporeal being that in "Amends" (3.10) takes on the likenesses of many of Angel's victims, forcing him to relive some of his worst crimes in gruesome detail. The First convinces Angel to kill himself, but Buffy, with whom he has forged an uneasy postromantic friendship, finds him and has time to convince him to stay alive. During the course of this encounter, the two also realize that their love, no matter how complicated and painful, deserves another try.

During this scene Angel asks Buffy, "Am I a thing worth saving? Am I a righteous man?" These questions, as they apply to virtually every character, pervade season three. Several characters encounter their dark side and are forced to ask questions about whether they are fundamentally good or evil. Buffy's righteousness is called into question when she deserts her friends and family, hides Angel, or goes on a shoplifting spree with Faith. Faith, through a series of unfortunate events and bad choices, eschews ethical behavior in favor of power. Willow and Xander face their own moral shortcomings as they begin a secret romance, thus cheating on Oz and Cordelia.

Anya, introduced in "The Wish" (3.9) as the vengeance demon Anyanka, has had nothing but a dark side for over one thousand years. After she grants a brokenhearted Cordelia's wish that Buffy had never come to Sunnydale, however, Giles is able to reverse the curse. As punishment for this failure, Anyanka is made mortal and must learn how to live with a soul and its attendant moral compass.

Finally, Giles struggles with his conscience, especially as it guides his actions toward Buffy. In "Helpless" (3.12) he follows the Watchers' Council's ancient custom of stripping his Slayer of her powers on her eighteenth birthday and putting her in a deadly situation that she must survive purely by her wits. In the end his fatherly feelings for Buffy motivate him to abandon this exercise, but not before Buffy has felt the sting of betrayal.

In each case these characters realize that they are not entirely righteous people, and each pays a price. Buffy hurts her friends, and Faith loses track of her conscience. Xander loses Cordelia, whose pain is so intense that, thanks to Anyanka, it almost destroys Sunnydale. Willow, who has been developing as a witch throughout the season, is able to reconcile with Oz, but in "Doppelgängland" (3.16) she encounters a version of herself so evil that she is forced to question her own capacity for evil—a theme that comes full circle at the end of season six.

And Giles not only hurts Buffy but, because he abandoned his duties in "Helpless," loses his post as her Watcher as well. This leads Wesley Wyndam-Pryce, an inexperienced Watcher from England, to Sunnydale to oversee Buffy and Faith. Although Giles keenly feels the loss of his job, his new status allows him to act more openly as a father to Buffy. The series explores parenthood repeatedly throughout the season, giving special emphasis to Giles and Buffy's increasingly familial connection. An episode that ironically underscores the importance of parental authority, "Band Candy" (3.6), begins with Buffy thoroughly resenting Joyce and Giles's attempts to control her schedule and her life. Soon enough, however, under the influence of some magically altered candy, Joyce and Giles, like all the other adults in town, begin acting like teenagers, and Buffy finds herself nostalgic for their parental behavior. They regain their maturity (but not before consummating their relationship). A few episodes later, in "Gingerbread" (3.11), Willow's heretofore unseen mother and Joyce are both bewitched into trying to burn Willow, Buffy, and a witch named Amy at the stake. Both episodes concern parental abdication—both magically induced but in Willow's mother's case chronic—and underscore how desperately Buffy and her peers need mature and loving parental figures.

Perhaps the most poignant portrayal of adolescent longing for a parent is Faith's relationship with the Mayor. She becomes not only his lieutenant but also his protégé and surrogate daughter. The Mayor manipulates Faith by playing on her hunger for a father and uses her longing for friends, as well as her desire for revenge against those who spurned her, to persuade her to poison Angel. In turn, after learning that a Slayer's blood is the only antidote to this deadly poison, Buffy tries to kill Faith so that she can bring her blood to Angel. Buffy fails and, in an erotically charged scene, lets Angel feed on her just enough to save himself without killing her.

In the final episodes of the season, Angel, realizing that their future is untenable, devastates Buffy by breaking up with her. In "The Prom" (3.20) Jonathan, the class nerd whom Buffy saved in "Earshot" (3.18), announces that Buffy has won the Class Protector award and gives her a beautiful umbrella. Xander reluctantly goes to the dance with Anya, and Cordelia, whose father has just been arrested for tax evasion, attends in a dress Xander secretly bought for her. The two reconcile as friends, and Cordelia shares a romantic dance with Wesley (though she later kisses him and finds they have no chemistry).

As graduation looms, the Scoobies find themselves fighting the Mayor, who is on his way to becoming a pure apocalypse-bringing demon. He plans to ascend to this state as he speaks at the Sunnydale High graduation, and the Scoobies realize that the only way to stop him is to enlist the entire senior class to fight him and the army of vampires who have come to feed on them during his ascension. In the memorable season finale (3.22), all the class members hide weapons under their gowns and, when Buffy gives them the signal, begin this battle. While the graduating seniors successfully fight off vampires, Buffy taunts the Mayor, who has turned into a giant demon-

snake, by telling him how she nearly killed Faith with the same knife he gave his protégé. He chases Buffy into the high school library, where the Scoobies detonate
enough explosives to destroy him and the high school.

In many ways the season is about coming of age. The destruction of the high
school is an apt metaphor for the fact that there is no going back to adolescence. And
season three shows Buffy changing from a teenage runaway to a mature woman who
rejects the oppressiveness of the Watchers' Council and successfully leads an army of
her peers against a monster. In the season's final scene, Oz says to the other Scoobies,
"Guys, take a moment to deal with this: we survived." Buffy assumes he means the battle with the Mayor, but he really means that they survived high school. The camera
zooms in on their yearbook, which says, "The Future Is Ours." Indeed, it is theirs
because they fought for and earned it.

Season Four
Number of Episodes: 22

Primary Villain: Adam

Scoobies: Giles, Buffy, Willow, Oz, Xander, Anya, Tara, and Riley

During season four, as Buffy and the Scoobies face life after high school, new moral
issues emerge: the need for balance, ambivalence about the self in relation to others,
and the challenges of coming of age. Buffy and Willow attend UC Sunnydale, where
Buffy meets and becomes involved with her handsome psychology teacher's assistant,
Riley Finn. Willow meets Tara, who, after Willow's breakup with Oz, becomes her new
love interest. Xander makes his way in the work world and continues his relationship
with ex-demon Anya, and Giles is adrift after having lost his jobs as Watcher and high
school librarian.

Riley and Maggie Walsh, the psychology professor he assists, are actually members
of a clandestine, government-sponsored demon-fighting organization called the
Initiative. Literally underground, the Initiative has good, if dangerously naive, intentions, and its presence on *Buffy* poses moral questions about the relative value of
modernity versus ancient thought. The Scoobies, of course, operate with a decidedly
premodern worldview. When they encounter the Initiative, with its high-tech
weapons and its scientific assumptions about the demons it captures, they question
the value of their own techniques and beliefs. At first the Initiative's methods seem
superior to the Scoobies' own: an army of strong men who fight demons with the lat-
est technology and then hold them in captivity in order to learn about them does
seem more effective than a group of kids with stakes and crosses. The Initiative's
worldview seems reasonable as well; speculation about demon dimensions seems trivial to them, because they regard those they capture simply as subterrestrials who are
nothing more than menacing creatures that need to be stopped and studied. (They
capture Spike, for example, and put a chip in his brain that makes it painful for him to
harm humans.)

When Buffy compares the countless demons she's killed to the seventeen Riley
has either killed or maimed, however, Riley and Professor Walsh must face the possibility that her supernatural, premodern approach is valid, and they invite her to join
the Initiative, which she briefly does. But Buffy's approach, which involves asking
lots of questions and poking around in top secret areas, is incompatible with the
Initiative's military chain-of-command style, and Professor Walsh unsuccessfully
tries to have Buffy killed. The professor has secrets that she doesn't want Buffy or
anyone else to know about, including the fact that she has been developing a

demon-robot-human hybrid, whom she calls Adam. However, Adam has his own diabolical plans. After launching a murder spree that begins with Professor Walsh herself, he hatches a plan to set the demons and humans in the Initiative free to fight a chaotic, bloody war so that he can use their body parts to create an entire race of hybrids like himself. Adam seems to embody all that is finally wrong with a modern, naturalistic approach to the supernatural. In "A New Man" (4.12) Ethan Rayne, a former friend of Giles's who continued to practice dark magic after Giles gave up the occult, tells Giles, "This new outfit, it's blundering into new places it doesn't belong. It's throwing the worlds out of balance. And that's way beyond chaos, mate." This is one of the series' earliest references to the importance of balance. The Buffyverse seeks a balance between good and evil, rather than one force permanently vanquishing the other.

Another moral question that pervades season four regards friendship and alienation. Can friends remain close and loyal, even if circumstances pull them in different directions? Having been quite literally displaced when the high school, their headquarters, was destroyed in "Graduation Day (Part Two)" (3.22), the Scoobies struggle with deeper feelings of displacement as well. When Buffy and Willow begin to study at UC Sunnydale, Buffy immediately feels lost and overwhelmed, while Willow thrives and delights in her on-campus boyfriend. Buffy is left to deal with yet another dilemma regarding her Slayer identity: How can she reconcile her powerful persona with that of a clueless freshman? In "The Freshman" (4.1) Buffy struggles with this as Sunday, the head of UC Sunnydale's vampire gang, capitalizes on Buffy's vulnerability in this new setting and beats her up, forcing Buffy to run away in decidedly un-Slayer-like fashion. Only when she receives help from Willow, Xander, and Oz does Buffy find the gumption to fight Sunday and regain her confidence.

After Buffy finds her place on campus, she struggles with other rites of passage as well. Her only sexual experience up to this point has been with Angel, and when she gets to college, she is easy pickings for Parker, the campus lothario, who loves her and leaves her. With Riley, however, she finds her first truly adult (and very physical) relationship. The depth and maturity of this intimacy, as well as Buffy's identity, is explored particularly well in "Who Are You?" (4.16), in which Faith, having awakened from her coma, discovers a magic object the Mayor left her that will allow her to switch bodies with Buffy. At first Faith views Buffy's life and body as toys. But after a night of true intimacy with Riley, and a moment of satisfaction after killing a vampire and saving its intended victim, Buffy's authenticity, depth, and morality rub off on Faith.

Willow, who begins the season blissed out at the prospect of higher learning and still in relationship with Oz, soon finds herself jealous of Oz's obvious attraction to Veruca, the lead singer of another band. Veruca turns out to be a werewolf, and in "Wild at Heart" (4.6) she has sex with Oz on two nights when they are both werewolves. She tries to seduce him into an amoral approach to their condition, encouraging him to abandon his werewolf's cage and run wild, even if it means hurting and killing people. When Willow finds Oz and Veruca naked together after a night as werewolves, she is devastated. Oz kills Veruca when they are both in wolf form and Veruca is about to kill Willow. Oz then decides to leave Sunnydale, and Willow, in order to gain some insight into and control over his condition.

As Willow's broken heart slowly mends, her friendship with Tara blossoms into romance. Although this is wonderful and exciting for Willow, her decision first to avoid introducing Tara to her friends and then to keep the romance a secret creates distance between her and the Scoobies.

While Buffy and Willow come of age on campus, Xander comes home to Sunnydale after a summer during which he meant to explore the United States but instead ended up washing dishes at a "fabulous ladies' nightclub" (and even filling in for a stripper). He returns to deal with life as a townie who must work in a string of thankless, low-paying jobs and live in his parents' basement. Xander has always struggled with feelings of inferiority, and this arrangement, as well as the fact that Willow is developing superpowers of her own as a witch, widens the chasm he feels between himself and his friends.

Finally, though Giles's new identity as a gentleman of leisure has its perks, it also has him questioning his value to the Scooby gang. He feels insecure about the nature of his relationship with these young people, especially Buffy. At first he pushes Buffy away, reminding her in "The Freshman" (4.1) that he is no longer her Watcher and encouraging her to go it alone against the vampires at UC Sunnydale. He quickly regrets this choice and soon offers not only his help but also his home to the Scoobies as a regular meeting place. Still, he struggles throughout the season with nagging doubts. Thinking of himself as a father figure to Buffy, he is disappointed, in "A New Man" (4.12), when he is the last to know that she has a boyfriend. To add insult to injury, he also has an ugly encounter with Professor Walsh, who tells him that Buffy "clearly lacks a strong father figure" and suggests that the independence he fosters and admires in her is "unhealthy" for such a young person. When Giles, usually the most stable member of the group, temporarily turns into a demon in "A New Man," it is a clever metaphor for the identity crisis he deals with all season. In "The Yoko Factor" (4.20) Giles is all too ready to believe Spike when he claims that Buffy now regards Giles as little more than "a retired librarian."

Like Giles, all the original Scoobies believe the lies Spike tells them in "The Yoko Factor." Willow believes her friends don't approve of her relationship with Tara; Xander concludes that they look down on him, hate his girlfriend, and have mocked him behind his back. After an ugly argument during which Giles gets stinking drunk, the Scoobies finally realize that Spike has played them (in order to help Adam, who had promised to remove his chip). They reconcile in "Primeval" (4.21), but not without acknowledging the real tensions that had made it so easy for them to be fooled. With this reconciliation comes the idea that the best way to beat Adam is to do a spell that incorporates all their strengths into one being: Buffy's strength, Giles's intellect, Xander's heart, and Willow's magical skill. When Buffy fights Adam, she is able to use magical power well beyond her own to remove his power supply and kill him. His death affirms both the value of friendship and the superiority of the Scoobies' premodern, supernatural approach to the Initiative's.

Although fans sometimes refer to season four as the show's weakest, it features several memorable episodes, including the Emmy-nominated "Hush" (4.10) and the dream montage "Restless" (4.22), which takes place immediately after Buffy, Giles, Willow, and Xander have defeated Adam. Feeling wired in the wake of the enjoining spell, the four plan a "vid-fest" at Buffy's house. Soon after claiming that they couldn't possibly sleep, they fall into a deep slumber. The rest of the episode depicts their dreams, during which some of the same mysterious figures appear to each of them and portend crises each will face in subsequent story arcs. Most significantly, Buffy encounters the First Slayer. Though she can barely speak, she manages to tell Buffy that Slayers should be alone. When Buffy protests that she wants her friends, the First Slayer insists, "No friends. Just the kill." Season five will explore this reminder of the dark side of slaying. In addition, Tara appears in the dream, reminding Buffy to "be back before dawn." Earlier in the season, in "This Year's Girl" (4.15), Faith has also appeared to Buffy in a dream, referring to "little sis coming." Both Tara's and Faith's dream messages turn out to be a reference to Dawn, Buffy's mysterious new sister, who appears in season five.

Season Five
Number of Episodes: 22

Primary Villain: Glory

Scoobies: Giles, Buffy, Willow, Xander, Anya, Tara, Riley, and Spike

More than any season before it, season five explores the spiritual and theological aspects of the Buffyverse. At the beginning of the season, Buffy realizes she needs to better understand the spiritual implications of being the Slayer. Just as Giles is about to tell her that he feels she no longer needs him and that he's going back to England, Buffy asks him to help her learn about past Slayers and find a way to control her darker impulses. Giles teaches Buffy to meditate and schools her in martial arts-like disciplines that allow her to maximize both her mental and physical abilities and exercise more self-control.

In the meantime Buffy suddenly has a new teenage sister, Dawn, whom everyone thinks has always been there. In "No Place like Home" (5.5) Buffy learns that thanks to the work of an ancient order of monks, Dawn is the embodiment of the mystical Key, which opens the portal between this world and the demon dimensions. The monks have made her the Slayer's sister so that Buffy will protect her from an evil, mind-sucking god called Glory who needs the Key so that she can return to the dimension where she once ruled.

In the Scoobies' romantic lives, Willow and Tara's relationship continues, as does Xander and Anya's. Both relationships become more serious, and Xander proposes to Anya at the end of the season. While Riley and Buffy remain together, he is convinced that Buffy does not love or need him. After a difficult confrontation with Buffy in "Into the Woods" (5.10), Riley accepts a military assignment in Central America, where he is under "deep cover" and therefore unreachable.

Buffy subsequently learns that Spike has fallen in love with her. Repulsed by his overtures, she befriends a handsome medical intern named Ben. Little does she know, however, that his body happens to be Glory's unwilling host. Buffy becomes acquainted with Ben during her frequent visits to the hospital, where Joyce undergoes successful surgery to remove a brain tumor. But six episodes later, in the landmark episode "The Body" (5.16), Buffy comes home to find her mother lying dead on the couch due to an aneurysm. Although the Scoobies can generally save lives or, failing that, avenge deaths caused by vampires, demons, or a god such as Glory, in this case they are desolate and dazed.

While Spike remains soulless and generally self-serving, the chip in his brain keeps him from harming humans but allows him to harm and kill demons. Thrilled to be able to kill something, he fights demons at every opportunity, thus forging an uneasy alliance with the Scoobies. These forays into fighting alongside the good guys ignite the faintest glimmer of decency in Spike, but it is his love for Buffy and, perhaps more profoundly, his protectiveness for Dawn that begin to transform him. Inexplicably moved by Dawn's predicament, saddened by Joyce's death, and drawn to Buffy, he begins acting selflessly out of loyalty to them, even enduring Glory's torture to protect Dawn (5.18).

In season five, viewers learn that the universe is made up of endless dimensions—some dark and horrific, some utopian, and others only slightly different from the one the Scoobies inhabit. The Scoobies encounter not only demons and monsters but also gods in "Triangle" (5.11) and the notion of mystical energy, since Dawn turns out to be the Key. In her use of crystals, meditation, and martial arts, Buffy strives to harness a similar sort of energy with the hope of achieving greater wisdom and power.

As Buffy seeks insight into this energy, she feels increasingly cut off emotionally from those around her. After Riley's departure and Joyce's death, she says to Giles in "Intervention" (5.18), "I'm starting to feel like . . . being the Slayer is turning me into stone. . . . To slay, to kill—it means being hard on the inside. Maybe being the perfect Slayer means being too hard to love at all." Concerned, Giles suggests that Buffy go on a vision quest. During the quest the First Slayer reappears to Buffy and tells her that death is her "gift." Having just lost her mother, Buffy thinks of death as anything but a gift; she takes umbrage at this remark just as she does with Spike's assertion in "Fool for Love" (5.7) that Slayers are "just a little bit in love" with death. Despite Buffy's resistance to the First Slayer's assertion, Joyce's death has already given at least some characters the gift of understanding their own mortality better and thus appreciating life more. Death clearly becomes a major moral and theological theme of this season; not only does Joyce die, but Buffy ultimately does as well. These deaths, though tragic, transcend tragedy, thereby exploring both Christian and Buddhist notions of death (both literal, physical death and other symbolic forms of death) as a wonderful release from the mortal coil.

In the episodes leading to Buffy's own death, Glory finally discovers that Dawn is the Key and captures her. Desperate, the Scoobies consider letting her kill Dawn, believing that she must be sacrificed to save the universe. In "The Gift" (5.22) Giles tries to convince Buffy that Dawn is not really her sister and explains that if they don't kill her before Glory gets to her, "every living creature in this and every other dimension imaginable will suffer unbearable torment and death, including Dawn."

As always, Buffy faces a moral dilemma that pits her interests against the greater good. This season's dilemma—to save Dawn or the universe—forces the search for a third way; but in this case, that search leads Buffy to realize what "death is your gift" means. The season's villain, Glory, is the most formidable evil the Scoobies have yet faced. Although she is not completely omnipresent, there does not seem to be any place the Scoobies can hide from her. She feeds on Tara's mind, rendering Tara insane, and kidnaps Dawn.

Buffy is not entirely surprised by this horrifying series of events. In "The Weight of the World" (5.21) she becomes catatonic and rehearses again and again the moment she realized that she would lose to Glory. In true Buddhist fashion, however, that moment of despair becomes one of surrender, transformation, and peace. Buffy knows she cannot survive Glory but realizes that in letting go of her own life, she can give the universe balance and stability and perhaps achieve something like nirvana for herself.

In the final episode ("The Gift," 5.22), all the Scoobies, including a lovesick and increasingly reformed Spike, try to no avail to save Dawn—whom Glory has taken to the top of a huge tower built by her mind-sucked minions, using Dawn's blood to activate the Key and open a portal to a demon dimension. During the battle the increasingly powerful Willow is able to reclaim Tara's mind from Glory. Buffy has an opportunity to kill Ben and thereby destroy Glory but refuses to kill a human being. Giles, acknowledging that he, unlike Buffy, is not a hero, does kill Ben, thus sparing the universe once and for all from Glory. Buffy, who has climbed to the top of the tower, finds Dawn bleeding and the sky filling with demons that have come through the open portal. She hugs Dawn and peacefully dives into the mystical portal, causing it to reseal. The episode ends with the devastated Scoobies surrounding Buffy's lifeless body as Buffy's voice expresses her last wishes for her friends. The final shot is of her tombstone, which reads, "Buffy Anne Summers, 1981-2001, Beloved Sister, Devoted Friend, She Saved the World. A Lot."

Season Six
Number of Episodes: 22

*Primary Villains: Warren, Jonathan, Andrew, and Willow—
and each major character's inner demons*

Scoobies: Buffy, Giles, Xander, Willow, Tara, Dawn, Anya, and Spike

The Scoobies' major moral question in season six, the series' darkest, is nihilism. Characters struggle throughout with their own dark sides and with a sense of futility. In the opening episode, "Bargaining (Part One)" (6.1), the Scoobies are trying to get on without Buffy. They use the Buffybot to make people and demons think she is still alive, and Willow and Tara move into the Summers' house to care for Dawn. Their slayage responsibilities and their grief overwhelm them, and after waiting months for the right time, the Scoobies try to resurrect Buffy. Although they feel some ambivalence about using powerful, dark magic to go against nature's laws, Willow is resolute and succeeds in bringing Buffy back.

Forced to claw her way out of her own grave, Buffy does not express gratitude for being returned to earth, and this hurts Willow deeply. Soon Buffy discloses to Spike that she thinks she was in heaven, that she felt total peace there, and that being back in this life is painful and utterly depressing. She keeps this fact from the Scoobies while going through the motions of caring for Dawn and being the Slayer.

In the early episodes, Buffy struggles mightily with finding a will to live. In the brilliant musical episode "Once More, with Feeling" (6.7), characters communicate through song the secrets and reservations they cannot speak. Buffy expresses her death wish in the song "Walk Through the Fire" and finally reveals to the Scoobies that they tore her out of heaven in "Something to Sing About." In a bid to wake from her numbing depression, she also kisses Spike.

Some of this episode's revelations have immediate repercussions for the Scoobies. Distraught about what she did to Buffy, Willow considers doing a spell that will make Buffy forget heaven. Incredulous, Tara tells Willow to stop trying to solve every problem with magic; she's angry about a spell Willow cast on her to make her forget a fight they were having about Willow's overdependence on magic. Tara suggests they break up, but Willow forestalls this by promising to go a week without using magic. However, Willow secretly keeps doing spells, sometimes to disastrous effect (in "Tabula Rasa," 6.8, all the Scoobies forget who they are). When Tara discovers Willow's continuing abuse of magic, she leaves Willow.

Meanwhile, Giles has decided to leave for England, largely because he sees Buffy depending on him in unhealthy ways; she expects him to discipline Dawn for her and to bail the family out financially. Although he is happy to help Buffy with her problems, he believes he must leave so that she will be able to move on to adulthood. Devastated by the news that he's leaving, she again finds solace by kissing Spike. Soon she and Spike are involved in an obsessive sadomasochistic affair whose intensity keeps Buffy from realizing that Willow has become dangerously addicted to magic. Bereft of Tara, Willow spirals out of control, endangering herself and Dawn while under the influence of her addiction.

Buffy and the others do not notice that Dawn is feeling neglected and has turned to compulsive shoplifting. Buffy is degraded by her relationship with Spike and a minimum-wage job at the Doublemeat Palace, a fast-food restaurant where she reluctantly works to make money and avoid the critical gaze of Child Protective Services. When Riley shows up in "As You Were" (6.15), finding her at the Doublemeat Palace and sleeping with Spike, Buffy becomes painfully aware of how low she has sunk, especially when she compares her life to Riley's wholesome, newlywed bliss. As he and his wife are about to leave Sunnydale, however, Riley downplays what Buffy refers to as her "incredible patheticness": "None of that means anything. It doesn't touch you. You're still the first woman I ever loved . . . and the strongest woman I've ever known." His affirmation encourages Buffy and gives her the strength to finally break up with Spike.

In "Hell's Bells" (6.16) Xander, spooked by disturbing visions of a possible future with Anya, flees on their wedding day, inspiring her to become a vengeance demon again. Soon after Xander flees, Anya and Spike have sex in a bid to forget their mutual pain, and the Scoobies see them, thanks to a hidden camera placed in the Magic Box. This leads both to hurt feelings and to the revelation of Buffy and Spike's affair. Buffy's friends forgive her for not telling them about the affair, and it seems she'll be able to move on. But when Spike shows up at Buffy's house to make amends, he attempts to rape her (6.19). Horrified by what he has done, he leaves town, promising himself that he'll give Buffy "what she deserves."

While the Scoobies deal with these personal demons, they also battle the pesky geek Troika: Warren, Jonathan, and Andrew. Using a combination of technology and magic, these three want to be supervillains who run Sunnydale. Initially little more than a nuisance, their high jinks take an ugly turn when they accidentally kill Warren's ex-girlfriend. Warren's sociopathic tendencies then take hold; when Buffy foils his attempt to rob an armored truck, he comes to her house with a gun, wounding her and killing Tara, who has just recently reunited with Willow. Willow, who had been magic-free ever since the frightening incident in "Wrecked" (6.10) when she almost killed Dawn, becomes so grief-stricken by Tara's death that she returns to dark magic, becoming powerful enough to destroy the world. Giles and Xander, with a combination of magic and love, are able to stop her but not before she has killed Warren.

Willow ends the season with a nihilist urge so powerful that she wants to obliterate not only her girlfriend's killer but the world as well. The combination of Willow's grief at Tara's death and the magic that is now an essential part of her fuel her murderous and world-destroying rage. When Willow brings the world within seconds of apocalypse, the only thing that is able to bring her back is the connection between the bit of humanity left in her and Xander's love. This finally vanquishes the dark magic that has been controlling her.

Although Buffy battles nihilism most overtly in the early part of the season, she struggles with it until the last episode ("Grave," 6.22). In the final scenes, however, Buffy realizes that she has regained the will to live and, impressed by Dawn's demon-fighting skills, that she should be showing Dawn the world rather than protecting her from it. Interestingly, the season begins and ends with Buffy literally crawling her way out of a grave. At the end of the season, however, she does so not in a state of confusion or panic but in a spirit of happiness and peace.

Like Buffy, many of the other characters must also choose between embracing or rejecting life. While Willow struggles with her world-destroying urges, Anya and Spike fight their own battles with darkness. Nihilism had been a way of life until their power to destroy life was taken away. Ironically, Anya, who is human and ensouled, chooses nihilism when she accepts D'Hoffryn's offer to make her a vengeance demon again. In contrast, Spike, who by virtue of his soullessness is inclined toward nihilism, chooses to endure many harrowing trials to win back his soul with the hope of a future with Buffy.

Xander's fear of a future with Anya (and a life that mirrors his parents') leads him to reject the life they were planning. Of all the choices the Scoobies make this season to either embrace or retreat from life, Xander's is perhaps the most ambiguous: on the one hand, he gives in to fear and runs away from making a life with the woman he loves; on the other hand, he makes this choice with the sincere hope of protecting himself and Anya from a miserable life and of creating the possibility of a better future for them both.

Unlike previous seasons, season six features more than one villain. The members of the Troika, or Evil Trio, were the primary villains, working throughout the season to foil the Scoobies and managing to do some serious damage. But Dark Willow emerges as the season's Big Bad; like the Master, the Mayor, Adam, and Glory, she garners enough power by the end of the season to bring about apocalyptic events. The third possibility is that the darkness within each character is the season's true Big Bad. The epic battle each individual fights is not with the geeks or with Dark Willow but with his or her own worst impulses.

This depiction of each character's dark side has not pleased all fans. Although some viewers have been fascinated by *Buffy*'s foray into heretofore uncharted territory, others have complained that the writers went too far. Sarah Michelle Gellar expressed displeasure with her character's choices during this season, and a large part of the show's fan base agrees that Buffy sinks to lows so uncharacteristic as to render her unrecognizable as a heroine. With masterful episodes such as "Once More, with Feeling," "Tabula Rasa," and "Hell's Bells," however, this season contributes greatly to the *Buffy* mythology and sets the stage well for season seven's exploration of power and redemption.

Season Seven
Number of Episodes: 22

Primary Villain: The First Evil

Scoobies: Buffy, Willow, Xander, Giles, Spike, Anya, Dawn, Andrew, Faith, Robin Wood, and the Potential Slayers

Season seven's most significant themes are power, moral accountability, and redemption. As Buffy tells Dawn in the opening line of the season, "It's about power"—its exercise and its exploitation. Who has power? How do they use it? How do they atone when they have abused it? Throughout the series the question of free will and accountability has been a thorny one. Most characters in the Buffyverse have been forced into a role not entirely of their choosing—whether they are vampire victims, Slayers, Watchers, or normal people in the thrall of a spell or a demon. Despite bad breaks, however, individuals are expected to rise to the occasion, displaying courage and self-sacrifice. In season seven the characters are held to different standards of accountability, depending on the free will they exercised when they committed heinous acts and their efforts to redeem themselves.

Although the season's major story arc revolves around the First Evil, the first six episodes explore Spike, Willow, Anya, Jonathan, and Andrew's search for redemption. In "Lessons" (7.1) the new Sunnydale High School is opened exactly where the old high school was, and this time the principal's office, not the library, is directly over the Hellmouth. On the first day of school, the manifestations of students who died at the school haunt Dawn in the basement. When Buffy comes to help, she finds Spike, who has obviously gone mad, living there. After Buffy saves Dawn and her schoolmates from the manifestations, the principal (a young, handsome man named Robin Wood), offers Buffy a job as a school counselor.

One of the most significant events of the first few episodes is Spike's disclosure to Buffy that he has a soul. Ever since she found him in the school basement, she knows that something is different about him but cannot figure out what it is. Spike is sometimes lucid and at other times speaks as though he were schizophrenic (for reasons made clear a few episodes later). In "Beneath You" (7.2) Buffy confronts Spike in an abandoned church about what is going on with him, so he finally explains, "I wanted to give you what you deserve, and I got it. They put the spark in me . . . and now all it does is burn." Though they do not rekindle their romance until the end of the season, Buffy and Spike share an emotional moment as she comes to terms with the transformation he has undergone for her. The episode ends with him resting on a crucifix, even though it, like his soul, burns him.

Meanwhile, Willow is staying with Giles in England; he and the members of a British coven are helping Willow learn how to control the powerful magic that is now part of her. In "Same Time, Same Place" (7.3) she returns to Sunnydale but unconsciously does a spell that places her in a different dimension from the other Scoobies, thus forestalling the frightening prospect of seeing them again after her murderous rampage. Willow's friends hold her accountable for killing Warren and nearly destroying the world, but they have forgiven her because she is repentant and has worked with the coven to rehabilitate herself by learning about ways to control her power. She also merits sympathy and forgiveness because of the extreme grief that led her to resume using magic toward the end of season six. Throughout season seven, Willow maintains an unwavering commitment to the appropriate use of magic, even though using magic at all makes her vulnerable to her dark side.

Anya, who accepted D'Hoffryn's invitation to be a vengeance demon again after being jilted by Xander at the altar, seeks redemption in two arenas. Initially, she metes out fairly innocuous punishment; when a young woman wishes that her boyfriend would turn into a frog, Anya makes him French. When she turns a young man into a large, burrowing worm monster, Xander convinces her to reverse the curse. She gets in trouble with D'Hoffryn for doing this; and after being egged on by Halfrek, an old friend of hers who is also a vengeance demon, she seeks to redeem herself in the demon world by unleashing a monster that tears out the hearts of a group of fraternity boys after they humiliate a girl. Again at Xander's behest, she is able to take this curse back and become human again, but it costs Halfrek her life.

Andrew and Jonathan return from their hideaway in Mexico because they have been haunted by something evil. They decide to return to Sunnydale to "make it right," as Jonathan says in "Conversations with Dead People" (7.7). Season seven begins with an ominous scene in Istanbul during which hooded men pursue a young woman and stab her to death. The phrase "from beneath you it devours" haunts various characters in dreams and visions, and in the first six episodes, many characters refer to a big evil approaching. That evil reveals itself in "Conversations with Dead People." The episode features Andrew, Dawn, and Willow's encounters with what Buffy soon realizes is the First Evil—the same force that tried to convince Angel to kill himself in "Amends" (3.10). Although it's incorporeal, it can manifest itself as any person who has died.

In "Never Leave Me" (7.9) the Scoobies realize that the First is grooming Spike as a sleeper agent. Although he has a soul and should not be killing people, Spike has commenced killing and siring vampires under the influence of the First Evil. Unlike others, whom the First persuades to commit acts of their own volition, Spike has been conditioned to kill when he hears a trigger—in this case an English folk song that his mother used to sing to him ("Lies My Parents Told Me," 7.17).

Spike's unique relationship with the First Evil speaks to the issue of moral accountability. Although both Spike and, for example, Andrew did horrible things under the influence of the First, Andrew is held accountable for his acts whereas Spike is ultimately forgiven. The difference, as Buffy says in "Never Leave Me" (7.9), is that "Spike didn't have free will." When the First took the form of Warren to convince Andrew to kill Jonathan, Andrew could have said no, but he was seduced by Warren's promises of godhood (and, it seems, by Warren himself) and actively chose to kill his best friend. Only in "Storyteller" (7.16) does Andrew fully accept the blame for this choice. In contrast, the First uses behavioral conditioning to get Spike to act unconsciously and completely against his will. Consequently, Buffy (and eventually the other Scoobies) is convinced that Spike is not guilty of these murders. Although he still must seek redemption for approximately 120 years of murder, these recent crimes are not added to the list. Arguably, when he sacrifices himself at the end of the series, he goes far in atoning for his evil deeds—a task that is taken up in the fifth season of *Angel.*

While these characters face the First (showing what they are morally made of), Giles appears in "Bring On the Night" (7.10) with three Potential Slayers. He reports that someone is trying to destroy the entire Slayer line and all their Watchers. From this point on, the Summers home is headquarters for the Scoobies and a growing army of Potential Slayers, as well as Andrew. The growing group of Potentials is confused, frustrated, and afraid about the seemingly hopeless task of fighting the First, especially after one of them is killed and Buffy is maimed by a Turok-Han supervampire in "Bring On the Night." As an indication of how connected they've become, in "Show Time" (7.11) Buffy, Willow, and Xander telepathically hatch a plan to boost morale: they bring the Potentials and a Turok-Han to a construction site where Buffy fights and kills the Turok-Han, thus showing the Potentials that they can have faith in her powers.

As the Potentials continue to train, Willow becomes involved with a Potential Slayer named Kennedy, and Buffy gets closer to Principal Robin Wood. On their first and only date, he reveals to her that he is the son of a Slayer. He knows his mother was killed by a vampire but doesn't know that, as Buffy learned in "Fool for Love" (5.7), the vampire was Spike. Raised and trained by his mother's Watcher, Robin is a skilled demon fighter with a vendetta against all vampires. Soon the First appears to Robin in his mother's guise and tells him that Spike is the vampire who killed her. When the First tempts him to kill Spike, Robin is easily persuaded and attempts to murder him. Buffy and Spike both hold him accountable for this but spare him any punishment beyond a warning, largely out of sympathy for his loss.

Meanwhile, another agent of the First—an evil, misogynist preacher named Caleb—appears in town in "Dirty Girls" (7.18), maiming a Potential Slayer who passes on to Buffy his message that he has something of hers. After using a locator spell to find him, the Scoobies and Potentials are overcome by his power; he kills two Potentials, breaks one of their arms, and puts out Xander's eye. Buffy tells the group they should go back to fight him again. Tired of Buffy's dictatorial leadership and believing that such a plan would be suicidal, the Scoobies and Potentials refuse to go and choose Faith, who has just returned to Sunnydale, to be their new leader.

Spike returns from searching an old monastery for information about Caleb. While there, he and Andrew learned about a secret room behind a statue of the Virgin Mary. A monk explains that Caleb had been excited when he found the secret place but enraged as he left; Spike reads the room's Latin inscription, which translates to "It is not for thee. It is for her alone to wield."

Under Faith's leadership the Scoobies and Potentials take several missteps. Andrew tells them that he and Spike suspect the secret room in the mission contained a weapon. They kidnap a Bringer, one of the First Evil's eyeless minions, and try to get useful information from him. Believing they know where Caleb is hiding the weapon, they learn that he has tricked them by leading them to a bomb. At the same time, Buffy finds Caleb, fights him, and takes possession of the weapon, a Slayer Scythe that she is easily able to pull from the rock in which it was embedded. She soon uses it to save Faith and the Potentials from the Turok-Han, who begin attacking them after the explosion.

In "End of Days" (7.21) Buffy meets an ancient woman in a tomb who introduces herself as the only remaining Guardian—the women who watch the Watchers. She explains the scythe to Buffy, telling her it was forged in that tomb and used to kill the last pure demon that walked the earth. Just as she is warning Buffy that the scythe does not guarantee her victory over the First and the Turok-Han, Caleb kills the Guardian. But Buffy uses the scythe to kill Caleb—an event that Angel shows up to watch. The two former lovers kiss passionately, but after giving Buffy a talisman that he believes will help her in battle, Angel leaves at Buffy's behest.

After saving Faith and the Potentials, Buffy is again at the helm of their motley organization. Though this time she does not switch bodies with Buffy, as she had in "Who Are You?" (4.16), Faith again experiences life through Buffy's eyes during her traumatic stint as the group's leader. In "End of Days" she debriefs with Buffy, saying, "My whole life I've been a loner. . . . Me, by myself all the time. I'm looking at you, everything you have, and, I don't know, jealous. Then there I am. Everybody's looking to me, trusting me to lead them, and I've never felt so alone in my entire life. . . . And that's you every day, isn't it?" Buffy acknowledges that being the Slayer is lonely, even with friends like the Scoobies.

Not long after this reconciliation, Buffy, Faith, the Scoobies, and the Potentials make a plan that viewers are not privy to until it is enacted in the final scenes of the series. After a season and, indeed, a series full of rumination about the Slayer's power and accompanying loneliness, Buffy and Faith work with Willow to find a spell that will disperse full Slayer power among all the Potentials.

In a final showdown with the First by way of the Turok-Han, the spell takes effect. Potentials around the globe are depicted gaining sudden power and confidence. Buffy's seven-year effort to overcome her loner status comes to fruition just in time for the new sisterhood of Slayers to fight the army of Turok-Han rising from the Hellmouth. Spike, who is wearing the talisman that Angel brought, casts sunlight on the Turok-Han, destroying them, himself, and all of Sunnydale. Every other Scooby except for Anya survives (including Andrew, much to his bewilderment), and they end the series contemplating what they will do next.

The series finale points to many of the themes that have always been integral to *Buffy*. Most of all, it shows that cooperation and friendship make individuals more powerful than they could ever be alone. Viewers leave the series knowing that evil will always be present and that it has not been and cannot be vanquished for all time. However, the courage of Buffy, her friends, and the Potential Slayers preserves the delicate balance between good and evil and ensures that evil cannot triumph.

'I'm Buffy the Vampire Slayer. And You Are . . . ?"

A Buffy Character Guide

Need an introduction or a quick refresher course on who's who in the Buffyverse? This guide introduces all of the major characters and some of the recurring minor characters on *Buffy*. It is arranged season by season to help you understand how the plot develops over time as various characters are introduced.

Characters Introduced in Season One

Buffy Summers

For the first fifteen years of her life, Buffy Summers was a typical Southern California girl. Popular at school and self-described as vacuous, she was dumbfounded when a member of the Watchers' Council told her that she was the Slayer. Her Slayer activity in Los Angeles predates the series; we see it in flashbacks. When the series begins, Buffy and her recently divorced mother have moved to Sunnydale after Buffy burned down her school gymnasium while fighting vampires. In Sunnydale Buffy grows from a teenager who wants to deny her calling to a mature young woman who has embraced her destiny, despite all the sorrow and misadventure it has wrought. As the seasons unfold, we see Buffy face the unimaginable: she gives her own life twice, is forced to kill her lover, grieves the sudden loss of her mother, is torn out of heaven, embarks on a destructive sexual relationship with a soulless vampire, and finally passes her powers on to scores of new Slayers. Throughout these trials, however, Buffy finds solace in her friendships as well as in her special powers. Time and again, Buffy's friends and family provide emotional, practical, and supernatural support, without which she would not survive. In the hellish alternate reality of "The Wish" (3.9), Buffy and her friends are instead enemies, and they all die; in "Primeval" (4.21), by contrast, their ability to magically meld into one being allows them to beat Adam, who would have been able to kill all of them individually. Ultimately, Buffy is not simply the Slayer but rather the Slayer who refuses to fight alone, fighting first alongside friends and finally alongside an army of Slayers.

Rupert Giles

Typically referred to as Giles, this character comes from a long line of Watchers and has known most of his life that mentoring a Slayer would be his destiny. As a young man in England, Giles resisted his calling, as seen in "The Dark Age" (2.8), just as Buffy occasionally resists hers. When he was in his early twenties, he called himself Ripper, took up with a group of friends interested in the occult, and began conjuring dark powers. His history haunts Giles throughout the series, especially when Ethan Rayne, an old friend who still embraces the dark arts, shows up in Sunnydale occasionally to create chaos. Despite the enduring implications of his youthful mistakes, Giles has been a faithful fighter for the good side for many years. When he comes to Sunnydale, ostensibly to take a job as a high school librarian, he has already become an accomplished scholar with vast knowledge of the demon world and the fight against evil forces. As his relationships with Buffy and the other Scoobies develop, viewers learn that he is not only committed to fighting demons but also to mentoring Buffy and her friends. The series quickly establishes a father-daughter bond between Giles and Buffy and deals often, most notably in "Helpless" (3.12), with the tension between Giles's duty to put Buffy in harm's way and his desire to protect her. His response to this dilemma eventually costs him his job as her Watcher (though he is reinstated during season five, with back pay). Though he leaves Sunnydale early in season six, he returns twice to help avert an apocalypse.

Willow Rosenberg

Willow is Buffy's best friend and the series character who undergoes the most dramatic transformation. In the first season, she is a meek young girl, a victim of all sorts of evils: Cordelia's cruelty, unrequited love for Xander, and the vampires from whom Buffy must consistently save her. Early on, Willow's primary assets are her dependability, loyalty, and academic skills. She develops a relationship with Oz, a sweet and unflappable musician, in seasons two and three, though he breaks her heart during their freshman year of college. Willow contributes a great deal in seasons one and two as a researcher, but her later dabbling in witchcraft eventually makes her a force to be reckoned with. After Jenny Calendar's death, Willow teaches her classes and learns about "techno-paganism" and Wicca in general from Jenny's files. It's the beginning of her transformation into a powerful witch. In "The Wish" (3.9) and "Doppelgängland" (3.16), we meet a Willow from another reality—a powerful, extraordinarily evil, pansexual vampire. Although her friends assure her that she is nothing like her doppelgänger, the appearance of Willow as a vampire portends a great deal about how Willow's character will develop. The alternative-reality Willow's lesbian tendencies are paralleled by Willow's discovery of her own lesbianism when she falls in love with Tara in season four, after Oz has left her. And when she allows dark powers to overtake her at the end of season six, she becomes Dark Willow, as powerful and nihilistic as the alternate-reality Willow. Having learned that she can neither fully use nor completely avoid magic, Willow spends the series' final season learning to use magic responsibly, although she is frightened by its power.

Xander Harris

Xander rounds out the foursome that viewers come to know as the original Scoobies. He and Willow have been lifelong friends and in the first two seasons are part of a love "rectangle" that features Willow pining for Xander, who pines for Buffy, who pines for Angel. Unlike Willow, Xander offers very little to the Scoobies in the way of academic skill, nor does he ever develop any sort of supernatural power, aside from his extensive knowledge of military weapons and strategy developed in "Halloween" (2.6). His heroism lies in his willingness to risk humiliation, injury, and even death to help his friends. In "Prophecy Girl" (1.12) he braves the Master's Lair to rescue Buffy, and in "Reptile Boy" (2.5) he endures humiliation bordering on terror at the hands of sadistic fraternity boys because he is concerned about Buffy. In "The Zeppo" (3.13) Xander, using only his wits, saves the high school and his friends from destruction without anyone ever knowing it. Beyond his sacrificial heroism, Xander contributes self-deprecating wit and unconditional love, a love that saves Willow and the world at the end of season six. As he points out to Dawn in "Potential" (7.12), the Scoobies who have special powers will "never know how tough it is . . . to be the one who isn't chosen. . . . I see more than anybody realizes because nobody's watching me." Dawn points out that his special power is seeing and knowing, an ability that is refined when Caleb puts Xander's eye out near the end of the series.

Angel (Angelus)

Sired by Darla in 1753, Angel, then known as Angelus, was a particularly cruel and powerful vampire who enjoyed feeding on people and psychologically torturing them.
Before siring Drusilla, he killed her family members one by one just to watch her suffer and go mad, and he convinced her that her clairvoyance meant that she was evil.
But in 1898 Romanian gypsies cursed him for his murder of a young woman. The curse
returned Angel's soul to him, and with it guilt for all the atrocities he had committed
since becoming a vampire. His anguished existence becomes more bearable when he
meets Buffy, and he experiences true happiness when he and Buffy consummate their
love. Unfortunately, this moment of happiness reverses the curse; Angel again loses his
soul and becomes the evil Angelus. He returns to feeding on humans, joins forces with
Spike and Drusilla, and takes pleasure in the suffering of his former friends, especially
Buffy. Jenny Calendar, a descendant of the gypsy tribe that originally cursed Angel,
tries to reinstate the curse, only to be murdered by Angel. At the end of season two,
however, Willow succeeds in restoring Angel's soul, but this unfortunately happens at
the moment when Buffy is forced to kill Angel to seal the entrance to hell. When
Angel returns from hell in season three, he and Buffy slowly rekindle their love, only
to realize at the end of the season that a future together is untenable. When they
break up, Angel moves to Los Angeles, though he appears briefly in seasons four, five,
and seven. Angel's adventures continue in the spin-off *Angel*.

Cordelia (Cordy) Chase

Cordelia starts out as the most popular and mean-spirited girl at Sunnydale High. At
first she welcomes Buffy, imagining that Buffy will fit into the popular clique. However,
when Buffy takes up with Willow and Xander, whom Cordelia regards as geeks,
Cordelia distances herself from Buffy. When she learns about Buffy's identity as the
Slayer, she rejects Buffy as a freak. However, fate intervenes time and again to place
Cordelia in the middle of the Scoobies' exploits, and she eventually becomes one of
them, even to the point of beginning a physical relationship with Xander that leads to
love. When she discovers Xander kissing Willow in the third season, Cordelia is devas-
tated, breaks up with Xander, and quits the Scoobies. Inadvertently, she summons
Anyanka, a vengeance demon, who in "The Wish" (3.9) creates a Buffy-free Sunnydale at
Cordelia's unwitting request. In the later episodes of season three, Cordelia gradually
rejoins the Scoobies, partly because of her infatuation with Buffy's new Watcher,
Wesley. At this point she has been humanized not only by heartbreak but also by a sudden loss of wealth after her father's arrest for tax evasion. After this season, her character joins Angel in Los Angeles, and she continues to develop on the *Angel* series.

Joyce Summers

Kept in the dark about her daughter Buffy's secret identity until the end of season two,
Joyce is introduced to viewers as a loving but frustrated mother who feels shut out by
her troubled daughter. Joyce uses every strategy imaginable to deal with Buffy: she
pulls up stakes and starts a new life in Sunnydale; when that doesn't work, she attempts
tough-love tactics. Her anguish about Buffy's sexual relationship with Angel and her
identity as the Slayer create a temporary rift in their relationship that partly motivates
Buffy to run away at the end of season two. As they rebuild their relationship in season
three, Joyce gradually accepts and comes to embrace Buffy's special calling and
becomes a sort of surrogate mother to the Scoobies. Under the influence of a spell,
she even has sex with Giles. She becomes more peripheral when Buffy goes to college,
but Joyce returns to center stage in season five. She acquires a "new" daughter, Dawn;
Buffy moves back home; and Joyce herself develops a brain tumor. Though she seems
to have been cured by surgery, Joyce dies unexpectedly from an aneurysm. The

Scoobies deal memorably with the gravity of this loss in "The Body" (5.16), reacting to this death very differently than to supernaturally caused death. After her death, Joyce reappears in Buffy and Dawn's dreams, fantasies, and delusions.

Jenny Calendar (Janna)

In the first season Jenny is Miss Calendar, the computer programming teacher at Sunnydale High. She soon becomes entangled in the Scoobies' activities and reveals herself as a "techno-pagan" (1.8). Her knowledge in this area proves helpful to the Scoobies, and soon she and Giles begin to date. Her direct, almost smart-alecky approach to their relationship contrasts with Giles's circumspect British approach; the two complement each other. But their hidden pasts block the road to true love. The first obstacle they encounter is a demon Giles summoned in his dark-magic days: though Jenny recovers when it temporarily possesses her, the experience makes her wary of Giles. As the two slowly rebuild trust, another bombshell drops: Jenny is a descendant of the gypsy tribe that originally gave Angel his soul back. She is in Sunnydale to make sure the curse stays in place. When Angel unwittingly breaks the curse by sleeping with Buffy, Jenny's identity is revealed, leaving the Scoobies feeling betrayed. Jenny tries to make amends by doing a spell that will reensoul Angel, but just as she is about to finish it, Angelus kills her and leaves her body in Giles's bed.

Jonathan Levenson

Jonathan first appears as an unnamed bit player in the first season (and in the unaired pilot episode), but he doesn't get much play until "Inca Mummy Girl" (2.4). An ancient Inca princess forestalls her own remummification by sucking the life out of people, and she almost kills Jonathan, who mistakenly thinks this beautiful girl simply wants to make out with him. This glimpse of Jonathan actually captures his essence: he is the awkward, gullible boy who wants love but gets hurt and humiliated instead. Viewers see him again when Cordelia's popular friends derisively suggest she date him after Xander spurns her, and in "Earshot" (3.18) Buffy just barely talks Jonathan out of suicide. Having recovered from his despair, he awards Buffy the Class Protector Award in "The Prom" (3.20), but unfortunately a troubled teen he meets in group therapy teaches him some magic. He uses this magic to very amusing effect in "Superstar" (4.17), in which he casts a spell that makes everyone in Sunnydale idolize him. He becomes a regular character in season six, when he teams up with Warren and Andrew to form the Evil Trio (also known as the Troika). Despite being cartoonishly geeky, these gifted inventors know enough magic to be a menace to the Scoobies. While Warren's sociopathic tendencies lead the trio to mayhem and murder, Jonathan remains ambivalent about the ethics of being a supervillain. He tries to help the Scoobies when Willow becomes evil at the end of season six; and when he and Andrew return from Mexico in season seven, Jonathan expresses a wish to make amends. Sadly, shortly after a speech during which he comes to terms with his difficult high school years, Jonathan is murdered by his best friend, Andrew.

Harmony Kendall

Harmony is first introduced as one of Cordelia's entourage of rich, savage, well-coiffed friends. Her only concern is popularity, and she is perfectly willing to turn on a friend if she thinks doing so will make her own social stock rise; when Cordelia's popularity nose-dives because of her brief dating relationship with the socially uncouth Xander, Harmony taunts Cordelia and humiliates her in public. On graduation day, Harmony is sired as a vampire, and in the fourth and fifth seasons she has an on-again, off-again relationship with Spike. She later appears on the spin-off *Angel* as Angel's executive assistant at Wolfram & Hart.

Season One Big Bad: The Master

The Master, Buffy's first-season nemesis, is a powerful vampire who has lived for approximately six hundred years. The leader of the Order of Aurelius, he came to Sunnydale in the 1930s to open the Hellmouth and allow full demons to roam the earth. However, his plan was foiled in 1937 when an earthquake trapped him between dimensions. Throughout Buffy's first season, he plots to restore himself to full power and unleash the Hellmouth's fury. In "Prophecy Girl" (1.12) Buffy bravely faces him, though she knows that a prophecy has predicted her death at his hands. Although he kills her, Xander revives her with CPR; Buffy is able to defeat the Master and close the Hellmouth.

Characters Introduced in Season Two

Kendra

After Buffy dies briefly at the end of season one, a new Slayer rises; and she appears in "What's My Line (Part One)" (2.9). A Caribbean beauty, Kendra has stowed away on an airplane to get to Sunnydale because she and her Watcher believed a catastrophic event was imminent. (Indeed, not only were Spike and Drusilla trying to cure Drusilla, but they had unleashed three powerful demon assassins, referred to as Taraka bounty hunters, to kill Buffy.) Kendra's disciplined, dispassionate approach to slaying at first makes Buffy feel inferior, especially when Giles seems gleeful to be with a Slayer who enjoys reading. Buffy realizes that she has more to worry about than feelings of inferiority when she learns that Kendra, who assumes that all vampires are evil, has left Angel to die. Buffy eventually sees that her own approach to slaying is healthier, both because she injects more passion and anger into her work and because she has some semblance of a normal life. Although Buffy has grown up with family and friends, Kendra left her family as a young child and does not socialize, instead spending all her time training with her Watcher. Kendra leaves Sunnydale after helping the Scoobies kill the Taraka bounty hunters, incorporating some of Buffy's wisdom into her approach. Unfortunately, when she returns in "Becoming (Part One)" (2.21), Kendra is killed by Drusilla, who mesmerizes her and slices her throat with long fingernails.

Daniel "Oz" Osbourne

Taciturn, wise, and kind, Oz first appears in "Inca Mummy Girl" (2.4) as the guitar player in the band Dingoes Ate My Baby. While Cordelia has a short-lived romance with the band's lead singer, Devon, Oz forms a more enduring attachment to Willow. He notices her from afar before finally meeting her in "What's My Line (Part One)" (2.9); during career day at school, a high-powered corporation tries to recruit them both to do computer programming. In "What's My Line (Part Two)" (2.10), he is shot as he pushes Willow out of the way of a Taraka bounty hunter's bullet. When she thanks him at the end of the episode, he makes clear that he is smitten with her, and she is charmed. Their romance builds slowly and sweetly but encounters its first major hurdle when Oz, infected by a bite from his young nephew, discovers that he is a werewolf. The Scoobies learn about this and discover that locking him up for three nights around the time of the full moon each month keeps him from harming anyone. Oz becomes a Scooby, and the relationship deepens between Oz and Willow until Willow and Xander begin having secret make-out sessions, one of which Oz and Cordelia discover during "Lovers Walk" (3.8). Oz eventually forgives Willow, and the two consummate their love just hours before their high school graduation. In season four they go off to college, and Oz is seduced by a female werewolf. He leaves Sunnydale and a devastated Willow in order to overcome his wolfish tendencies. Thinking he has succeeded, he returns later in season four, only to learn that Willow is involved with Tara and that he has less control over the werewolf within than he thought. At this point he leaves Sunnydale and returns only in Willow's dream in "Restless" (4.22).

Season Two Big Bads:

Spike ("William the Bloody")

Spike, along with his girlfriend Drusilla, was initially season two's villain. (He first appears in 2.3.) He and Drusilla take over the Master's Lair, killing the Anointed One, engineering various destructive schemes, and restoring Drusilla to full health. Although the Scoobies are unable to stop Spike and Drusilla from finding her cure, Buffy manages to injure Spike, leaving him confined to a wheelchair. Soon after, Angel loses his soul and becomes Drusilla's consort, infuriating Spike. Viewers learn that Spike's sire was Drusilla, whose sire was Angel, whose sire was Darla, and that this foursome lived for a time as a diabolical family, traveling the world to feed on its inhabitants. Longtime rivals, then-soulless Angelus baits Spike during season two, and Spike shrewdly convinces Buffy to ally with him to save the world from the Armageddon that Drusilla and Angel are attempting to bring forth. Spike leaves with Drusilla at the end of season two, returns briefly in "Lovers Walk" (3.8), and appears regularly in seasons four through seven. Spike, who was named William before being sired, chose life as a vampire after the woman he loved spurned him. Although a self-serving vicious killer, he remains a true romantic and an especially insightful student of human behavior. During "Lovers Walk" he memorably says to Buffy and Angel, "I may be love's bitch, but at least I'm man enough to admit it." After getting over Drusilla, Spike eventually falls deeply in love with Buffy. Though he remains soulless until the end of season six, a chip planted in his head in season four forces him to stop harming people. This and his love for Buffy are the beginning of his redemption, which is furthered dramatically when he sacrifices his life at the end of the series. His character then reappears on the spin-off series *Angel*.

Drusilla

Drusilla, Spike's sire and paramour, was sired by Angel (Angelus) after he had murdered her family and driven her mad. When she arrives in Sunnydale with Spike, Drusilla suffers not only from madness but also an unspecified illness that is sapping her strength and her ability to kill. She and Spike find a cure, and she returns to full strength, which for Drusilla includes clairvoyance. In "Becoming (Part One)" (2.21) viewers learn that Drusilla has always been a "seer" and that before he sired her, Angel posed as a priest and convinced her during confession that her clairvoyance was evidence of her evil. When Angel loses his soul, he taunts Spike by moving in on Drusilla, which leads Spike to abduct Drusilla and take her from Sunnydale at the end of season two. She eventually leaves Spike but appears again in seasons five and seven; she also appears in the *Angel* series.

Characters Introduced in Season Three
Faith

When Kendra dies, a Slayer named Faith is called. She arrives early in season three and is instantly popular with the Scoobies as well as Buffy's mother, Joyce. A tough high school dropout, she tells funny, colorful stories and seems to enjoy being a Slayer, unlike Buffy. Although Faith's bravado turns out to be a cover for her grief and horror at having witnessed her Watcher's death, she initially does some good. Her recklessness continues, however, and in "Bad Girls" (3.14) Faith persuades Buffy to adopt her approach to slaying and to life. When Faith accidentally kills a human, she insists that it is not a big deal and that Slayers are above the law. Buffy, of course, cannot agree. Faith then pretends to be rehabilitated, but she secretly forges an alliance with Sunnydale's evil Mayor. Soon the Scoobies discover that she works for him as, among other things, an assassin. When Faith nearly kills Angel (and only the blood of a Slayer will save him), Buffy tries to kill Faith and bring her to Angel as an antidote. Faith escapes but is comatose for eight months. When she awakens, she vengefully pursues Buffy and learns that the Mayor left her a special object that will enable her to switch bodies with Buffy. Living Buffy's life has the surprising effect of reawakening Faith's conscience. She leaves Sunnydale and goes to Los Angeles. On the *Angel* series, she eventually turns herself in to the police, does time in prison, and escapes just in time to help the Scoobies and Potential Slayers ward off Sunnydale's final apocalypse at the end of *Buffy*'s season seven.

Anya Emerson (formerly Anyanka)

A 1,120-year-old vengeance demon named Anyanka appears in season three in the guise of a high school student to grant Cordelia's wish that Buffy had never come to Sunnydale. Horror ensues, but Giles is able to reverse the curse; as a result, Anyanka finds herself stripped of her demonic attributes and doomed to live as Anya, a human. After a failed attempt to become a demon again, Anya accepts her fate and tries to make the best of it by asking Xander to the prom. After their less than wonderful date, Anya nonetheless feels connected to Xander and asks him to flee Sunnydale with her to avoid the Mayor's ascension. After Xander refuses, Anya leaves for the rest of season three but comes back to town in season four. She continues to pursue Xander, who haplessly lets her. Both irritated and charmed by her tactless but often refreshingly honest observations and literal language, Xander falls into a serious relationship with Anya, declaring his love for her in "Into the Woods" (5.10). The two later become engaged, but Xander leaves her at the altar in season six. This leads her back into the vengeance demon business, from which she is just barely able to extricate herself in season seven. After a brief attempt to return to life as a vengeance demon, Anya reconciles with Xander late in season seven. She dies in the series finale, saving Andrew's life as they fight the Bringers together. Anya is full of contradictions: she is a jaded veteran of the demon world who exhibits childlike innocence and curiosity regarding her newly acquired humanity. She is one of the series' funniest characters and often one of the most touching.

Quentin Travers

A high-ranking member of the Watchers' Council, Quentin Travers first appears in "Helpless" (3.12) when he forces Giles to give Buffy the Cruciamentum test on her eighteenth birthday. This cruel test, typical of the Council's dictates, requires the Watcher to use drugs to remove an unknowing Slayer's powers and then trap her with a vampire in order to test her resourcefulness and ability to improvise. Though Buffy passes the test, Giles does not, and Travers fires him for being too attached to his Slayer. This incident makes Buffy distrustful of the Council and its orders, and Travers's subsequent behavior does not change her opinion. He assigns an inexperienced Watcher, Wesley Wyndam-Pryce, to take Giles's place, then tries to kidnap Faith, and threatens Giles with deportation. In season seven he is killed when the servants of the First Evil destroy the Watchers' Council building.

Wesley Wyndam-Pryce

Sent by the Watchers' Council to replace Giles as the Watcher for Buffy and Faith, Wesley Wyndam-Pryce's inexperience and ineptitude undermine his authority. Before arriving in Sunnydale, he has confronted a vampire only in "controlled circumstances" and frequently panics when attacked. Buffy and Giles continue to behave as if Wesley had never arrived, patrolling and planning how to defeat the Mayor without his input. Wesley suffers another failure when Faith decamps to the Mayor's team. Wesley's only friend among the Scoobies is Cordelia, due to mutual attraction rather than any skill on Wesley's part. He does manage to redeem himself by bravely volunteering to help in the fight against the Mayor at the end of season three but is still pretty ineffective. By taking part in the battle against the Mayor, Wesley defies the Council, which promptly fires him. Wesley then joins Angel Investigations in Los Angeles, where he develops his skill as a fighter as well as his knowledge of demons and becomes a valuable addition to Angel's team.

Gwendolyn Post

Gwendolyn Post arrives in Sunnydale to be Faith's Watcher in "Revelations" (3.7). Her uptight manner and criticisms of Giles's training method don't impress the Scoobies, but Faith slowly warms up to her new Watcher. Having witnessed the death of her previous Watcher and lacking any parental figures, Faith wants to believe that Mrs. Post truly cares for her. Unfortunately, Mrs. Post is a rogue Watcher who is scheming to obtain the powerful Glove of Myhnegon. She pits Buffy and Faith against each other until Faith realizes that her Watcher has turned. Buffy and Faith defeat Mrs. Post, but the damage is done: this betrayal leaves Faith even more alone and ripe for the Mayor's fatherly attention.

Season Three Big Bad: Mayor Richard Wilkins III

Mild-mannered, funny, and obsessive about cleanliness, Sunnydale's Mayor appears to be an unlikely candidate for a Big Bad, but he proves to be a formidable foe. Throughout season three he meticulously lays plans for the Ascension, when he will become a pure demon-snake and devour all of Sunnydale. With Faith by his side as a hired assassin and cherished surrogate daughter, the Mayor schedules his Ascension for graduation day, when he will be the commencement speaker at Sunnydale High. His plans are foiled by the senior class, who attack with the weapons they've hidden under their graduation gowns, and by Buffy, who destroys the Mayor in snake form when she blows up the high school.

Characters Introduced in Season Four

Tara Maclay

Willow meets Tara early in season four at a meeting of the UC Sunnydale Wiccans. They instantly recognize that they are the only serious witches in the group, and their blossoming friendship is a bright spot in Willow's post-Oz life. A shy stutterer, Tara also happens to be a powerful, knowledgeable witch who inherited her abilities from her late mother. As Tara and Willow's relationship turns romantic, Willow avoids introducing Tara to the Scoobies; when she does, she lets them assume Tara is simply her friend. In "New Moon Rising" (4.19), however, both Buffy and a heartbroken Oz learn the truth about Tara and Willow, and in "The Yoko Factor" (4.20) Xander and the others learn as well. After Willow chooses Tara over Oz, their relationship becomes one of the healthiest any of the Scoobies ever enjoy. In "Family" (5.6) Tara's deeply dysfunctional family appears and, claiming that she's a demon, tries to take her away. When Buffy declares that the Scoobies are Tara's real family, Tara revels in a level of acceptance and love she has never experienced; as she and Willow dance at Tara's birthday party at the end of the episode, their levitation is a metaphor for their joy. Sadly, this is cut short when the hell god Glory feeds on Tara's mind, leaving her insane. Willow is able to reverse the effect of this in the season-five finale, but the sixth season shows their relationship in trouble as Willow becomes addicted to magic and begins manipulating Tara with spells. Tara's nonjudgmental nature and strong moral compass allow her not only to support her estranged girlfriend as she recovers from magic addiction but also to serve as Buffy's sole confidante regarding her sexual relationship with Spike. Tara is killed at the end of season six by a stray bullet from Warren's gun, and her death leads to Willow's grief-stricken transformation into a vessel of dark magic.

Riley Finn

Buffy and Willow meet Riley, their psychology teaching assistant at UC Sunnydale, in "The Freshman" (4.1). The three become friends, and soon Riley and Buffy begin to date. A seemingly normal guy from Iowa, Riley is a far cry from Angel, and Buffy is drawn to him and the possibility of a healthy, stable relationship. Unfortunately, the two both have secret identities. In "Doomed" (4.11) they come clean about their roles in the fight against demons. Riley is part of the vast underground military operation called the Initiative. Ostensibly created to capture, study, and neutralize the threat of what the group calls subterrestrials, the Initiative is up to all sorts of even more secret activity. It has pumped medicines into Riley's body, implanted a chip in his brain, and hidden a camera in his bedroom. Naive about the degree to which he is being manipulated and monitored, he continues to fight demons and even recruits Buffy into the Initiative. When Riley's boss, Professor Maggie Walsh, tries to kill Buffy and her demon-human hybrid then destroys the entire Initiative, Riley temporarily cuts off his affiliation with the government. For a portion of season five, he becomes a full-time Scooby but struggles with feeling inferior to Buffy and thinking that she does not truly need or love him. These struggles motivate him to solicit vampire prostitutes to suck blood from his body. He finally decides to reenlist with the military and leave Sunnydale, and Buffy, to join a secret mission in Central America. Riley comes back for one episode in the sixth season and brings his wife, much to Buffy's disappointment. He gives Buffy a pep talk, however, and his encouragement gives her the strength to finally end her affair with Spike.

Season Four Big Bad: Adam

A hybrid of demon, human, and robot parts, Adam is the creation of Professor Maggie Walsh, Buffy's psychology professor, who secretly leads the Initiative. When Adam awakens in "The I in Team" (4.13), Professor Walsh is the first person he kills; he goes on to murder many more people in his quest for domination and annihilation. Buffy stops him for good in "Primeval" (4.21) when she taps into her friends' abilities to create an über-Buffy who is able to remove Adam's uranium-core power source.

Characters Introduced in Season Five

Dawn Summers

Buffy's younger sister appears out of nowhere at the end of "Buffy vs. Dracula" (5.1). Although she has just been introduced, all the other characters treat her as if she has always been around. In "Real Me" (5.2) Dawn provides the voice-over for the episode, reading entries from her diary that reveal her as a typical fourteen-year-old girl who admires but is jealous of her older sister. In episode 5.5 Buffy realizes that Dawn's existence (and everyone's memory of her) is the result of a spell. At first she thinks that Dawn herself is evil, but Buffy soon realizes that Dawn is under the same spell as everyone else and that Dawn is actually a mystical Key that unlocks the portal between this and the many demon dimensions in the universe. An ancient order of monks has made her into the Slayer's sister so that Buffy will protect her from Glory, a hell god who wants the Key so that she can return to her own dimension. At the end of season five, Buffy sacrifices herself to save Dawn and the world, and at the beginning of season six, Dawn is no longer the Key. From this point on, she deals with the burden of being the youngest Scooby and with Buffy's attempts to protect her by excluding her from all Scooby activities. Dawn deals with Buffy's vacillation between neglect and overprotection by becoming a kleptomaniac. At the end of season six, Buffy finally realizes that her approach to raising Dawn has been wrong and that she should show her the world rather than protect her from it. In season seven Dawn is an integral part of the fight against the First Evil and even temporarily believes she is a Potential Slayer. When Buffy tries to get Dawn out of Sunnydale to protect her from its destruction, Dawn makes her way back, fights the Turok-Han, and rides out of town on the bus with the rest of the survivors.

Warren Mears

In "I Was Made to Love You" (5.15) the Scoobies learn that a fellow Sunnydale High alumnus named Warren has created a beautiful female robot, April, to be his girlfriend. He enjoys her complete devotion less than he expected, however, and abandons her in his college dorm room while he leaves for spring break with his new girlfriend, Katrina. Unfortunately, April comes looking for him, and when Katrina finds out about her, she is repulsed and leaves him. Viewers do not see Warren again until the beginning of season six, when he has joined forces with Jonathan and Andrew to form the Evil Trio. Warren capitalizes on Jonathan's vulnerability and Andrew's impressionability, tricking and seducing them into acts much more evil than either would have undertaken alone. At the end of "Gone" (6.11), for example, Warren lets them believe he is using the invisibility ray gun to reverse Buffy's invisibility when in fact he is trying to kill her. Soon enough, he does kill someone: Katrina is killed after his attempt to control her mind and enjoy her servitude fails. He successfully bullies Andrew and Jonathan into framing Buffy for Katrina's murder. After Buffy foils his attempt to rob an armored truck and humiliates him in the process, he seeks revenge by walking into her backyard and shooting her. Buffy recovers from her wounds, but Warren accidentally kills Tara, whose death unleashes Willow's fury. Warren dies when Willow magically skins him alive, but in season seven the First Evil appears in his guise to convince Andrew to do its bidding. And in an ironic spell cast by Amy, Willow finds herself turning into Warren when she begins her first romance after Tara's death.

Season Five Big Bad: Glory

A hell god who wishes to return to the horrific dimension from which she has been expelled, Glory spends season five searching for the Key, a ball of mystical energy that enables the opening of many dimensions. She does not realize until near the end of the season that the Key has been hidden inside of Dawn, a human, to protect it from Glory's evil plan. When Glory was discharged from her home dimension, part of her punishment was that she was doomed to share a body with a human, a medical intern named Ben. Having a part-time human body limits Glory's power and is a source of great frustration for her; she copes with her mental instability by sucking the minds out of human beings for energy. At the end of the season, Buffy injures Glory, who morphs into Ben. But because Ben is a human and Buffy is bound by the Slayer code to protect all humans, it is Giles who kills Ben, thereby ensuring that Glory cannot return.

Characters Introduced in Season Six

Season Six Big Bads: The Evil Trio or Troika:

Warren
See Season Five.

Jonathan
See Season One.

Andrew Wells

The third member of the Evil Trio or Troika, Andrew is the brother of Tucker, the malcontent who tried to unleash hellhounds at Buffy's senior prom (3.20). Throughout season six the Scoobies refer to him as "the other one," and only after he becomes their hostage early in season seven do they learn his name. Neither as pathological as Warren nor as morally ambivalent as Jonathan, Andrew is an impressionable character looking for someone he can follow uncritically. This moral flaw leads him to murder Jonathan when the First Evil, disguised as Warren, convinces him to do so. After Willow finds Andrew trying to buy pig's blood, she apprehends him, and his attempts to be a Scooby member instead of a Scooby hostage succeed in the final episodes of season seven when he makes several valuable contributions to the fight against the First Evil and its minions. A geek who has exhaustive knowledge of Dungeons and Dragons, Wonder Woman, and the *League of Extraordinary Gentlemen*, Andrew has obvious crushes on Warren and Spike and shows no sexual interest in women. Although his lines are howlingly funny (particularly his speech when he thinks he is about to die in the series finale), in "Storyteller" (7.16) Andrew explores the limits of humor and narrative: he makes a solemn documentary about Buffy called *Buffy, the Slayer of Vampires*. Although the entire episode is played for laughs, it is clear that Andrew is still rationalizing his past as a supervillain and his murder of Jonathan. When Buffy takes him to close the Seal of Danzalthar, which is the entry to the Hellmouth, he keeps telling her different versions of Jonathan's death. Fed up, she says to him, "Stop! Stop telling stories. . . . You make everything into a story so no one's responsible for anything because they're just following a script." Sobered, Andrew ends his documentary with no jokes and no resolution. Despite his belief that he will (and probably should) die in the final showdown with the Turok-Han and the Bringers, Anya saves his life as they fight side by side.

Characters Introduced in Season Seven

Principal Robin Wood

When Sunnydale High School reopens at the beginning of season seven, Buffy meets the handsome new principal, Robin Wood, on the first day of school. He promptly offers her a job as a guidance counselor. While working at the high school, Buffy slowly begins to suspect that the principal is more than he seems. On their first and only date, he reveals that he is the son of a previous Slayer, and he soon joins Buffy and the Scoobies in their struggle against the First Evil. Once in the inner circle, the First Evil manipulates him by telling him that Spike is the vampire who killed his mother. Robin tries to stake Spike, but Spike defeats him. Despite this behavior, Robin remains a valued part of the Scooby gang and survives the final battle against the First Evil.

Season Seven Big Bad: The First Evil

In many ways the First Evil, introduced in the episode "Amends" (3.10), proves to be Buffy's trickiest and most intriguing opponent. Its inability to assume corporeal form is balanced by a disconcerting ability to appear in the form of any person who has died: Spike; Warren; Jonathan; Robin Wood's mother, Nikki; even Buffy herself. The First Evil, the origin of all evil, uses its persuasive powers to convince people on earth to do its bidding; it compels Spike to begin siring vampires and goads Andrew into killing Jonathan, his best friend. The First also employs various henchmen to do its bidding, including an army of über-vampires, a host of Bringers (servants who methodically murder off the world's Watchers and Potential Slayers), and Caleb, a misogynistic and preternaturally strong priest. In the series finale, Buffy does not kill the First Evil, which is impervious to physical harm. She does, however, seriously weaken its power by magically sharing her own power with all of the remaining Potential Slayers and allowing Spike to use a talisman that destroys the army of über-vampires.

Keeping the Faith

An Interview with Eliza Dushku

In seasons three, four, and seven, Eliza Dushku electrified audiences with her portrayal of Faith, the rogue Slayer who went bad and then fought for redemption. In September 2003 she took time out of her busy shooting schedule for the TV series *Tru Calling* to sit down over a meal in Vancouver and talk about Faith, faith, life, and Buffy.

J.R. *How did you first get involved with* Buffy?

E.D. Sarah Michelle Gellar and I had the same manager, who got me in my first movie when I was ten years old. She'd had a handful of the same clients for years—me, Sarah Michelle Gellar, Adrien Brody, Brittany Murphy. Some pretty stellar people. I thought it was a show about, you know, vampires. I didn't watch it. I had never been into science fiction so much.

When I first made an audition tape for the show, I'd just graduated from high school. I was about to enroll in my mom's university [Suffolk in Boston, where her mother is a professor], and this came up. My mom had just put my brother through NYU, and I wanted to make some money to put myself through college.

The character was described as "biker girl meets trailer park." She was from the wrong side of the tracks, just tough, wild. I literally remember going to the mall in my hometown, wanting to go all out to create what they described on the page. So I bought this black leather vest and put safety pins all over it and did all this silver jewelry and red lipstick. I wore black makeup to be a biker girl and mixed in this kind of tough, street, in-your-face, hard-as-nails attitude—but clearly keeping in mind that this would be kind of a facade. An exaggerated character or situation.

[At the audition] they wanted to see a couple of punch moves to see if I was physical. And I showed them that I was physical, because I was a little bit of a tomboy and a wild kid. And that was it, and they called me to come out and do those five shows.

J.R. *What else did you do to prepare to play this character?*

E.D. I had stepped out of the business for the last two years because I wanted to finish high school and go to college. I wasn't really trained as an actor and had never taken an acting class. Ever since I was young, people would say, "She has good instincts." I could think of someone that I knew who these things had happened to, and that [technique] worked fine in movies. But in TV you're in a small box, so you have to overexaggerate the emotions and the behavior. After the first shoot, Joss and the producers weren't feeling my rhythm, and Joss wasn't seeing what he wanted. The first episode was hard to get through. I had five people directing me in that last scene with Kakistos, and I was really self-conscious and uncomfortable.

I needed kind of a tune-up, I guess. They wanted me to go see this coach. I didn't like the way the coach tried to pull emotions out—by breaking you down and getting into your head. For me it's just acting. I'm not going to tap into my own life. My life comes first, my life and my soul. But the work is making that real.

Finally, I think it came down to me being directed by one person, and that was Joss. We somehow just clicked and took off with it. And all these different colors started to come out of the character.

J.R. *What kind of initial direction were you given about playing Faith?*

E.D. On the first show, there was Kakistos and that final scene where Faith's terrified of this guy who killed her Watcher. Basically, Joss said, "He killed the only person that ever loved you, and with that all the strength you had or thought you had. You've always been so tough with everyone else, and he's the one thing you can't face, the thing you've always most feared." In that scene, where Kakistos beats her down, and she fights back, Joss really wanted that to resonate and have intensity and emotion. He wanted that feeling that this guy ripped out everything Faith had ever loved.

After that, now Faith was in Sunnydale, in this strange place, and has just fought the biggest thing she's ever been afraid of. Well, now what? So she puts that on her list of things she's done. She's a loner and she doesn't have a family, so she decides to stay in Sunnydale for a while. So she starts to try to socialize and tells Buffy's friends these stories about wrestling alligators. She starts to see that even though she can tell [these great] stories, that Buffy's friends are really loyal and love her [Buffy]. No one has ever really helped Faith—helped her with her homework and watched her go to school and unconditionally loved her. When she realizes what that [love] is, she starts to kind of test that and try to steal Buffy's friends, which is a really cowardly thing to do. Faith was the bravest coward that I've ever played or that I've ever seen written.

So she started to unfold as a young woman, with a depth and range of emotions. And I just started to peel them out of her, you know? Joss was steering the ship. I just thank God for Joss. It's awesome when you've got a great writer, and you're just regurgitating their knowledge and their smarts on-screen. When people tell me how much they love Faith, I really can't take much credit for that. It's the writing.

I'm starting to understand it all more as I get older. I was really young then. And when I went back [in the seventh season], I kind of had a deeper connection.

J.R. *What was it like to return for that seventh season?*

E.D. I actually worried a lot when I came back: "Joss, is Faith still cool? Is she too soft? Is she still wild and crazy?" And Joss said, "You are her, a little bit. She's grown, and you've grown." He went back to the idea of the character—Faith's life, whoever she is, it's organic.

When I got to the last episode, we were saying, "How in the hell is Joss going to do this?" This show means so much to so many different kinds of people. How do you please everyone? How do you end it?

Before I read the script, I was thinking the whole time of how to say to Joss: "Well, you gave it your best effort." I was going to be really nice to Joss, thinking he was going to be under a lot of pressure. And then when I turned the last page, I went "Oh! *That's* how you do it! That's how you end one of the most profound shows in the history of television. You give the power to every potential Slayer on the planet and empower every girl." He did it!

I'm not the most emotional person, though I'm a little more now than I was five years ago. But when I went into rehearsal for that episode, I gave Joss one of those uncomfortable, spur-of-the-moment hugs. And I said, "Man, that was so beautiful. I'm so proud of you and in awe of you. You rock." And Joss knew what I was saying when I said he rocked. We were simpatico with that.

J.R. *The scene that I'll never forget is of the little girl standing up to bat on the baseball diamond— the one who's so timid and scared. And then she gets that power, that gleam in her eye, and looks ready to whack it out of the park.*

E.D. I still get chills about it. I'm not a gusher, but I was really blown away by that episode. And by that as a cap to the show. I was like, "Joss, you did it, man. You really did it."

J.R. *What did you appreciate most about the show and about working with Joss Whedon?*

E.D. He's such a genius. Everything he puts on paper, you first look at it and say, "Oh, this is just a TV show for teenagers." And then you look again and see that it's *so* much more. There are so many hidden messages.

It's amazing. . . . In season three there was a line about Little Miss Muffet counting down from 730. The writers knew two years in advance that Dawn was coming as Buffy's sister and that she would represent the end of the world. Three hundred sixty-five days times two equals two years from now: Buffy's going to have a sister she doesn't know about yet and will face the end of the world. And when they threw that line in, people on the Internet just went crazy. Two people online actually figured it out that early. It's just a trip. It made it almost a game, a challenge. It sucked people in. Joss was always one step ahead of the rest with all of his ideas and stories. It was so thought out, and that's what he was always known for.

I know why I did *Buffy*, and it was really because it stirred something within me, and I just *so* connected with the people. I mean, I'd been in the business for years, but it was a different level in terms of how realistically he wanted to portray these girls and their different values and struggles and triumphs and failures and emotions. That's why I was always grateful when they wanted to let me back into the story line.

I'm probably a little biased, but I think that with Joss, what you see is what you get. It's either a case of a guy who had really good luck and really good instincts, or it's something bigger. And in his case it's definitely something bigger. He is so intuitive and so respectful of women. I think that he goes down in history as one of those men who understood women and did women justice. He took the time to think about it deeply and make it real.

J.R. *What were the best aspects of playing Faith, in terms of your development as an actress?*

E.D. Probably mixing the strength with the weakness and mixing vulnerability with toughness. Sometimes it would be easy to run in and do these fight scenes. I get to look like I'm beating up seven guys with my leather jacket, and I've got all these cute catchphrases. But then I have a moment to slow it down and let something deeper come out.

I think Buffy and Faith taught each other so much. They were such opposites of each other, yet they were really in the same predicament and the same place. They were almost like sisters or something. It was powerful, you know? And again, it's funny how art imitates life. I really find that more and more. It's almost like therapy. It's a great outlet for me in my own personal life to see it played out.

My relationship with Sarah was the same way, art imitating life in a way. We had a real chemistry that was similar to Buffy and Faith. [*laughs*] I was like, "Hey! This is fun! Let's have fun!" And she'd say, "This is my *job*. This is work. There's responsibility, and there are consequences. You can't hook up with these hot guys! We *work* with them. You cannot hook up with our costars." It was a real dynamic that we had, that just started to come out in the show.

J.R. *What were your favorite scenes to play?*

E.D. The scene with Angel in the alley ["Five by Five," A1.18] was really a great opportunity—as an actor and for Faith and also just for me. I got to go all out, no holds barred. Everyone says to punch a pillow or scream out loud when you're feeling emotional. I'd kind of feel silly doing that, but when I actually got to take all of the confusion and pain and fear and reach that desperate level, it was totally cathartic. It wasn't my favorite scene in terms of fun, but it was cathartic.

J.R. *What about the episode where you and Buffy switched bodies?*

E.D. We both really wanted to go for it. And it was kind of funny, because we didn't see each other doing it while we were filming it. I felt a little bit apprehensive to try some different things [to imitate Sarah/Buffy], because it was Sarah's set. But for both of us, there had to be, and there was, an enormous amount of trust in the show and in Joss and in the story and in the message. It was humbling and challenging, but it was great. What a great thing to have them live each other's lives for a day.

J.R. *What was your own religious or spiritual background?*

E.D. I'm in a mode in my life where I was raised Mormon, but I kind of fell out of Mormonism when I was like ten or eleven years old. I was one of those kids who saw religion in the same category as superstition, almost. I was always questioning and wanting proof.

One thing I've always loved about Mormonism is that Mormons really help each other out. You can't deny that. They back each other up and help each other in the worst times. There's a real humanitarian theme in Mormonism that I love. But growing up, I hated feeling that there was a big bearded man in the sky who was going to punish me if I did or thought anything wrong. And I hated all the guilt. It was too much, especially for children, I think.

When I used to go to church, I felt out of place. I don't know whether it had to do with the fact that my parents were divorced. At church all the girls' daddies were in the priesthood, and I didn't have that, and I felt like a bad seed. I also questioned a lot of things. I remember being six or seven in Sunday school saying that all this Adam and Eve stuff sounds like a great fairy tale, but hasn't it been scientifically proven that we descended from monkeys? I had a full-blown debate with my Sunday school teacher about Adam and Eve. The teacher wasn't prepared for the kind of precocious little shit that I was. And I got kicked out of Sunday school that day.

Also, I had family members that were homosexual. When I was fourteen, I got kicked out of Mormon girls' camp for talking about a gay family member. It wasn't like I lived a wild Hollywood lifestyle, but I'd just spent three months in Australia shooting a movie, and we had three drag queens on our set. I saw this whole other world, and then I found out that one of my closest family members was gay. I was tripped out by that, but it was great. And then I went to Mormon girls' camp and said that boys kiss and there's nothing wrong with that. It's not like I was being graphic. But the head of the camp came to me that night and said she prayed that my family member could pull himself out of that deep dark hole of homosexuality, but she said I couldn't talk about homosexuality while I was there.

I know that Mormons aren't all in one category, and not all of them feel that way. That was just one woman. I have no malicious or bitter feelings toward Mormons. I go to church with my Mormon grandparents when we visit them, because I love them. My grandma is the best woman I know on the planet. Along with my mom.

J.R. *What do you think about spirituality now?*

E.D. I believe in the basics—they don't sound very profound. Treat other people how you want to be treated. I'm not calling myself an atheist anymore. I know that there must be a higher power, and there must be something greater and bigger than me, than what I've seen. I believe in people . . . and my family . . . and my mother. And whatever my mother has told me and can teach me, I'm pretty much a believer. My mom's my hero. My parents divorced when I was born. My mom's a teacher, a feminist, a humanitarian. She's such a brave, awesome woman.

Eliza Dushku with her "hero," mom Judy Dushku.

Not to get all foofy, but my brother and two friends and whoever's on set, we all kind of shared this book at one time called *The Four Agreements* [by Don Miguel Ruiz]. It's simple in a way, but it's really amazing and thought-provoking. It's kind of a self-help book. The first chapter is about the domestication of the planet, about what is good in us and what is taught to us. How as children we're domesticated and taught by our parents. How we're taught about what is good and right and wrong. One of the agreements is not to take anything too personally. (When my brother gave it to me, he put a paper clip in that chapter just for me!) Another is to do everything the best you can do it. Another is to be meticulous and be careful with your words, with what you say.

When you look at the core of religion and spirituality and life and good and evil, right and wrong, there are things that can be spelled out in a very black-and-white way, but nothing's like that; everything is gray. As human beings we're packed with so much emotion. Most of us really have a strong conscience and want to do right. And when we go wrong, we want to learn from it. All you can do is learn from your day to day [experience] and from yourself and from your parents and be affected by life.

With Faith, one of the things that made her so appealing to people is that she's got all of the bad girl attributes. She's next to Buffy, this blonde, blue-eyed, good girl from a good family. And then there's Faith: dark. A "bad" girl. But then you find that she goes so much deeper than that and that Faith is not just evil. You find that she can change. People were surprised that they could still love Faith and feel compassion and empathy for her after she'd done such awful things. But what we hate most in other people is often what we hate the most about ourselves. The writers did a really good job of making her flawed. The show runs the gamut of the human emotions.

J.R.   *What have your interactions with fans been like? Why do you think that fans are so passionate about this show?*

E.D.   I've gone to two *Buffy* posting-board parties, which were intense. Some people just live, eat, breathe, and die this show. It's flattering and at times frightening. [*laughs*] But this is why we play, to reach people and affect people. At the end of the day, we want to thank people for being so enthusiastic and loyal. But my name is Eliza, and I play a *character* named Faith! I'm thrilled that I could bring so much therapeutic energy to people's lives, but at the same time, I tell them, "Go talk to Joss." We're just actors. There's a firm, thick, long line in the sand for me about where my character ends and my life begins. They're not the same.

Probably the most poignant connections and messages that I've received from fans are the ones from girls. The envelopes come, and they're thick. You open it up, and it's white lined paper, front and back, and it's seven pages long. I read my fan mail when I have time to go through it. I mean, it's one thing when someone writes and just wants a signed picture. But when someone writes you a letter by hand, and it's a fourteen-year-old girl from God knows where, and it's her story, you should take it seriously. I've read probably twenty of them that say, "I was being abused by a teacher, a stepfather, a brother, a neighbor. And the first day that Faith made it to my TV box, I started standing up for myself. If Faith has the power to stand up for herself, so can I." That stuff *trips me out*. You can't ask for any better or greater kind of verification than that. Again, I don't write it, but I'll be their hero girl, because that's amazing.

J.R. *Does it make you feel a lot of pressure to be a role model?*

E.D. Not really. I'm twenty-two years old, and I'm not perfect. One of the things that I think they're relating to is that the character I play wasn't perfect. So I don't feel that they're pressuring me, Eliza, to be Superwoman. They're following the show, and connecting with it.

J.R. *Why did you decide not to do a Faith-based spin-off?*

E.D. I started Faith when I was seventeen years old. It's been five years, and sometimes you just have to move on. I've changed a lot since I started that character. When I started Faith, I was just out of high school, and high school was hell for a girl who was an actress in Hollywood movies. The other kids really put me through it. I made it, and it made me stronger. But I'm a little more recovered from high school at this stage. And even though Faith also changed and learned a lot, it was time to move on.

I've said it once, and it's been plastered everywhere: sometimes you have to take the road less traveled and try something new. I wanted to stand on my own two feet a little bit, and I didn't want to be in Buffy's footsteps—not that those aren't great footsteps to follow. This show seemed like a new chapter, a different book. There are a lot of the same themes and values though—death, relationships, women, and families. It makes it more than a TV show when you feel you're dealing with heavy life issues that everyone can relate to.

Notes

Introduction

The characterization of *Buffy the Vampire Slayer* as "the most original, witty, and provocative television show of the last two decades" is from Boyd Tonkin, "Farewell Buffy, and Fangs for the Memories," *Independent*, May 21, 2003, http://news.independent.co.uk/uk/media/story.jsp?story=408046.

The "Barbie with a Kung Fu grip" quote is from Joss Whedon in an interview with *The Onion A.V. Club*, Sept. 5, 2001, http://www.theonion avclub.com/avclub3731/avfeature_3731.html.

For an example of a thoughtful article about why a Christian might reject *Buffy* for its nontheistic worldview, see Gina Dalfonzo, "Buffy Fades to Black," http://www.boundless.org/2002_2003/features/a0000763.html. However, I do not agree with Dalfonzo's assessment that because Whedon is an atheist, the Buffyverse can never compare to some of the genius fantasy of a Christian writer like Tolkien. Without an understanding of how God fits into reality, Dalfonzo implies, "at best all you've got is a pop-culture phenomenon that ultimately trivializes the great themes it tries to deal with."

The *Relevant* quote is from Jason Boyett's beautifully written article "Finding God in the Darker Side of Prime Time: Lessons from *Buffy* and *Angel*," in *Relevant*, May-June 2003, p. 66. Shaun Narine has an interesting article on *Buffy* and metaphysics at http://www.the-buzz.com/b_7_13a.html.

The first Marti Noxon interview, with *Prevue Magazine*, is found at http://www.prevuemagazine.com/Articles/TheVault/589. The second, which discusses Joss Whedon's "yearning for belief," is located at http://www.buffy.nu/article.php3?id_article=172. Marti Noxon was also asked about the Buffyverse's idea of heaven in "Question Time," an interview in *The Official 2003 Buffy the Vampire Slayer Yearbook* (London: Titan Towers, 2003). "Oh my God, that's a big question," she said. "I'd imagine it as a place with lots of cheesecake" (p. 32).

The *Buffy the Vampire Slayer* movie, written by Joss Whedon and directed by Fran Rubel Kuzui, starred Kristy Swanson as Buffy; Donald Sutherland as her Watcher, Merrick; and Paul Reubens (Pee-Wee

Herman) as a villainous vampire. According to the Internet Movie Database, the 1992 film grossed a disappointing $16.6 million at the box office and received mixed reviews. However, it quickly became a cult video-rental favorite, and its popularity spawned the television series. See http://www.imdb.com/title/tt0103893/business.

Sarah Michelle Gellar's thoughts on God are from *The Door*, issue 183, Sept.-Oct. 2002, which cited the Scottish *Daily Record*.

For more on Generation X and Generation Y spirituality, see Lynn Schofield Clark, *From Angels to Aliens: Teenagers, the Media, and the Supernatural* (New York: Oxford University Press, 2003). Chapter Two, "Touched by a Vampire Named Angel," specifically focuses on how the spirituality of *Buffy* and *Angel* appeals to—and reflects—the values of today's young people. To better understand the Zen notion of privileging experience over teaching, see Brad Warner, *Hardcore Zen: Punk Rock, Monster Movies, and the Truth About Reality* (Boston: Wisdom, 2003). For more on *Buffy* and relationships, see Marguerite Krause, "The Meaning of *Buffy*," in *Seven Seasons of* Buffy: *Science Fiction and Fantasy Writers Discuss Their Favorite Television Show* (Dallas: BenBella Books, 2003), pp. 97–108.

Rabbi Kushner's etymology of the word *religion* is found in *The Lord Is My Shepherd: Healing Wisdom of the Twenty-Third Psalm* (New York: Knopf, 2003), p. 15. The Oscar Wilde quote comes from *The Critic as Artist* in *The Complete Works of Oscar Wilde* (London, 1923), vol. 5, p. 209. The "what's to come" quote is spoken slightly differently by various characters—Tara in "Restless" (4.22), Dracula in "Buffy vs. Dracula" (5.1)—but the idea is the same.

Chapter One

The references to 730 have been dissected and analyzed on *Buffy* bulletin boards and in chat rooms, but Whedon has stated that the number referred to the number of days remaining before Buffy's death. "Some fans figured it out," he said. "Seven three oh is exactly two years in days. Two years until the next climax. Whatever she's talking about will be resolved." See Candace Havens, *Joss Whedon: The Genius Behind* Buffy (Dallas: BenBella Books, 2003), p. 42. Note that the finale of season four, the dream episode "Restless" (4.22), shows Buffy's clock displaying the time 7:30. Tara tells Buffy that the clock is completely wrong, suggesting that at that point in the series Buffy only has one year left to live, not two.

For more on "Innocence" (2.14), see the episode analysis in Nikki Stafford's *Bite Me! An Unofficial Guide to the World of* Buffy the Vampire Slayer, rev. ed. (Toronto: ECW Press, 2002), pp. 212-214. Stafford notes that "Innocence" was the most-watched *Buffy* episode ever, with 5.2 million people tuned in to find out what happened with Buffy and Angel. Arthur Lender quoted Joss Whedon in "San Diego, Day Three: Joss Whedon Talks *Buffy, Fray,* and More,"http://www.comicbookresources .com/news/newsitem.cgi?id=2573.

Buddhist art sometimes depicts Tara, a bodhisattva who shares wisdom with others, with seven eyesall to watch over her devotees. The philosopher Nagarjuna called her the "compassionate Savioress from *samsara* [suffering]." Like other bodhisattvas, her entire reason for being is to help others. As Peg Aoli points out in "Skin Pale as Apple Blossom," an homage to the character and beauty of the television Tara, Tara's last words also recall the painful moment in the fifth season when Willow is frantically trying to find an appropriate shirt to wear after Joyce's death. That essay is found in *Seven Seasons of* Buffy, p. 45.

The Dalai Lama's idea that all persons desire happiness, not suffering, is from *The Art of Happiness: A Handbook for Living* by the Dalai Lama and Harold C. Cutler (New York: Riverhead Books, 1998). The Philo quote dates back to the first century and is widely cited on the Internet.

The role of the bodhisattva is explored generally in *The Bodhisattva Vow: A Practical Guide to Helping Others* (Glen Spey, N.Y.: Tharpa Publications, 2003). Chögyam Trungpa Rinpoche's book *The Heart of the Buddha* (Boston: Shambhala, 1991) also contains a helpful chapter. In Kim Boykin's book *Zen for Christians: A Beginner's Guide* (San Francisco: Jossey-Bass, 2003), we find this version of the basic bodhisattva vow:

> However innumerable all beings are, I vow to save them all.
> However inexhaustible my delusions are, I vow to extinguish
> them all.
> However immeasurable the Dharma teachings are, I vow to
> master them all.
> However endless the Buddha's Way is, I vow to follow it com-
> pletely [p. 142].

For more on the Buffy-Dawn relationship, see Shaun Narine's article "'Be Back Before Dawn': Neglect, Abandonment, and the Sister-Slayer Relationship" at http://www.the-buzz.com/b_7_12a.html.

Chapter Two

Christopher Golden and Nancy Holder comment on demons' inability to change in *The Watcher's Guide* (New York: Pocket Books, 1998), p. 138.

For more on Spike's gradual transformation, see Mary Alice Money, "The Undemonization of Supporting Characters in *Buffy*," in Rhonda Wilcox and David Lavery, eds., *Fighting the Forces: What's at Stake in* Buffy the Vampire Slayer (Lanham, Md.: Rowman & Littlefield, 2002), pp. 98–107.

Joss Whedon's remark about change is found in Scott Andrews's article "The Chosen Ones" in *Starburst* online, http://www.visimag.com/starburst/280_feature.htm.

Whedon's quote about Seth Green and Amber Benson is from Candace Havens's biography *Joss Whedon: The Genius Behind Buffy*, p. 43. James Collier's comment is from his article "*Buffy the Vampire Slayer:* Change Is Good" in the online magazine *teevee*. The Marti Noxon quote is found in her interview with *Prevue Magazine* cited earlier.

James South provides some very good thoughts on Willow's evolution in his essay "'My God, It's like a Greek Tragedy': Willow Rosenberg and Human Irrationality," in James South, ed., Buffy the Vampire Slayer *and Philosophy: Fear and Trembling in Sunnydale* (Chicago: Open Court, 2003), pp. 131–145. James Collier's article "*Buffy the Vampire Slayer:* Change Is Good" explores how the series rejected trite formulas and embraced new artistic directions.

Thich Nhat Hanh's thoughts on how impermanence makes everything possible are in *No Death, No Fear: Comforting Wisdom for Life* (New York: Riverhead, 2002), p. 41. Lama Surya Das provides valuable reflections on spiritual growth in *Letting Go of the Person You Used to Be: Lessons on Change, Loss, and Spiritual Transformation* (New York: Broadway Books, 2003), pp. 6, 27–28. The Heraclitus quote is analyzed in Charles H. Kahn, *The Art and Thought of Heraclitus: An Edition of the Fragments with Translation and Commentary* (New York: Cambridge University Press, 1979), p. 168.

Chapter Three

Madeleine L'Engle's quotation is from the foreword to Johann Christoph Arnold's book *Be Not Afraid: Overcoming the Fear of Death*

(Maryknoll, N.Y.: Orbis Books, 2003), p. xi. Arnold's book is filled with wisdom and comfort for those who are facing their own death or that of a loved one. Thich Nhat Hanh's quote is from *No Death, No Fear*, p. 45. Philip Yancey's quote is from *Rumors of Another World: What on Earth Are We Missing?* (Grand Rapids, Mich.: Zondervan, 2003), p. 38. Lama Surya Das's thought is taken from *Letting Go of the Person You Used to Be*, p. 104. Sarah Michelle Gellar spoke about the sixth season's darkness in Jeff Jensen's article "The Good-Bye Girl," *Entertainment Weekly*, Mar. 7, 2003, p. 21. For more on how Buffy's experience of the afterlife affects her return to mortality, see Shaun Narine's article "Metaphor and Metaphysics in 'Buffy'" at http://www.the-buzz.com/b_7_13a.html.

Marti Noxon's "dark night of the soul" quote is found in her interview with *Prevue Magazine* cited earlier. The Dalai Lama's ruminations on death are found in *Advice on Dying and Living a Better Life*, translated and edited by Jeffrey Hopkins (New York: Atria, 2002), pp. 51-52.

Chapter Four

The Thomas Moore quotation comes from "Spiritual Anger" in his book *The Soul's Religion: Cultivating a Profoundly Spiritual Way of Life* (New York: HarperCollins, 2002), p. 102.

For more on Faith, see Greg Forster's essay "Faith and Plato: 'You're Nothing! Disgusting, Murderous Bitch!'" in Buffy the Vampire Slayer *and Philosophy*. Elyce Rae Helford makes some observations on Buffy and Kendra in her essay "'My Emotions Give Me Power': The Containment of Girls' Anger in *Buffy*" in *Fighting the Forces*, pp. 18-34.

The dialogue from Glory is taken from "The Weight of the World" (5.21). Although the episode's title seems to refer most clearly to Buffy's desire to cave in to the terrible responsibility of being the Slayer and possibly having to sacrifice Dawn, it also has resonance with Glory's newfound spark of humanity, which causes her to feel the heavy weight of human emotion.

Rage is just one of the emotions or circumstances that can bring out a vampire's real countenance. Lust, hunger, or passion can also. We see this in the first-season episode "Angel" (1.7), when the sexual heat of kissing Buffy for the first time causes Angel to transform into a vampire.

The insights on anger as a living thing are from Thich Nhat Hanh's book *Anger: Wisdom for Cooling the Flames* (New York: Riverhead, 2001), pp. 85 and 119. I am grateful to Kelly Hughes for pointing out how her favorite character, Xander, often gets it right.

Chapter Five

My argument that Buffy's use of humor demonstrates her sense of power and control entirely disagrees with an article by Elyce Rae Helford, who claims that Buffy uses humor to diffuse her anger and uphold a "ladylike" identity. Helford's gender argument does not account for the fact that it is Xander, not Buffy, who most often employs sarcasm (especially the self-deprecating kind) in order to redirect anger. See Helford, "'My Emotions Give Me Power'," in *Fighting the Forces*, pp. 18-34.

"Fightin' Quips" is found at http://vrya.net/bdb/quips.php. The examples about the power of language are taken from Karen Eileen Overbey and Lahney Preston-Matto, "Staking in Tongues: Speech Act as Weapon in *Buffy*," in *Fighting the Forces*, p. 73. As the authors point out, language's power is most obvious in its absence: "Hush" (4.10), often regarded as the most terrifying episode of *Buffy*, imagines a world where we are robbed of the ability to speak.

Steve Wilson's article is "Laugh, Spawn of Hell, Laugh," in Roz Kaveney's edited collection *Reading the Vampire Slayer: An Unofficial Critical Companion to* Buffy *and* Angel (London: Tauris, 2002), p. 81. The G. K. Chesterton quote is from David Heim, "A Joking Matter," in *Christian Century*, Aug. 9, 2003, p. 27. The *Door* article naming Buffy as theologian of the year, cited earlier, appeared in its Sept.-Oct. 2002 issue.

Chelsea Quinn Yarbro's essay "Lions, Gazelles, and Buffy," is found in *Seven Seasons of* Buffy, p. 53. The Pema Chödrön quote comes from the revised edition of *Start Where You Are*, as found in *The Compassion Box: Powerful Practices from the Buddhist Tradition for Cultivating Wisdom, Fearlessness, and Compassion* (Boston: Shambhala, 2003), p. 154.

One of the most interesting aspects of the Buffyverse, which is unfortunately beyond the scope of this book, is the intense fascination that die-hard fans have with the show. This is evident in the many witty, entertaining Web sites in which fans create new scenes and even whole episodes for the show. Although the series has been canceled, fans on the Internet have already written seasons eight and nine. Some of these episodes are at least as funny as any that were actually produced for television.

Chapter Six

Rhonda Wilcox's essay "'Who Died and Made Her the Boss?': Patterns of Mortality in *Buffy*" in *Fighting the Forces*, pp. 3-17, is an excellent exploration of themes like friendship, shared power, and loneliness in the series. Also, Jessica Prata Miller's outstanding essay "'The I in Team': Buffy and Feminist Ethics" in Buffy the Vampire Slayer *and Philosophy*, pp. 35-48, offers more on the ethic of cooperation in the series. Overbey and Preston-Matto's essay "Staking in Tongues: Speech Act as Weapon in *Buffy*" in *Fighting the Forces*, pp. 73-84, contains some examples of how Buffy's friends help her. See especially pp. 81-82.

Thomas Hibbs argues that friendship is the key to the season-six finale in "Buffy's War: Good and Evil 101," *National Review Online*, May 24, 2002, http://www.nationalreview.com/comment/comment-hibbs 052402.asp). Ralph Waldo Emerson wrote "A friend is a person with whom I may be sincere. Before him, I may think aloud" in the essay "Friendship" (1841). Kathleen Tracy's observations about "The Wish" can be found in *The Girl's Got Bite: The Original and Unauthorized Guide to Buffy's World, Completely Revised and Updated* (New York: St. Martin's Press, 2003), p. 189. For terrific additional reading on how Xander helps Buffy, see Roxanne Longstreet Conrad's hilarious send-up of *The Screwtape Letters,* "Is That Your Final Answer . . . ?" in *Seven Seasons of* Buffy, pp. 5-18. Strong general thoughts on Buffy and her friendships can be found in Joelle Renstrom's article "Is the Slayer Destined to Be Alone? Is the Mission All That Matters?" in *The Buzz* online, http://www.the-buzz.com/ b_7_19a.html; see also Sharon Ross's essay "'Tough Enough': Female Friendship and Heroism in *Xena* and *Buffy*" in *Action Chicks: New Images of Tough Women in Popular Culture*, edited by Sherrie A. Inness (New York: Palgrave, 2004), pp. 231-255.

Marti Noxon's quote about finding meaning in the journey itself and the companions on the journey is from a CBC Radio interview with IDEAS producer Mary O'Connell. The transcript can be found at http://www.buffy.nu/article.php3?id_article=235. For more on intimacy as a precursor of enlightenment, see Norman Fischer, *Taking Our Places: The Buddhist Path to Truly Growing Up* (San Francisco: Harper-SanFrancisco, 2003), p. 35.

The translation of *'ezer kenegdo* as "an equal helper" comes from Carol Meyers, *Women in Scripture: A Dictionary of Named and Unnamed Women in the Hebrew Bible, the Apocryphal/Deuterocanonical Books, and the New Testament* (Boston: Houghton Mifflin, 2000), p. 81.

Fans of the show will note that Buffy does not always welcome others into her inner circle. She adopts a different tack with romantic relationships. At the end of "Never Kill a Boy on the First Date" (1.5), for example, Buffy tells Owen that she can't have a relationship with him, despite her earlier insistence to Giles that such a thing would be possible. In fact, throughout the series Buffy tends to gravitate toward boyfriends with superpowers: Angel, Riley (who is a human but a trained and chemically enhanced warrior), and eventually Spike. She has very few "normal" boyfriends, as much as she pines for them; those relationships rarely last because of her unique responsibilities as the Slayer.

Chapter Seven

The quote from Lynn Schofield Clark comes from her fascinating book *From Angels to Aliens*, p. 49. David Brin's article "Buffy vs. the 'Old-Fashioned Hero,'" which originally appeared in Salon, is found in *Seven Seasons of* Buffy, pp. 1–4. For more on the comparison between Buffy and Kendra, see Zoe-Jane Playden, "'What You Are, What's to Come': Feminisms, Citizenship, and the Divine" in *Reading the Vampire Slayer*, p. 127. For a fine interpretation of Professor Walsh, see Madeline Muntersbjorn, "Pluralism, Pragmatism, and Pals: The Slayer Subverts the Science Wars," in Buffy the Vampire Slayer *and Philosophy*, p. 95. I am grateful to Roz Kaveney, who in a private conversation pointed out the intriguing wordplay surrounding Riley Finn's title (Agent Finn) and his evolving moral agency.

In "Dating Death," Jennifer Crusie points out that Buffy's resistance to the patriarchal, almost slavish system in which the Slayer is a mere pawn of the Watchers' Council is directly connected to Buffy's remarkable longevity as the Slayer. See her essay in *Seven Seasons of* Buffy, pp. 85–96, especially her insights on p. 95.

David Fury is quoted in Keith Topping's book *Slayer: An Expanded and Updated Unofficial and Unauthorised Guide to* Buffy the Vampire Slayer (London: Virgin Books, 2002), p. 289.

Norman Fischer's thoughts on spiritual maturity are found in *Taking Our Places*, p. 2. Richard Foster's contributions are taken from the twentieth-anniversary edition of his classic book on spiritual formation, *Celebration of Discipline: The Path to Spiritual Growth* (San Francisco: HarperSanFrancisco, 1998), pp. III and 185.

Chapter Eight

Joss Whedon's comments about "I Only Have Eyes for You" (2.19) are found in an interview on the second-season DVD. I am grateful to Holly Welker for reminding me about the powerful theme of forgiveness in this often-overlooked episode.

Since forgiveness comes from a place of strength rather than weakness, it's not surprising that the seventh season—which Buffy opens by telling Dawn that "it's about power"—is all about forgiveness as well. Many of the examples from this chapter (Anya, Andrew, Spike, and Willow) are taken from that season, in which various characters confront the ramifications of power and require forgiveness for abuses of that power.

The quote about hatred not being able to put an end to hatred is from the Dhammapada, translated by E. Easwaran (Tomales, Calif.: Nilgiri Press), verse 5.

For more on the randomness of vampire sirings in the Buffyverse, see Gregory Erickson, "'Sometimes You Need a Story': American Christianity, Vampires, and *Buffy*," in *Fighting the Forces*, p. III. Timothy Beal's vampire chapter in *Religion and Its Monsters* (New York: Routledge, 2002), provides some helpful history on Dracula tales. *The Monster Book* by Christopher Golden, Stephen R. Bissette, and Thomas E. Sniegoski has a brief history of early vampire legends (New York: Simon Pulse, 2000), p. 141. Most notably, it claims that people who were thought to be "at risk" for transforming into vampires after burial (those who had been murdered or who were born with certain physical deformities) were interred with various sacred objects to prevent them from leaving their coffins as vampires. In *Vampire Legends in Contemporary American Culture* (Lexington: University of Kentucky Press, 2002), p. 14, however, William Patrick Day notes that the more typical early vampire legend has the vampire as a sexual predator rather than an unforgiving avenger.

In Exodus 21:24, the law states that recompense can be exacted in the form of "eye for eye, tooth for tooth, hand for hand, foot for foot, burn for burn, wound for wound, stripe for stripe." In Matthew 18:22, Jesus instructs Peter that he should forgive "seventy times seven" times.

Archbishop Tutu's quote on forgiveness comes from his book *No Future Without Forgiveness*, an excerpt of which is posted at Beliefnet.com at http://www.beliefnet.com/story/39/story_3904_1.html.

I'm grateful to my editor, Julianna Gustafson, for pointing me toward the full implications of Spike's draping himself over the cross early in season seven.

The beautiful scene in which Buffy holds Willow's hands and takes on her pain is very reminiscent of the Tibetan Buddhist practice of *tonglin*, where individuals put compassion into practice by attempting to physically and spiritually take others' pain into themselves.

Jesus' comment about the one without sin casting the first stone is found in John 8:7. The Hannah Arendt quote is from *The Human Condition* (Chicago: University of Chicago Press, 1970).

Chapter Nine

Buffy has taken criticism from many Wiccans for its rather strange portrayal of witchcraft, which the show calls Wicca but which bears only superficial resemblance to the earth-centered paganism that practitioners call by the same name. For the record, Wicca is a bona fide religion practiced by neo-pagans, many of whom are also practitioners of other religions—think of Willow's continuing self-identification as someone who still observes Jewish rituals enough by the fifth season that she keeps a "big honkin' menorah" in her window at Hanukkah; 5.16). Although Wicca is tremendously diverse, most Wiccans profess that the earth is sacred, and they worship at least one of many gods and goddesses connected to the earth or some element of nature. Real Wiccans have protested various elements of the show, including its odd (and inconsistent) insistence that Wiccans are called "Wiccas" and its occasional flubbing of the names and responsibilities of various deities. For more on this, see Christie Golden, "Where's the Religion in Willow's Wicca?" in *Seven Seasons of* Buffy, pp.

159-166, or Seanan McGuire, "Witchcraft on *Buffy*" in *newWitch*, Autumn 2002, pp. 19-20.

Oscar Wilde's thoughts are found in *Intentions* (London, 1891).

The New Testament story of the man blind from birth is found in John 9.

The notion that magic is a stand-in for sensuality as well as power comes from Joss Whedon's commentary in the fourth-season DVD featurette.

Thomas Hibbs explores noir themes of transgression and its consequences in "*Buffy the Vampire Slayer* as Feminist Noir" in Buffy the Vampire Slayer *and Philosophy*, p. 55. James South discusses Willow's evolution in his essay "'My God, It's like a Greek Tragedy'" in the same volume, pp. 131-145. For more on the use of magic in the Buffyverse, see Tanya Krzywinska, "Hubble-Bubble, Herbs, and Grimoires: Magic, Manichaeanism, and Witchcraft in *Buffy*," in *Fighting the Forces*, pp. 178-194.

Chapter Ten

Nikki Stafford points out in *Bite Me!* (p. 353) that the Big Bad of the sixth season was not so much Willow or the Troika as the inner enemies each character faced.

For more on how our cultural stories about vampires reflect our own ambiguities and secret anxieties, see William Patrick Day, *Vampire Legends in Contemporary American Culture*, p. 5. See also the final chapters in Timothy Beal's outstanding book *Religion and Its Monsters*. Monsters, Beal says, reflect both our deepest fears and our most intense desires.

In *The Girl's Got Bite*, Kathleen Tracy interprets Xander's comment in episode 3.21 to mean that he's worried about losing Buffy's spirit and nature, not her physical life. The observation about Faith representing Buffy's dark side is found in Diane De Kalb-Rittenhouse's essay in *Fighting the Forces*, "Sex and the Single Vampire: The Evolution of the Vampire Lothario and Its Representation in *Buffy*," p. 147.

Jung's story of the righteous man and his family is found in *C. G. Jung Speaking: Interviews and Encounters* (Princeton, N.J.: Princeton University Press, 1977), p. 158. Another version of the story is recounted on p. 161.

Joss Whedon's comment about people believing themselves to be righteous is found in the voice-over DVD commentary for "Wild at Heart" (4.6).

For more on the continuity between Willow and Dark Willow, see James B. South, "'My God, It's like a Greek Tragedy,'" in *Buffy the Vampire Slayer and Philosophy*, pp. 131-145. Laura Resnick discusses Angel's saga in her essay "The Good, the Bad, and the Ambivalent," in *Seven Seasons of* Buffy, p. 56.

Chapter Eleven

Thomas Hibbs's insight about Angel's path to redemption is found in "*Buffy the Vampire Slayer* as Feminist Noir," in Buffy the Vampire Slayer *and Philosophy*, pp. 58-59. The fact that Charles Dickens is Joss Whedon's favorite author comes from Candace Havens's biography *Joss Whedon: The Genius Behind* Buffy, p. 41. The comparison to Job is drawn from Job 42:6, where Job despises himself and repents "in dust and ashes." For more on general themes of redemption in *Buffy* and *Angel*, see Tanya Krzywinska, "Hubble-Bubble, Herbs, and Grimoires," in *Fighting the Forces*, p. 184; see also in the same book, Mary Alice Money, "The Undemonization of Supporting Characters in *Buffy*," p. 104.

Shaun Narine examines the redemption of Willow and Faith in "'We Are All Who We Are': Change and Redemption in *Buffy*," posted on March 22, 2003, at http://www.the-buzz.com/b_7_16b.html. In the fourth-season DVD, Joss Whedon discusses the "Who Are You?" episode (4.16), noting that although switching bodies gives Faith the ultimate opportunity for revenge, she finds herself changed by the experience. In the fourth-season featurette, Marti Noxon also discusses how Faith is transformed by the love she finds when she walks in Buffy's shoes.

Shaun Narine's comment about Faith being improved by the California penal system is found in "We Are All Who We Are," cited above.

Faith is not the only character who tries to choose suicide over redemption. As we saw in Chapter Eight, when Anya is confronted with the enormity of the fraternity murders she has committed in the seventh season, she simply wants out; she tells D'Hoffryn that she will give her life to reverse her vengeance spell and revive the students. It's a tremendous sacrifice on her part, but it's also a way to end her pain, a fact that is not lost on the livid D'Hoffryn. He executes another vengeance demon in her stead, forcing Anya to face her misery.

Angel allowed Faith to live because he wanted her to taste freedom from guilt and pain; D'Hoffryn permitted Anya to live because he wanted her to wallow in guilt and pain. Either way, the message is clear: as Andrew would say, redemption is hard. Death is too easy a way out.

For examples of fan fiction about Spike's ongoing redemption, see http://www.allaboutspike.com, particularly the section "Why Redemption?" Also helpful is "The Redemptive Force of Love: Spike and the Hero's Journey" by Magpie, found at the same site. David Fury's thoughts on Spike are taken from "The Sound of the Fury: Part II of an Exclusive Interview with Writer and Co-Executive Producer David Fury" in the online fanzine *City of Angel,* http://www.cityofangel.com/BehindTheScenes/btvs3/fury3/html.

Angel producer Kelly A. Manners says in the *Angel* season-one DVD featurette that the spin-off series develops "an alcoholic metaphor with Angel. Angel's a guy one drink away from going back to his evil roots."

Epilogue

William Patrick Day's comments are taken from *Vampire Legends in Contemporary American Culture,* p. 165. For more on Christian and *The Pilgrim's Progress,* see John Spalding, *A Pilgrim's Digress: My Perilous, Fumbling Quest for the Celestial City* (New York: Harmony, 2003), p. xix.

A Guide to Buffy's Seven Seasons

Sarah Michelle Gellar's statement on the darkness of the sixth season is found in Jeff Jensen's article "The Good-Bye Girl," p. 21. Fans' mixed reactions to the sixth season are legendary; for a snapshot of this, visit http://www.jumptheshark.com for fans' assessment of when they think *Buffy* went downhill. Although the highest number of votes at press time were from loyal fans who feel that the series never "jumped the shark" (went into irrevocable decline), the majority of those who believed that *Buffy* had indeed declined dated their ennui to one of the most unpopular story arcs of the series, the murder of Tara at the end of the sixth season. Fans and critics were furious at the writers' decision to kill Tara, with *Boston Herald* entertainment critic Mark Perigard calling it "another cruel twist in a cold season" ("The Friday Rant," May 10, 2002, p. S34).

Acknowledgments

One of the major themes of *Buffy the Vampire Slayer* is that although going it alone is very brave and macho and all that, you'll have much more success—and more fun—if you move forward with others of like-minded purpose. This book would have not happened without the encouragement, gentle criticism, and (failing that) swift kicks in the butt from many friends and colleagues. First, I'd like to thank Susan Elia, my college roommate, fellow writer, and good friend, who forwarded timely articles and *Buffy* news and commented on many chapters in this book. Kerry Ose, my friend and research assistant who wrote this book's season and character guides, was an invaluable source of *Buffy* knowledge and literary connections. Kelly Hughes has been a tireless supporter through every stage of the book's creation, Mark Pinsky offered advice about writing about the entertainment industry, Roz Kaveney graciously agreed to meet with me when I was visiting London and discussed some of the redemptive themes on *Angel*, and David Lavery helped me mine the fascinating maze of academic work on *Buffy*. Judith Weisenfeld of Vassar College provided helpful insights about religion and popular culture—and more important, did not laugh at me when I told her that I had just seen my first episode of *Buffy* and thoroughly enjoyed it. Ed Kawakami, Holly Welker, Rhonda Wilcox, and Marcia and Sarah Ford lent their inexhaustible knowledge of *Buffy* episodes. I owe my thanks also to the audiences at the Cornerstone Festival and the Sunstone Symposium, who listened to early portions of these chapters in the summer of 2003.

I am grateful to Judy Dushku, whom I interviewed for my undergraduate thesis many years ago and who has been a mentor to so many young women. With this book she helped me once again, responding to a paper I presented and putting me in touch with her lovely and talented daughter Eliza. Thanks to Eliza for graciously taking the time out of her busy shooting schedule to be interviewed for the book and to Jim Coleman for providing a photo.

My agent, Linda Roghaar, was enthusiastic about this project from the start, and the folks at Jossey-Bass could not have been more delightful to work with. In particular, Julianna Gustafson, my hip young editor, has been a dream, encouraging me at key points and helping me to write for a popular audience. Chandrika Madhavan, the assistant editor, assiduously tracked down the photos for this book, helped with the character and season guides, and commented on every chapter. Both of them have gone above and beyond their editorial duties and have made the entire process enormous fun. I owe thanks to other people at Jossey-Bass and Wiley, including Catherine Craddock, Geneviève Duboscq, Andrea Flint, Heather Florence, Paula Goldstein, Sachie Jones, Mark Kerr, and Sandy Siegle.

I am also grateful to the many dedicated *Buffy* and *Angel* fans who have taken the time to post opinions on episodes or discuss the show's spiritual themes in chat rooms. And of course, I deeply appreciate the writers and creators of both shows, who have raised the bar for TV as art.

Most of all, I thank my family. I appreciate the fact that my mom taught me to value strong, resourceful, funny women and that she has been so supportive of my writing projects. I am grateful to my husband, Phil Smith, who first began watching episodes of *Buffy* because he wanted to share in this project with me and then was generous enough to get thoroughly hooked for his own sake. This book is dedicated to our daughter, Jerusha. She's much too young to watch this stuff, but my prayer is that she'll grow up to be as strong, wise, and giving as Buffy. Though I could do without that sassy Slayer sarcasm.

Winchester, Kentucky
February 2004

Jana Riess

The Author

After saving the world as a Brownie, Jana Riess went on to earn a master of divinity degree from Princeton Theological Seminary and a Ph.D. in religion from Columbia University. When she's not watching *Buffy* or *Angel*, she's writing books (*The Spiritual Traveler: Boston and New England*) or working her day job as the religion book review editor at *Publishers Weekly*. Her favorite character is Giles. Or maybe Spike. Or actually, it's Buffy. Yeah, definitely Buffy.